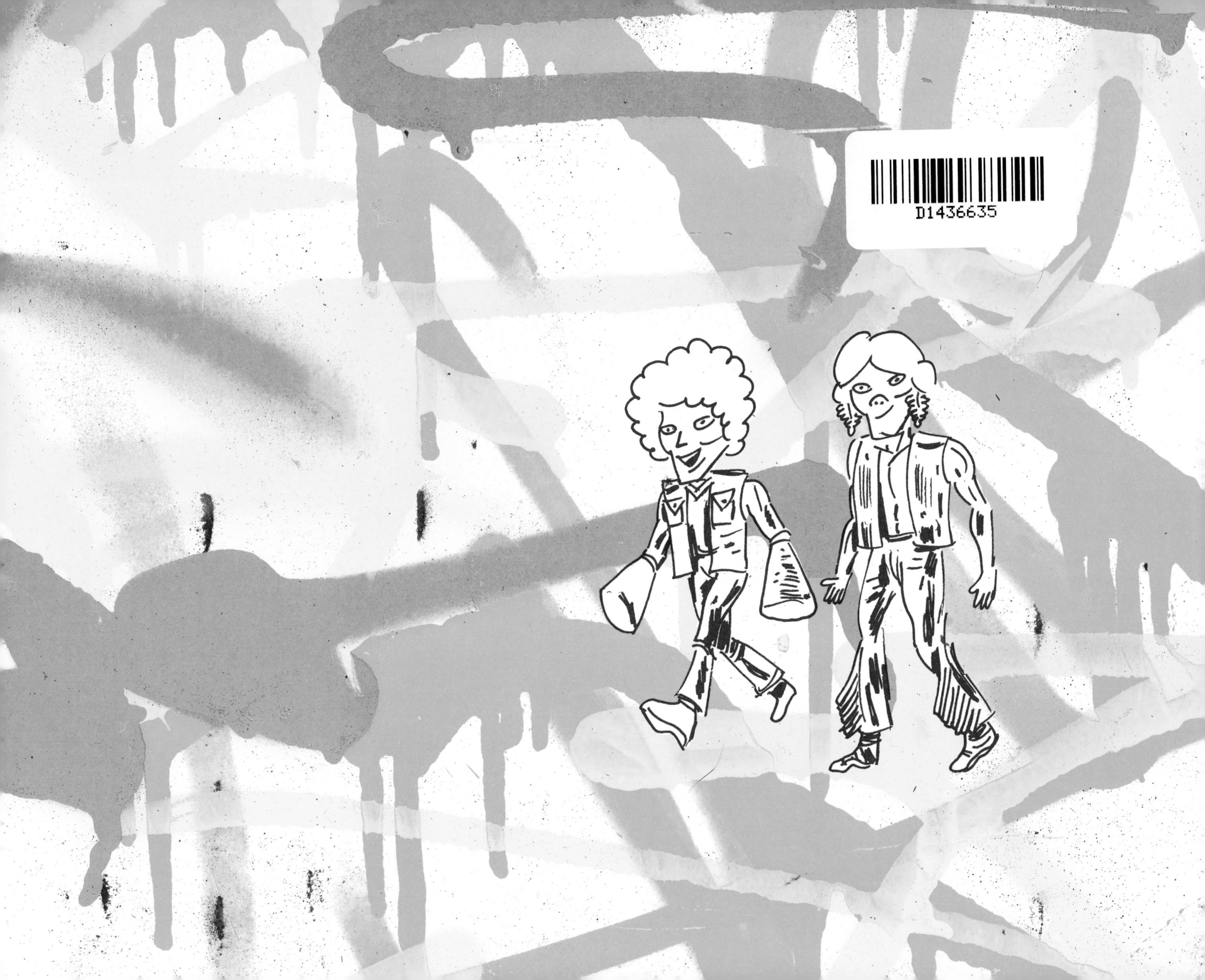

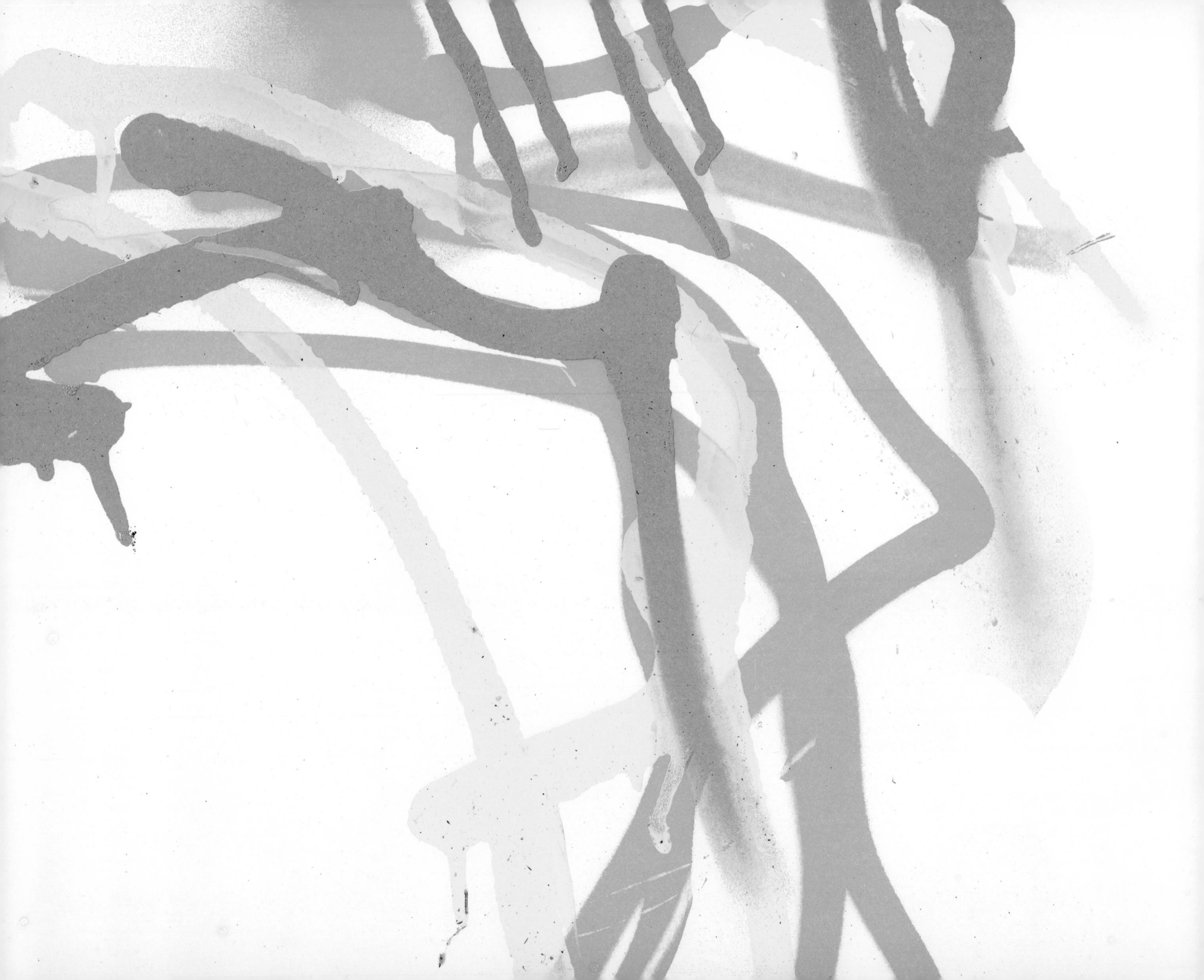

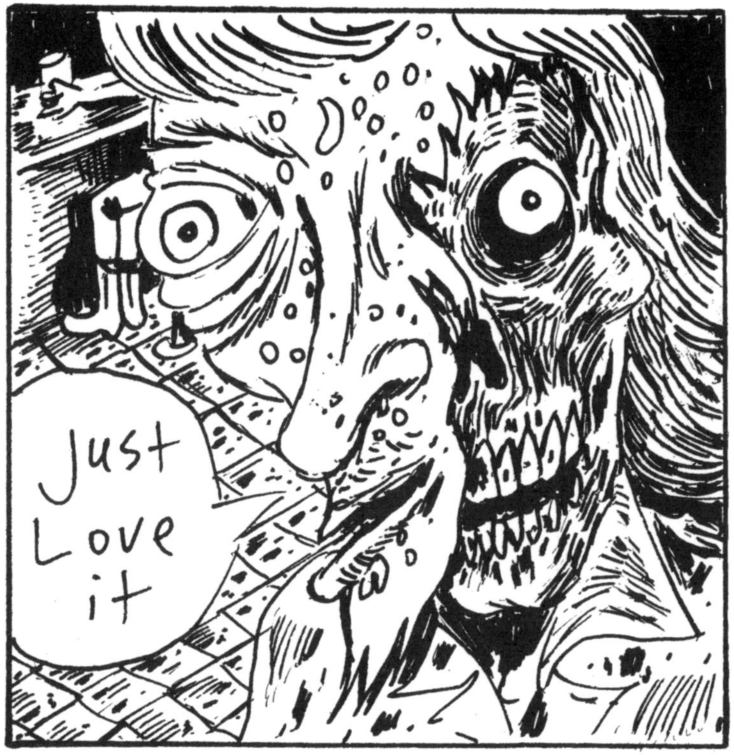
Just Love it

PUKE FORCE

BRIAN CHIPPENDALE

drawnandquarterly.com

First hardcover edition: January 2016. Printed in China.

Library and Archives Canada Cataloguing in Publication
Chippendale, Brian, author, illustrator
    Puke Force / Brian Chippendale
ISBN 978-1-77046-219-9 (bound)
    1. Graphic novels. I. Title.
PN6727.C45P85 2015   741.5'973   C2015-902370-X

Published in the USA by Drawn & Quarterly, a client publisher of Farrar, Straus and Giroux;
orders: 888.330.8477
Published in Canada by Drawn & Quarterly, a client publisher of Raincoast Books;
orders: 800.663.5714
Published in the United Kingdom by Drawn & Quarterly, a client publisher of Publishers Group UK;
orders: info@pguk.co.uk

REMINDER

EACH PAGE SHOULD
HAVE A PANEL READING
GUIDE, BUT FOR OPTIMAL
EFFECT PLEASE READ IN A
SNAKE-LIKE FASHION. THIS
COMIC WAS DRAWN 2009 —
2015 IN THE COMFORT AND
DISCOMFORT OF THE HILARIOUS
ATTIC, PROVIDENCE RHODE ISLAND.
PORTIONS WERE ORIGINALLY PUBLISHED
ON PICTUREBOXINC.COM (R.I.P.)
THANK YOU DAN NADEL. THANK YOU
JUNGIL HONG. THANK YOU TOM DEVLIN.
THANK YOU DRAWN AND QUARTERLY.

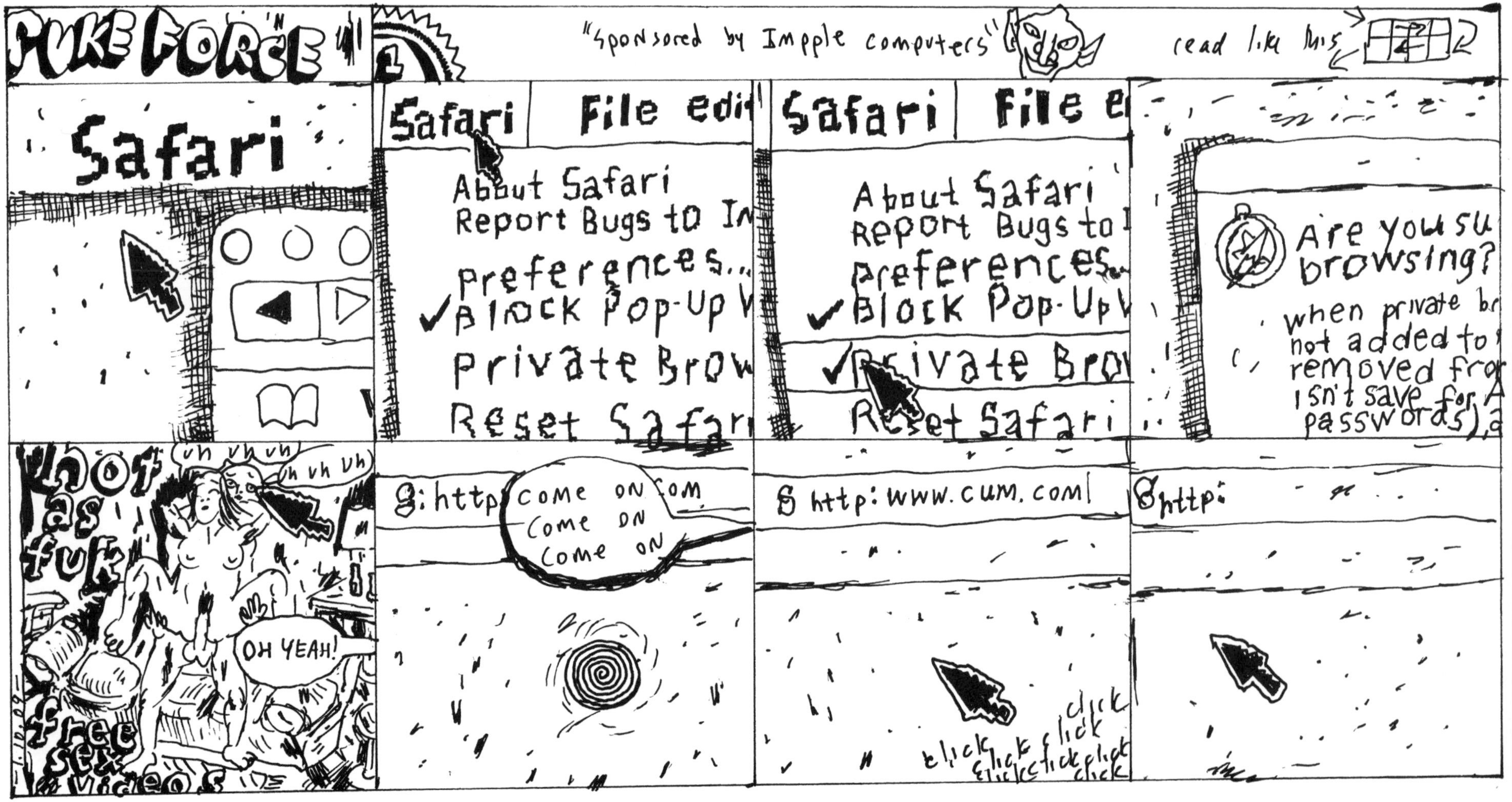
PUKE FORCE
"sponsored by Impple computers"
read like this
Safari
Safari File edit
About Safari
Report Bugs to In
preferences...
✓Block Pop-Up W
private Brow
Reset Safari
Safari File e
About Safari
Report Bugs to I
preferences...
✓Block Pop-Up W
✓Private Brow
Reset Safari
Are you su
browsing?
when private br
not added to
removed fro
isn't save for A
passwords), a
hot as fuk
uh uh uh
uh uh uh
OH YEAH!
free sex videos
1.10.09
http:
come on
come on
come on
http: www.cum.com
click click click click click click click
http:

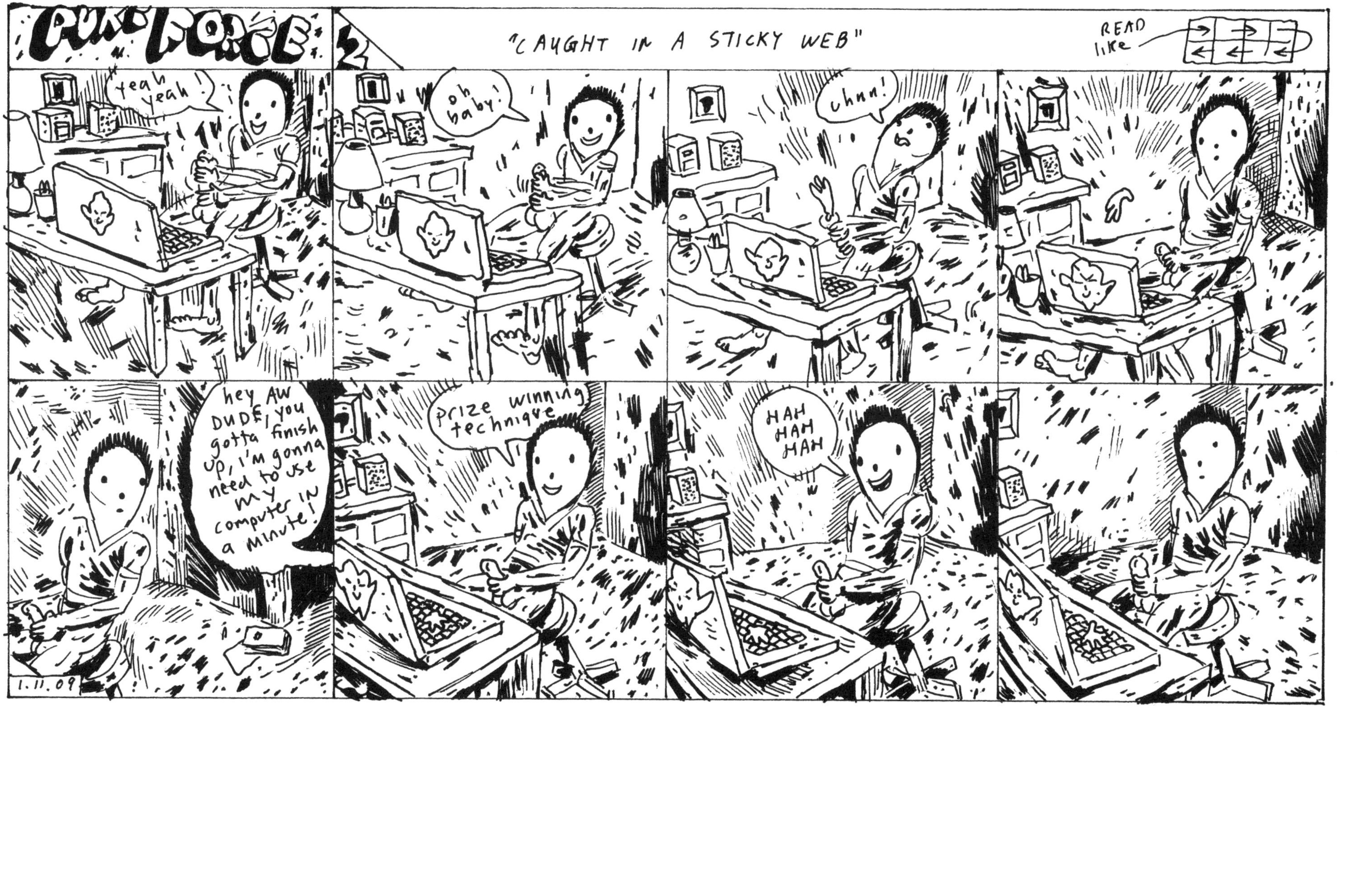
PUKE FORCE
2
"CAUGHT IN A STICKY WEB"
READ like
yeah yeah!
oh baby!
uhnn!
HAH HAH HAH
prize winning technique
hey AW DUDE, you gotta finish up, I'm gonna need to use my computer IN a minute!
1.11.09

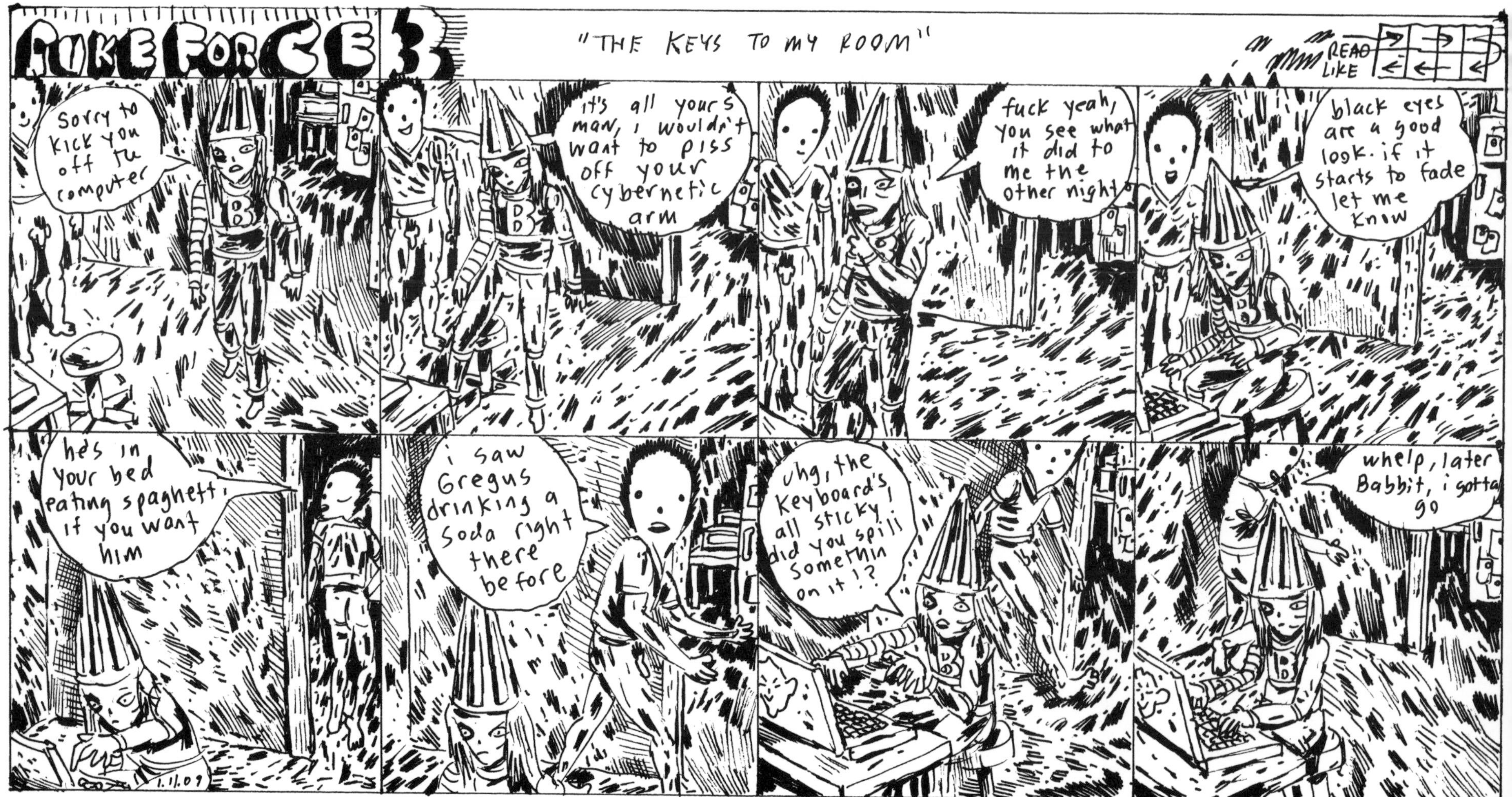
PUKE FORCE 3
"THE KEYS TO MY ROOM"
READ LIKE
Sorry to kick you off the computer
it's all yours man, i wouldn't want to piss off your cybernetic arm
fuck yeah, you see what it did to me the other night
black eyes are a good look. if it starts to fade let me know
whelp, later Babbit, i gotta go
uhg, the keyboard's all sticky! did you spill somethin on it!?
i saw Gregus drinking a soda right there before
he's in your bed eating spaghetti if you want him
1.11.09

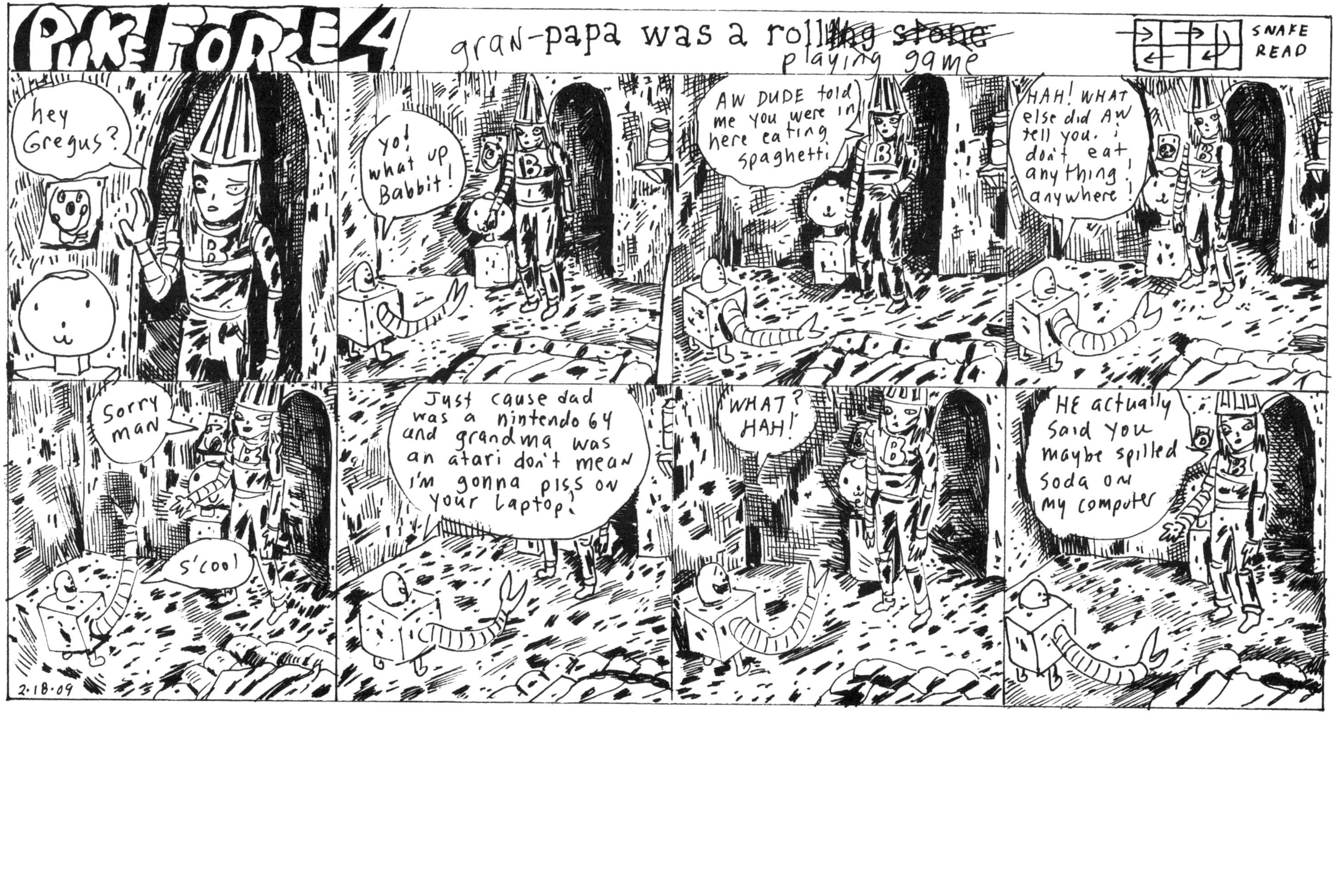
PUKE FORCE 4
gran-papa was a rolling stone playing game
SNAKE READ
hey Gregus?
yo! what up Babbit!
AW DUDE told me you were in here eating spaghetti
HAH! WHAT else did AW tell you. i don't eat anything anywhere!
HE actually said you maybe spilled soda on my computer
WHAT? HAH!
Just cause dad was a nintendo 64 and grandma was an atari don't mean i'm gonna piss on your laptop!
Sorry man
s'cool
2.18.09

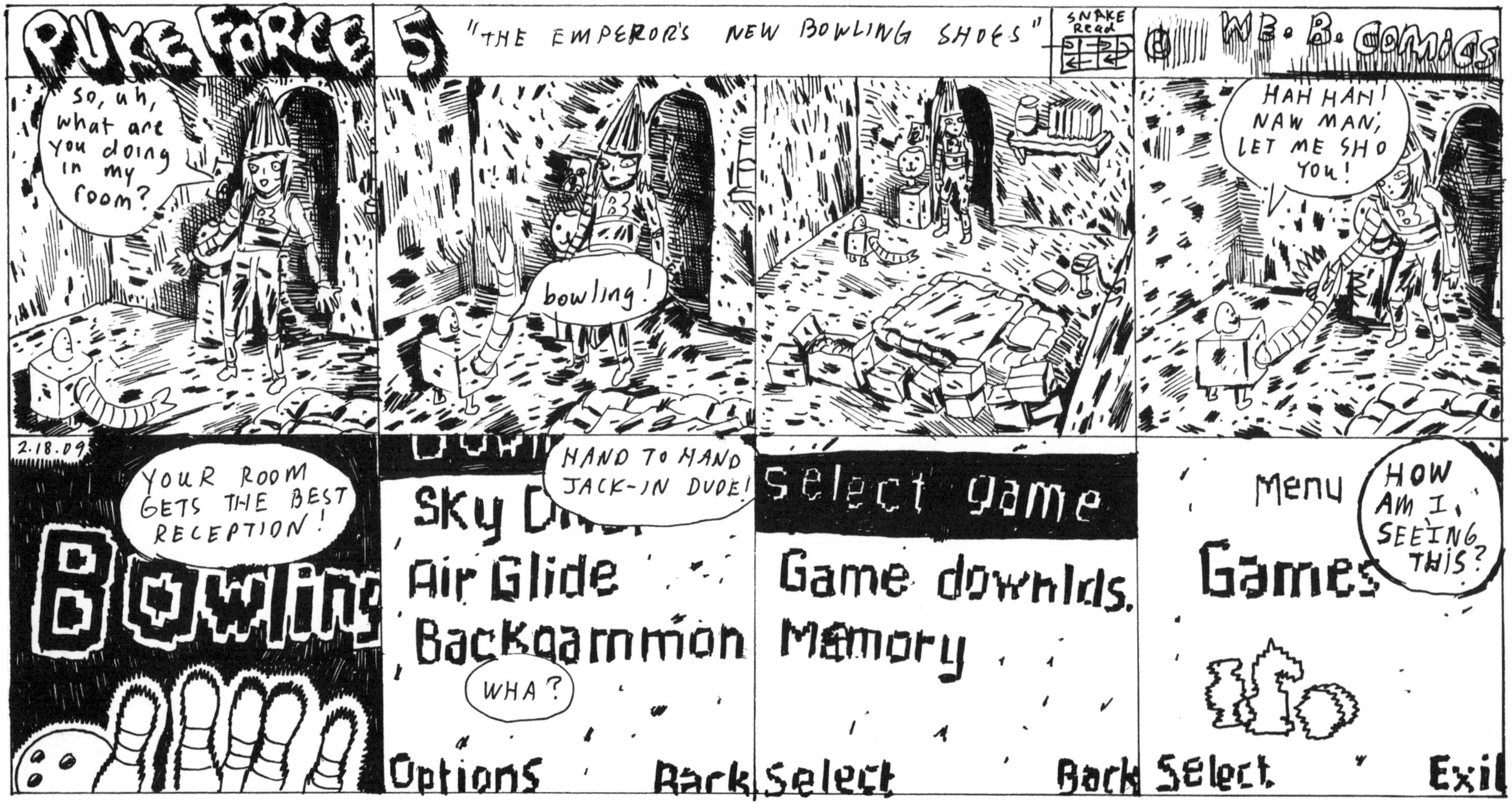
PUKE FORCE 5
"THE EMPEROR'S NEW BOWLING SHOES"
SNAKE Read
© WE. B. COMICS
So, uh, what are you doing in my room?
bowling!
HAH HAH! NAW MAN, LET ME SHO YOU!
2.18.09
YOUR ROOM GETS THE BEST RECEPTION!
Bowling
HAND TO HAND JACK-IN DUDE!
Sky Diver
Air Glide
Backgammon
WHA?
Options
Back
Select game
Game downlds.
Memory
Select
Back
Menu
HOW AM I SEEING THIS?
Games
Select
Exit

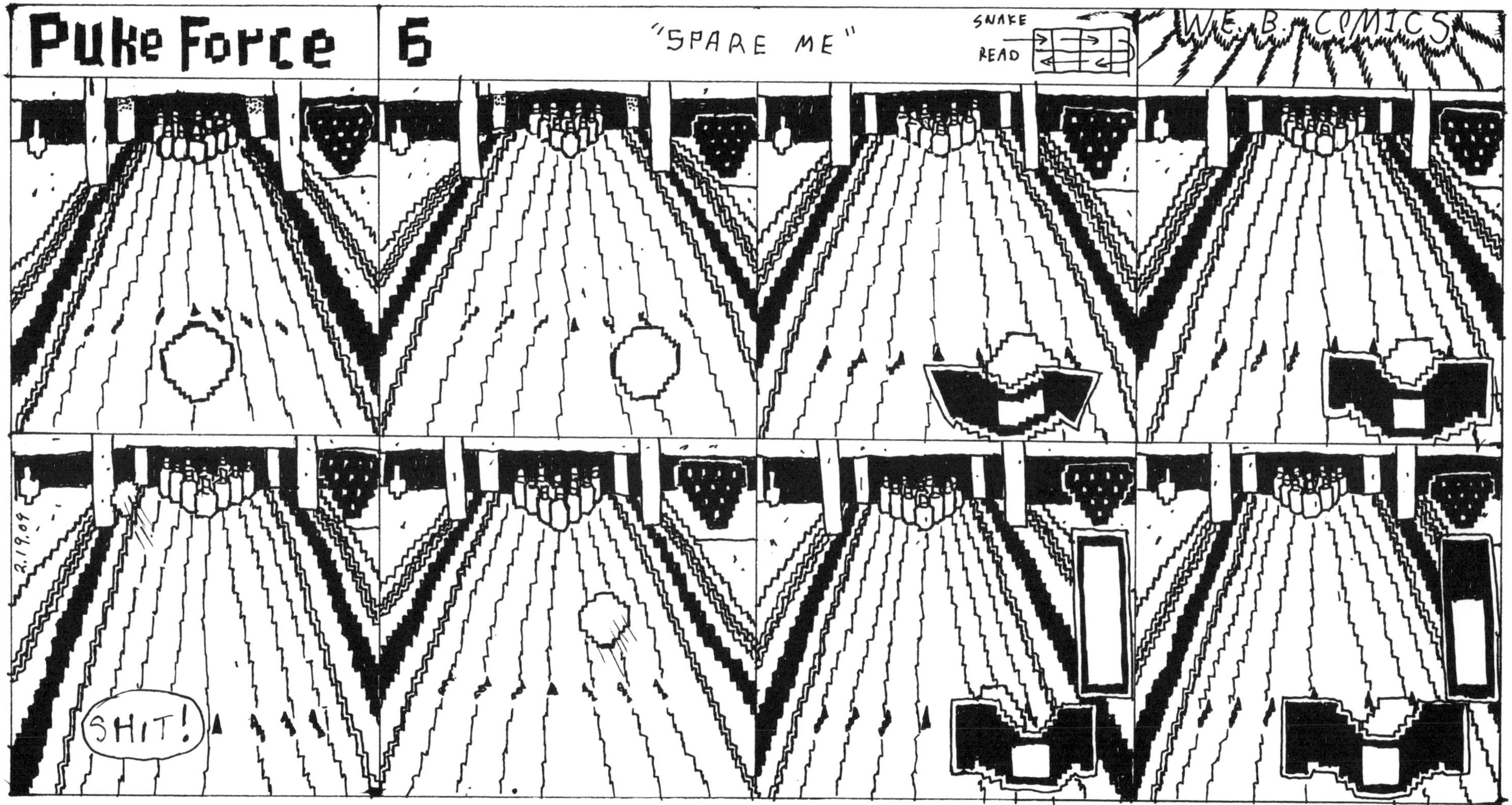
Puke Force
6
"SPARE ME"
SNAKE READ
W.E.B. COMICS
2.19.09
SHIT!

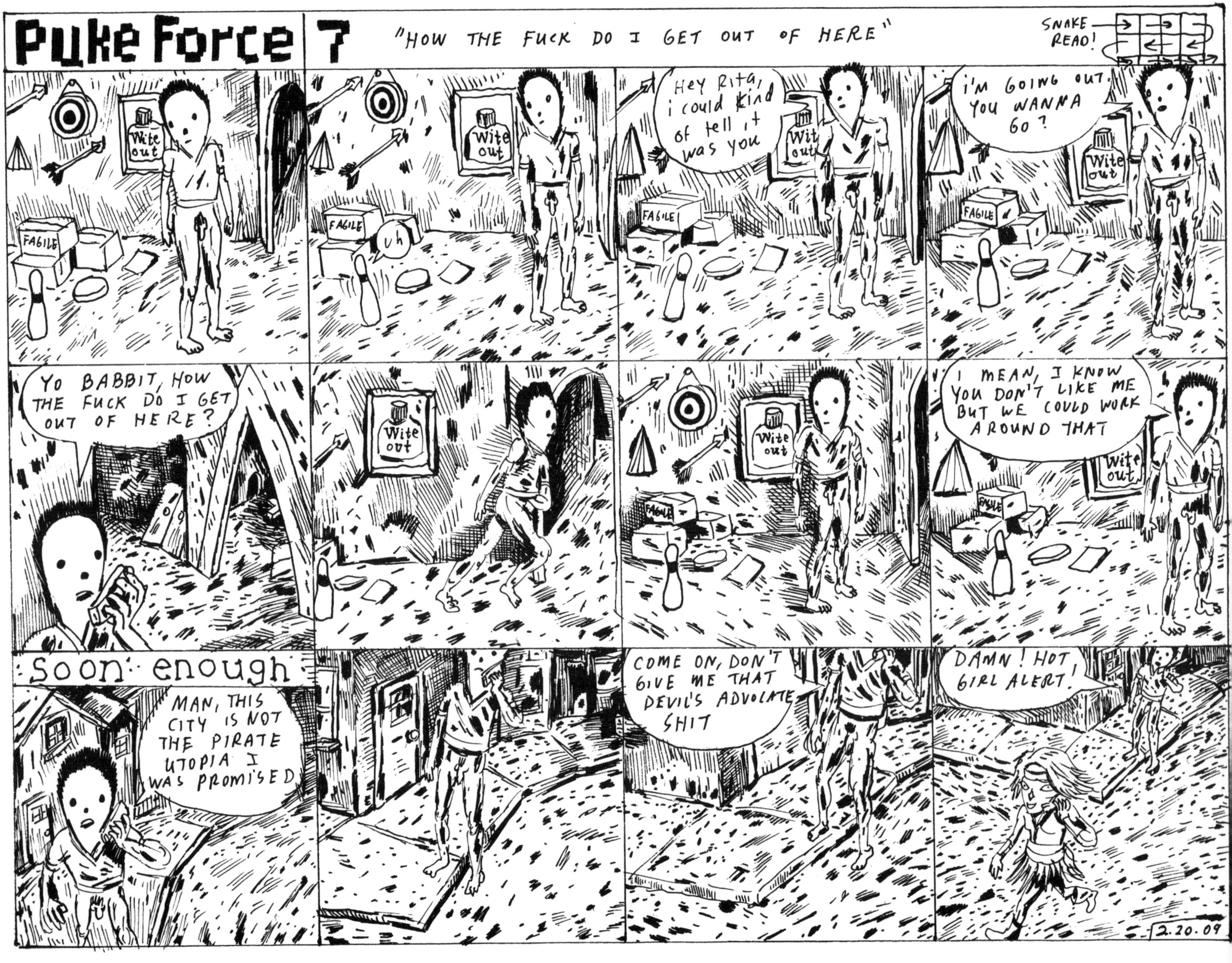
Puke Force 7
"HOW THE FUCK DO I GET OUT OF HERE"
SNAKE READ!
FAGILE
Wite out
uh
Hey Rita, i could kind of tell it was you
I'M GOING OUT. YOU WANNA GO?
YO BABBIT, HOW THE FUCK DO I GET OUT OF HERE?
I MEAN, I KNOW YOU DON'T LIKE ME BUT WE COULD WORK AROUND THAT
Soon enough
MAN, THIS CITY IS NOT THE PIRATE UTOPIA I WAS PROMISED
COME ON, DON'T GIVE ME THAT DEVIL'S ADVOCATE SHIT
DAMN! HOT GIRL ALERT!
2.20.09

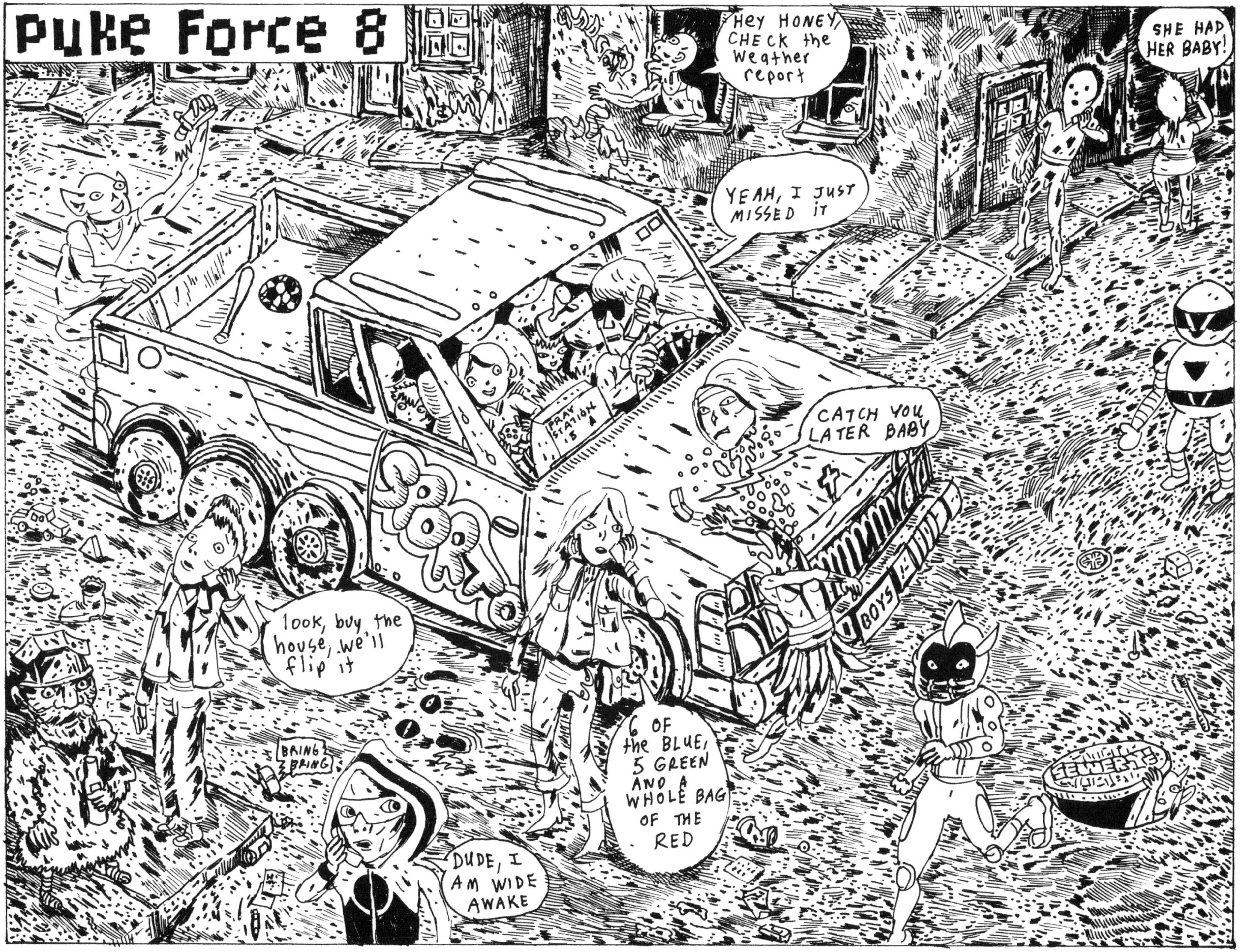
Puke Force 8
Hey Honey, CHECK the weather report
SHE HAD HER BABY!
YEAH, I JUST MISSED IT
CATCH YOU LATER BABY
look, buy the house, we'll flip it
6 OF the BLUE, 5 GREEN AND A WHOLE BAG OF THE RED
BRING BRING
DUDE, I AM WIDE AWAKE
BOYS

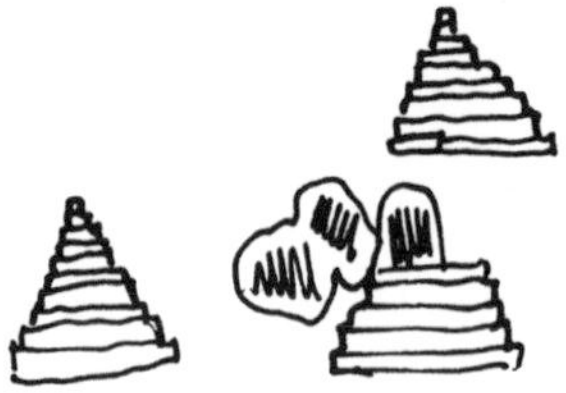

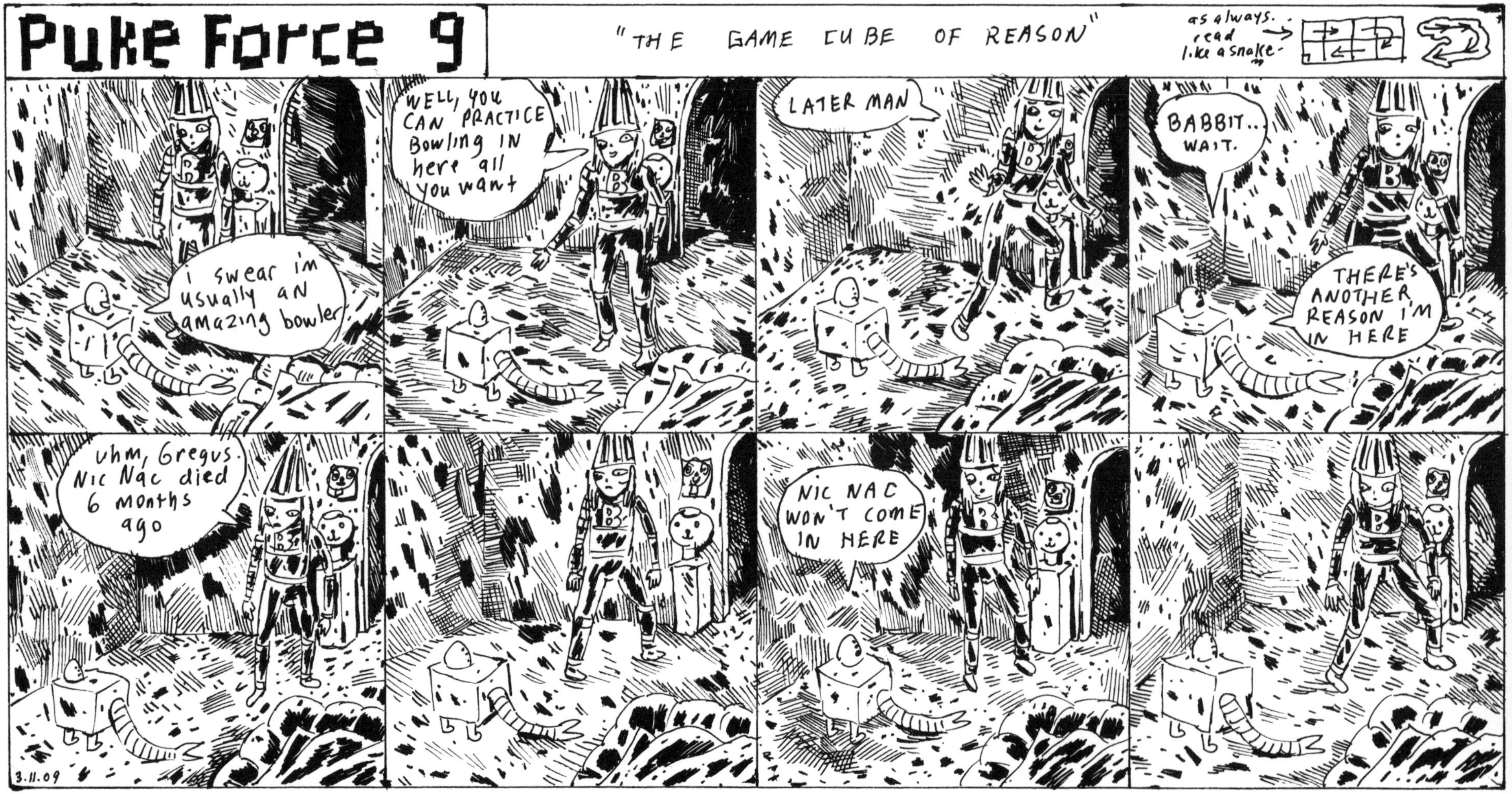

Puke Force 9
"THE GAME CUBE OF REASON"
as always. read like a snake
I swear I'm usually an amazing bowler
WELL, YOU CAN PRACTICE Bowling IN here all you want
LATER MAN
BABBIT.. WAIT.
THERE'S ANOTHER REASON I'M IN HERE
NIC NAC WON'T COME IN HERE
uhm, Gregus Nic Nac died 6 months ago
3.11.09

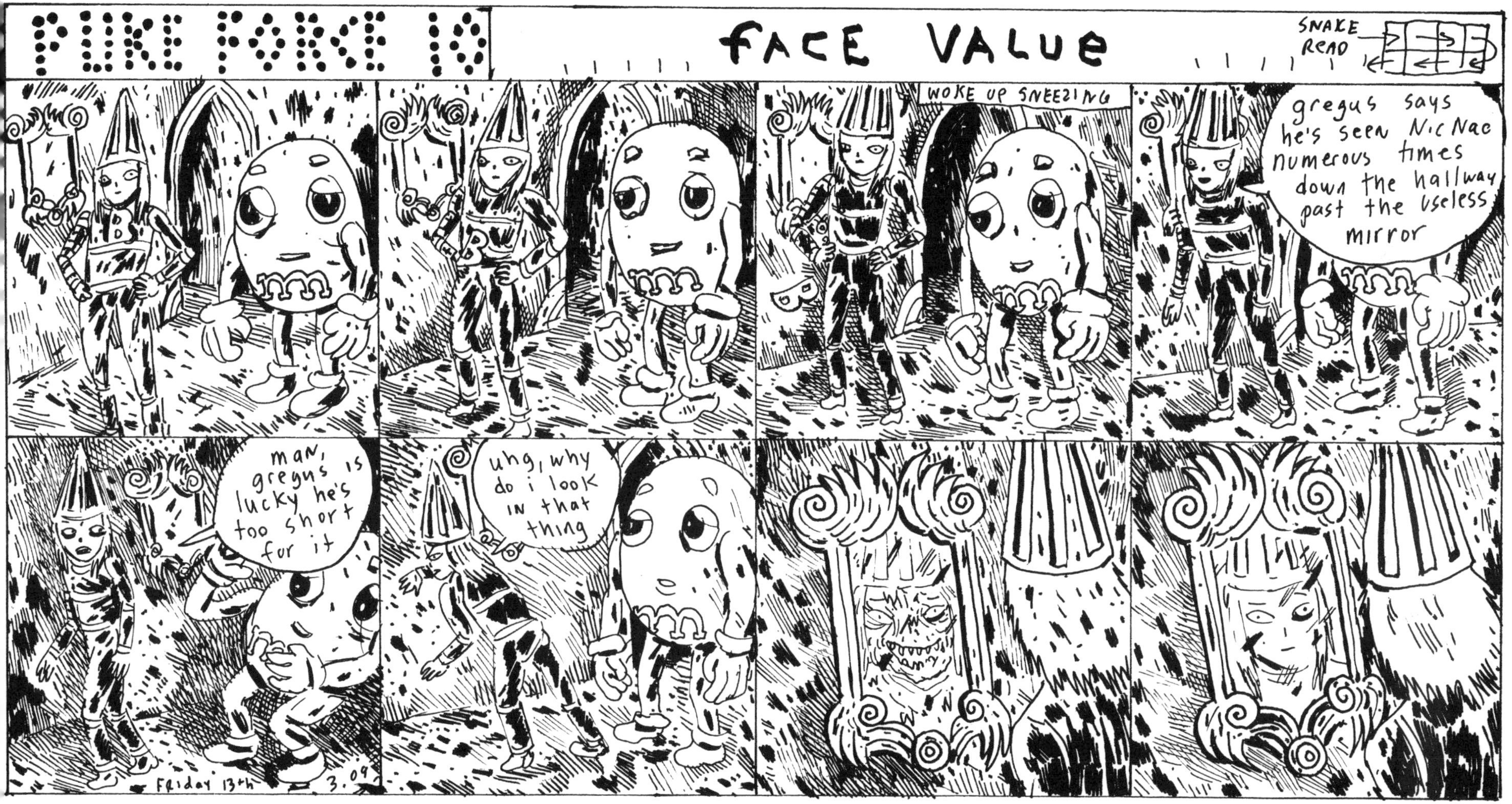
PUKE FORCE 10
FACE VALUE
SNAKE READ
WOKE UP SNEEZING
gregus says he's seen NicNac numerous times down the hallway past the useless mirror
man, gregus is lucky he's too short for it
FRiday 13th
3.09
uhg, why do i look in that thing

psyched

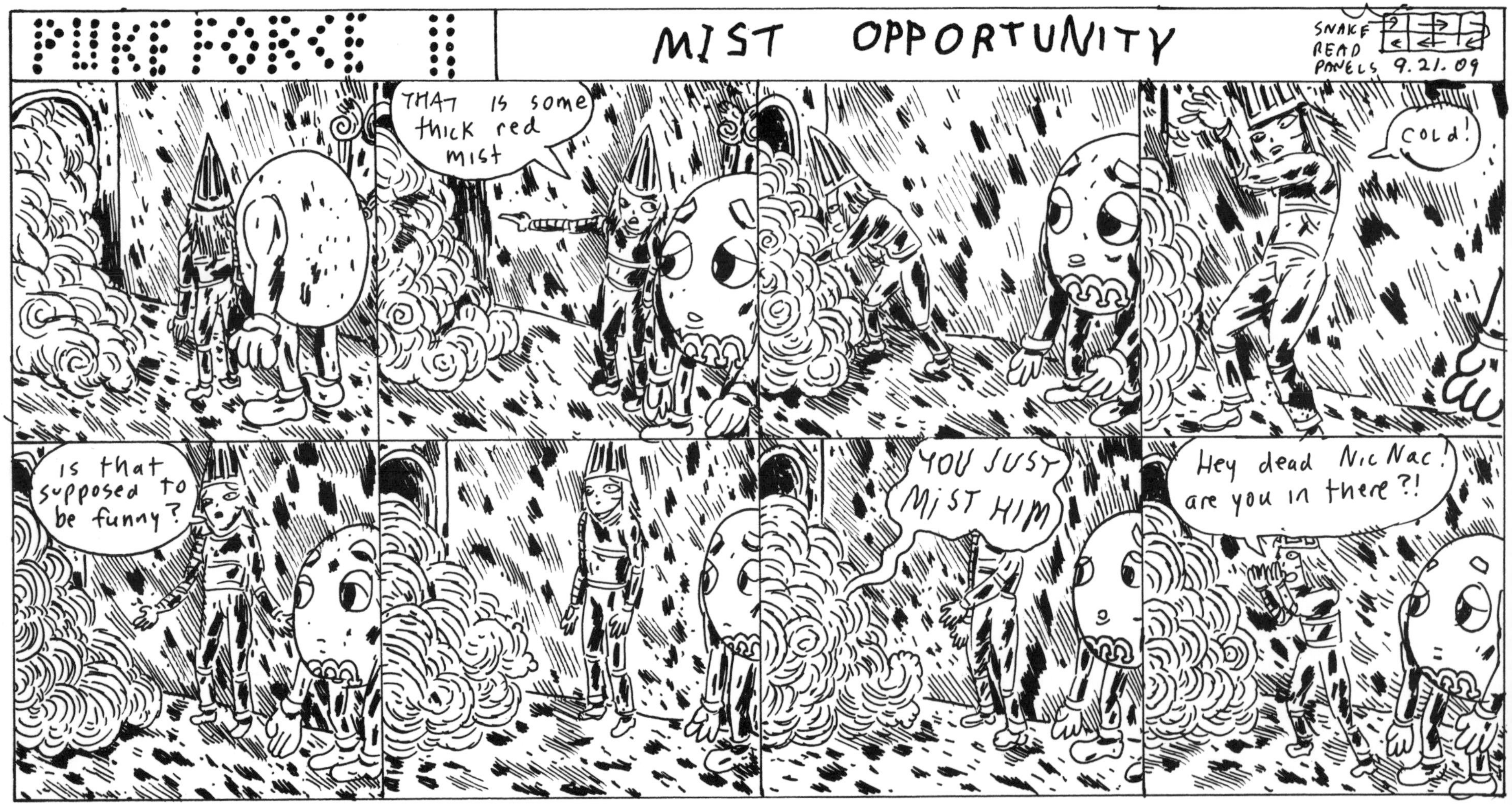
PUKE FORCE II
MIST OPPORTUNITY
SNAKE READ PANELS
9.21.09
THAT is some thick red mist
COLD!
Hey dead Nic Nac! are you in there?!
YOU JUST MIST HIM
is that supposed to be funny?

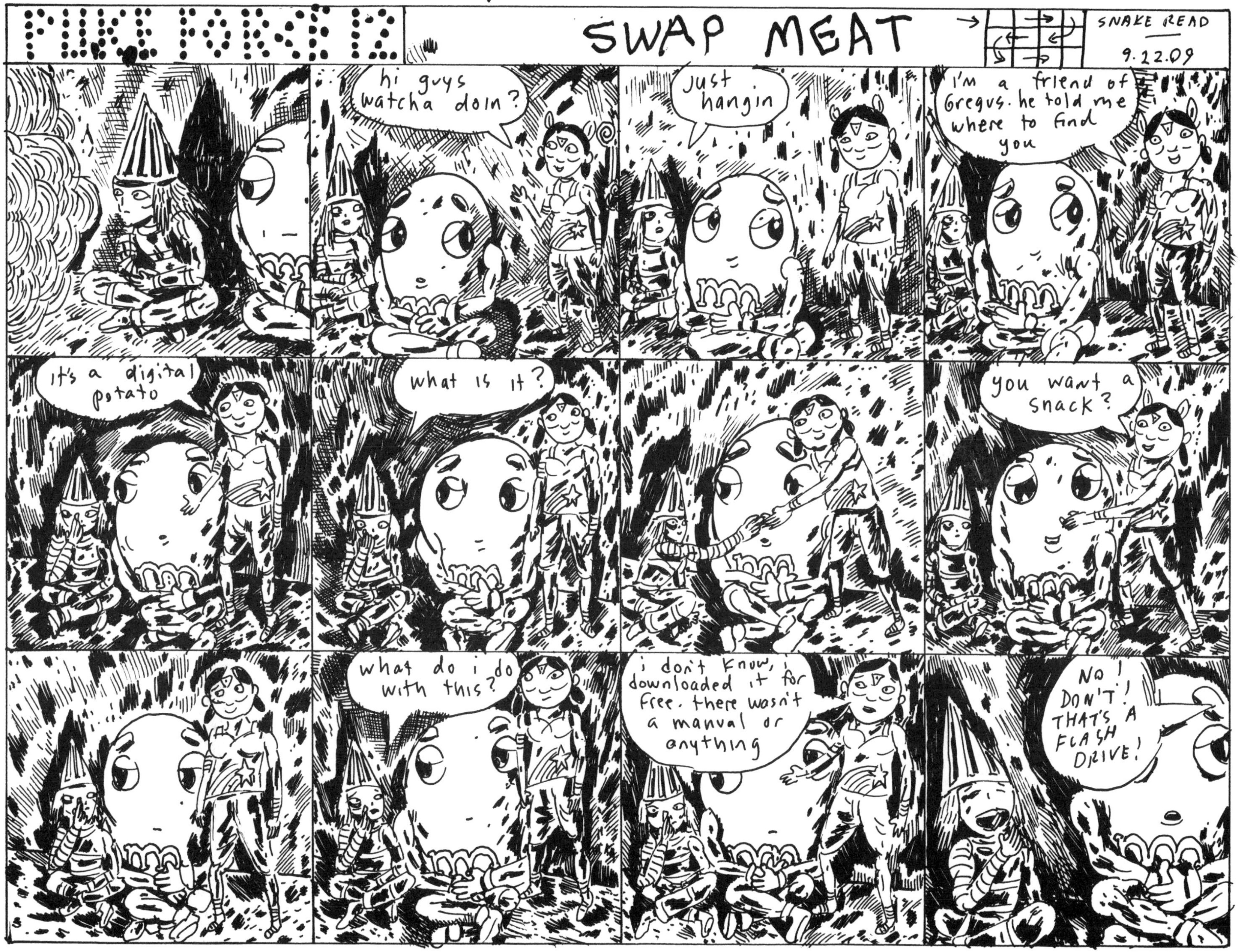
PUKE FORCE 12
SWAP MEAT
SNAKE READ
9.22.09
hi guys watcha doin?
just hangin
I'm a friend of Gregus. he told me where to find you
you want a snack?
what is it?
it's a digital potato
what do i do with this?
i don't know, i downloaded it for free. there wasn't a manual or anything
NO! DON'T! THAT'S A FLASH DRIVE!

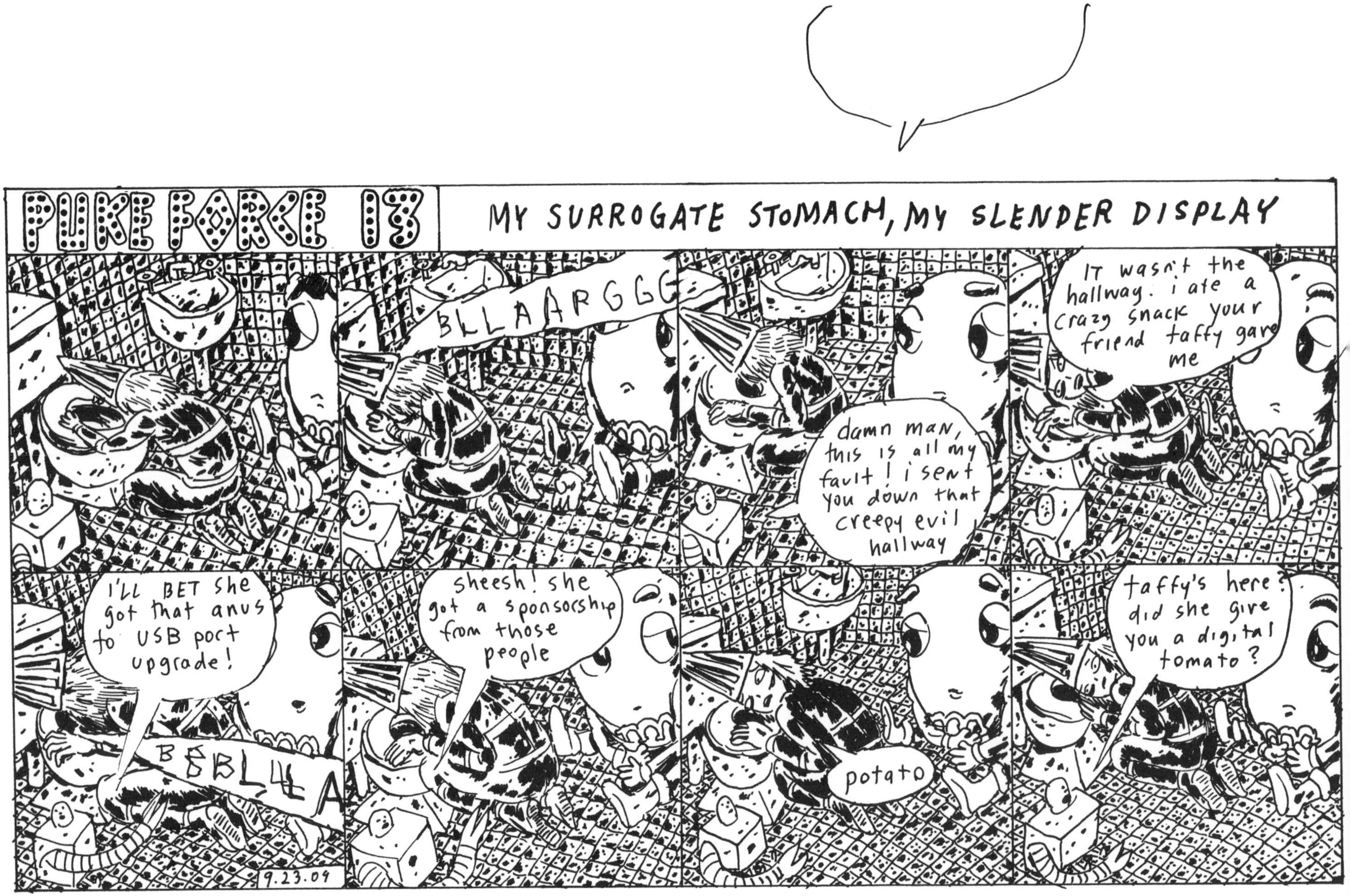
PUKE FORCE 13
MY SURROGATE STOMACH, MY SLENDER DISPLAY
BLLAARGGG
damn man, this is all my fault! i sent you down that creepy evil hallway
IT wasn't the hallway. i ate a crazy snack your friend taffy gave me
I'LL BET she got that anus to USB port upgrade!
BBBLLLA
9.23.09
sheesh! she got a sponsorship from those people
potato
taffy's here? did she give you a digital tomato?

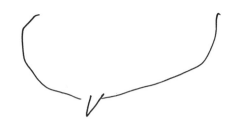

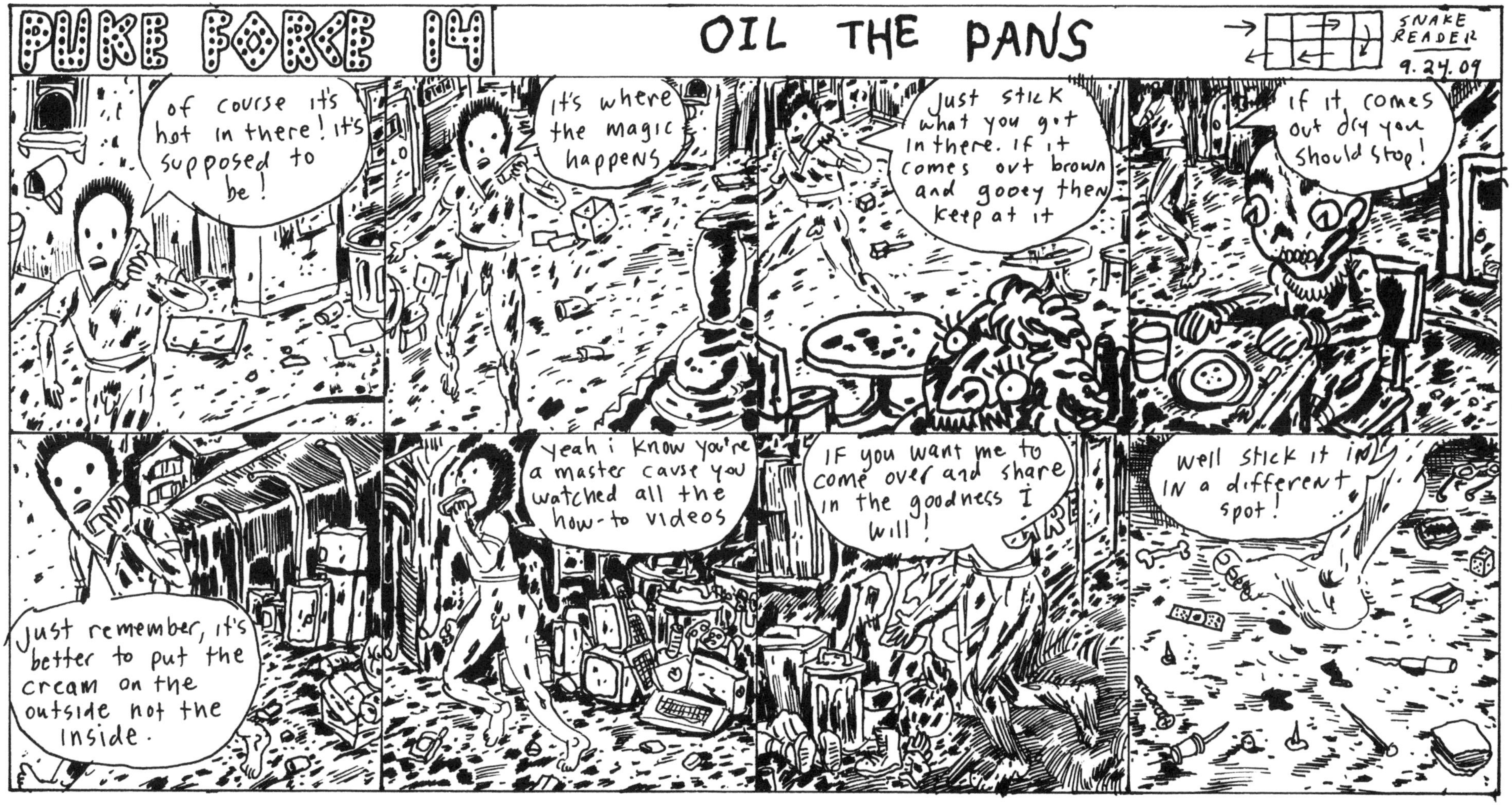
PUKE FORCE 14
OIL THE PANS
SNAKE READER
9.24.09
of course it's hot in there! it's supposed to be!
it's where the magic happens
Just stick what you got in there. If it comes out brown and gooey then keep at it
If it comes out dry you should stop!
well stick it IN IN a different spot!
IF you want me to come over and share in the goodness I will!
Yeah i know you're a master cause you watched all the how-to videos
Just remember, it's better to put the cream on the outside not the inside.

STILL

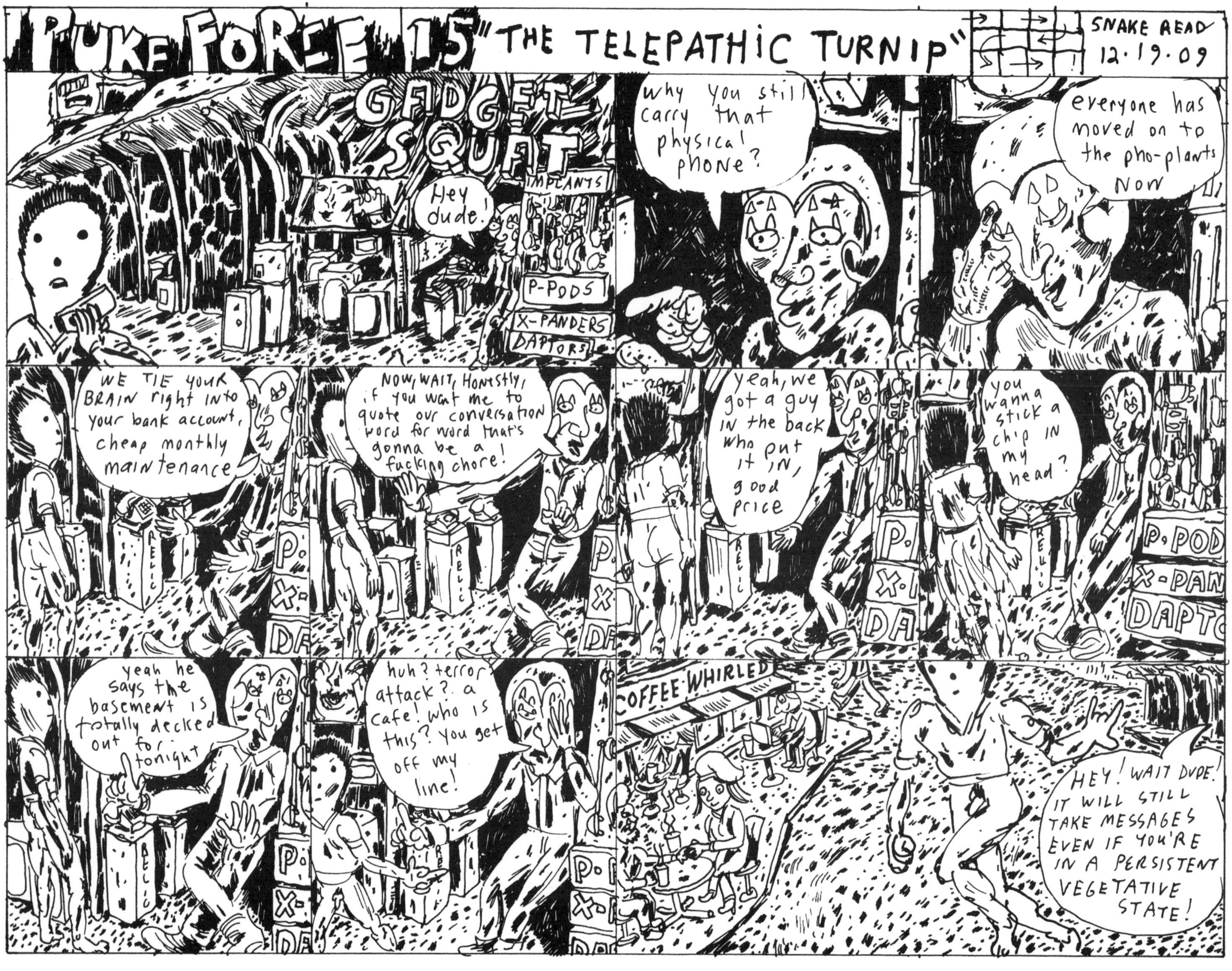
PUKE FORCE 15 "THE TELEPATHIC TURNIP"
SNAKE READ
12·19·09
GADGET SQUAT
IMPLANTS
P-PODS
X-PANDERS
DAPTORS
Hey dude!
why you still carry that physical phone?
everyone has moved on to the pho-plants now
WE TIE YOUR BRAIN right into your bank account, cheap monthly maintenance
RELIC
NOW, WAIT, Honestly, if you want me to quote our conversation word for word that's gonna be a fucking chore!
yeah, we got a guy in the back who put it in, good price
you wanna stick a chip in my head?
P-POD
X-PAN
DAPTO
yeah he says the basement is totally decked out for tonight
huh? terror attack? a cafe! who is this? you get off my line!
COFFEE WHIRLED
HEY! WAIT DUDE! IT WILL STILL TAKE MESSAGES EVEN IF YOU'RE IN A PERSISTENT VEGETATIVE STATE!

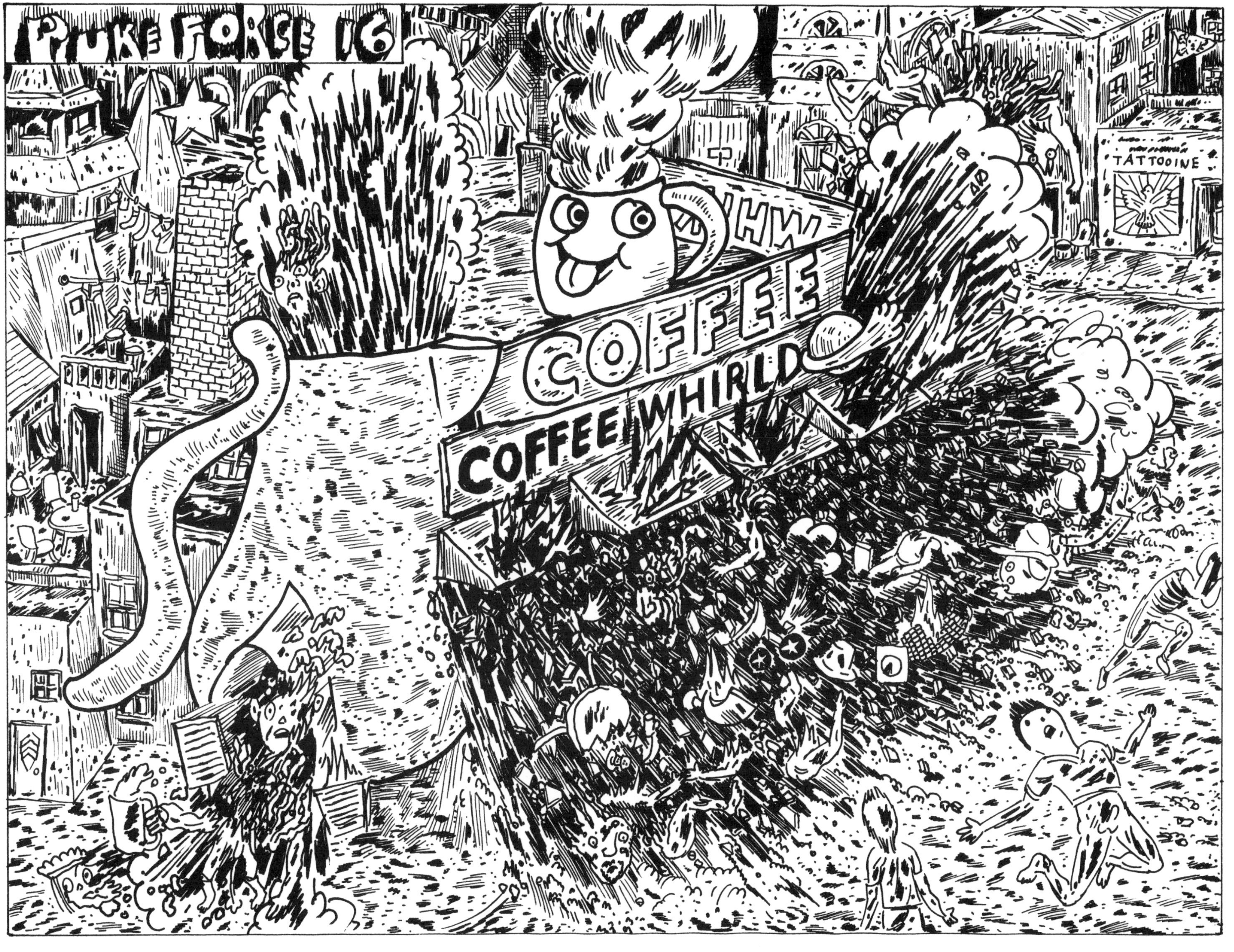
PUKE FORCE 16
TATTOOINE
COFFEE
COFFEE WHIRLD

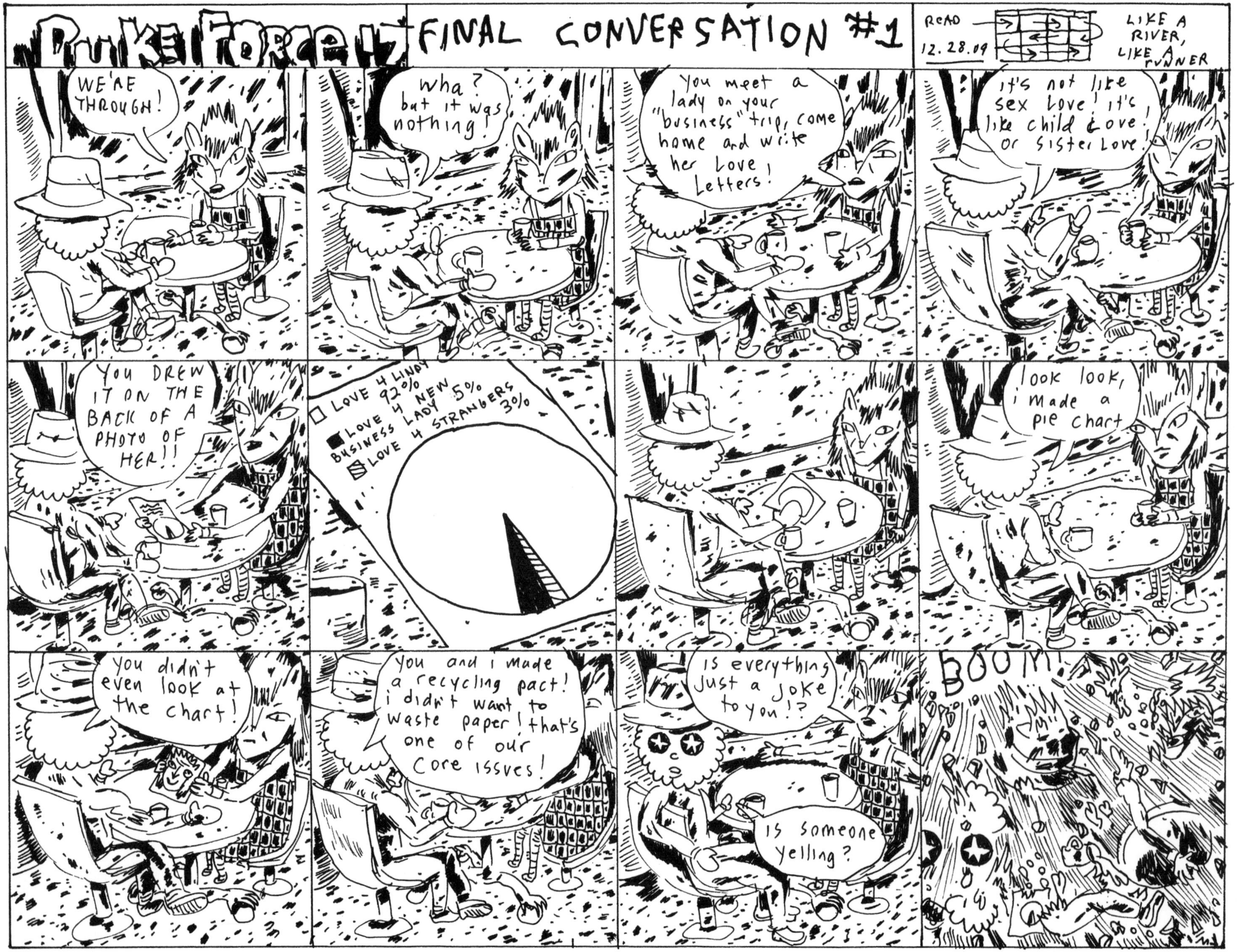
PUKE FORCE 17
FINAL CONVERSATION #1
READ 12.28.09
LIKE A RIVER, LIKE A RUNNER
WE'RE THROUGH!
Wha? but it was nothing!
You meet a lady on your "business" trip, come home and write her Love Letters!
it's not like sex love! it's like child love, or sister love!
look look, i made a pie chart
LOVE 4 LINDY 92%
LOVE 4 NEW BUSINESS LADY 5%
LOVE 4 STRANGERS 3%
YOU DREW IT ON THE BACK OF A PHOTO OF HER!!
you didn't even look at the chart!
You and i made a recycling pact! i didn't want to waste paper! that's one of our core issues!
is everything just a joke to you!?
is someone yelling?
BOOM!

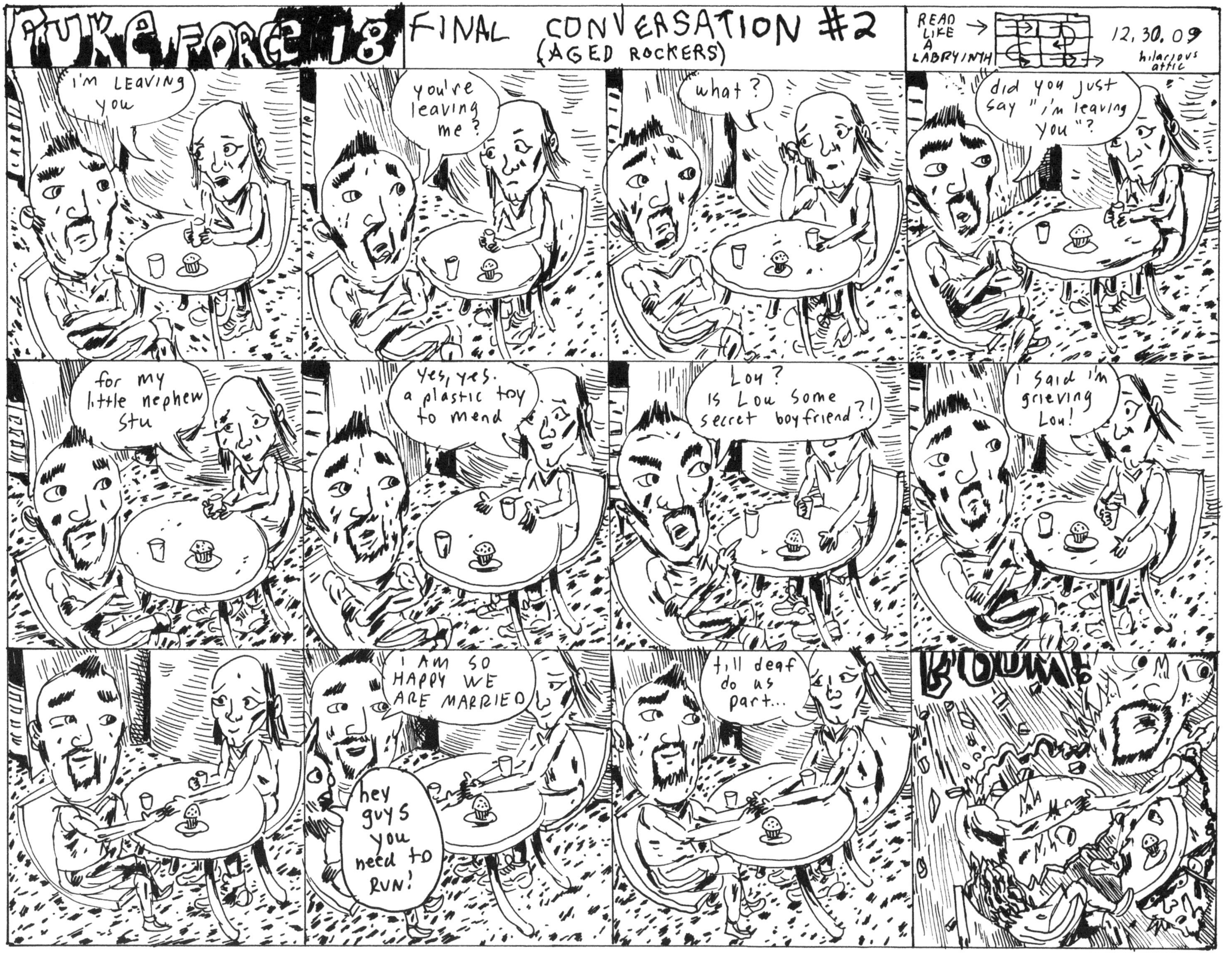
PUKE FORCE 18
FINAL CONVERSATION #2
(AGED ROCKERS)
READ LIKE A LABRYINTH →
12.30.09
hilarious attic
i'm LEAVING you
you're leaving me?
what?
did you just say "i'm leaving you"?
I said i'm grieving Lou!
Lou? Is Lou some secret boyfriend?!
Yes, yes. a plastic toy to mend
for my little nephew Stu
I AM SO HAPPY WE ARE MARRIED
hey guys you need to RUN!
till deaf do us part...
BOOM!

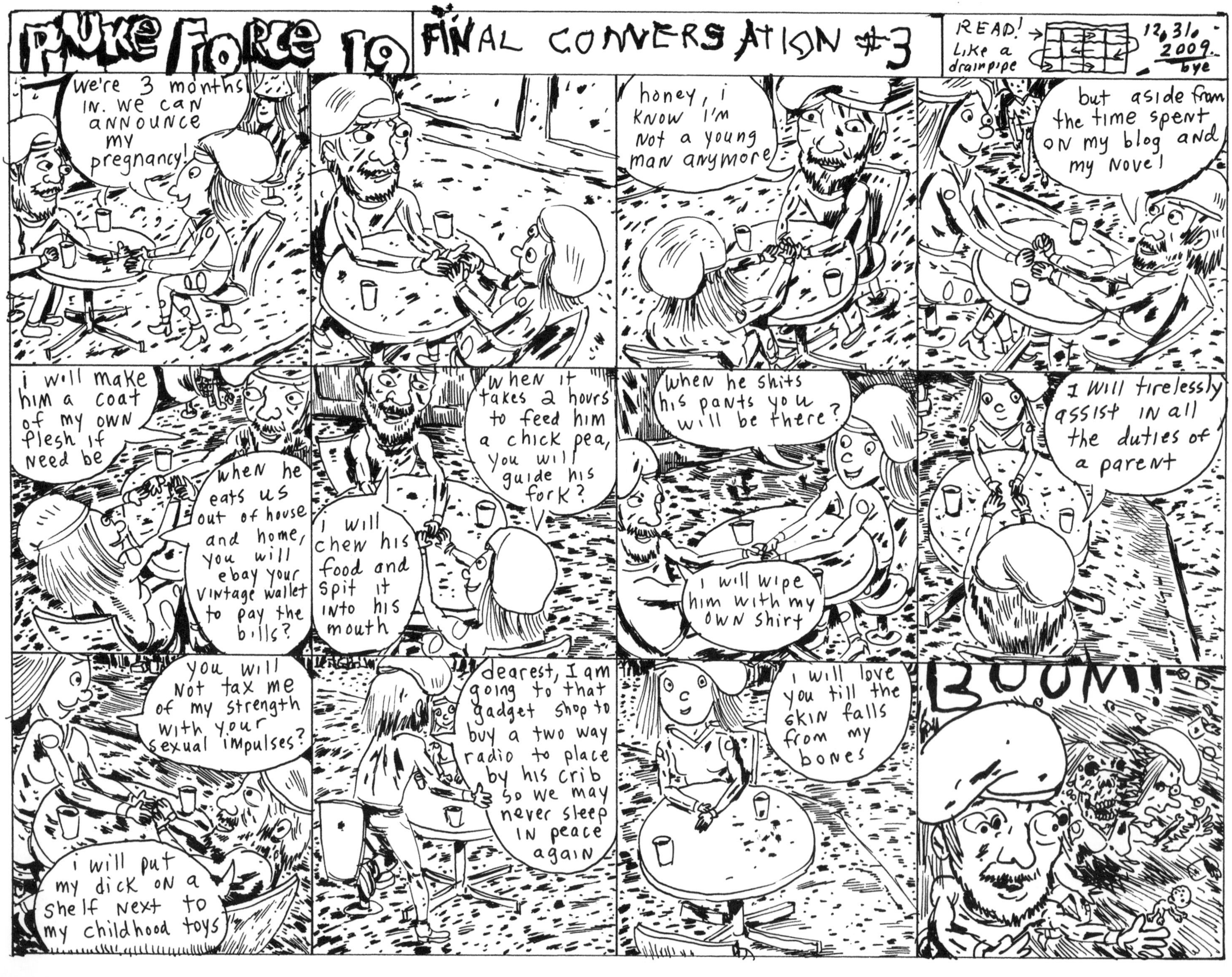
PUKE FORCE 19
FINAL CONVERSATION #3
READ! Like a drainpipe
12, 31, 2009. bye
we're 3 months in. we can announce my pregnancy!
honey, i know i'm not a young man anymore
but aside from the time spent on my blog and my novel
I will tirelessly assist in all the duties of a parent
when he shits his pants you will be there?
i will wipe him with my own shirt
when it takes 2 hours to feed him a chick pea, you will guide his fork?
i will chew his food and spit it into his mouth
when he eats us out of house and home, you will ebay your vintage wallet to pay the bills?
i will make him a coat of my own flesh if need be
you will not tax me of my strength with your sexual impulses?
i will put my dick on a shelf next to my childhood toys
dearest, I am going to that gadget shop to buy a two way radio to place by his crib so we may never sleep in peace again
i will love you till the skin falls from my bones
BOOM!

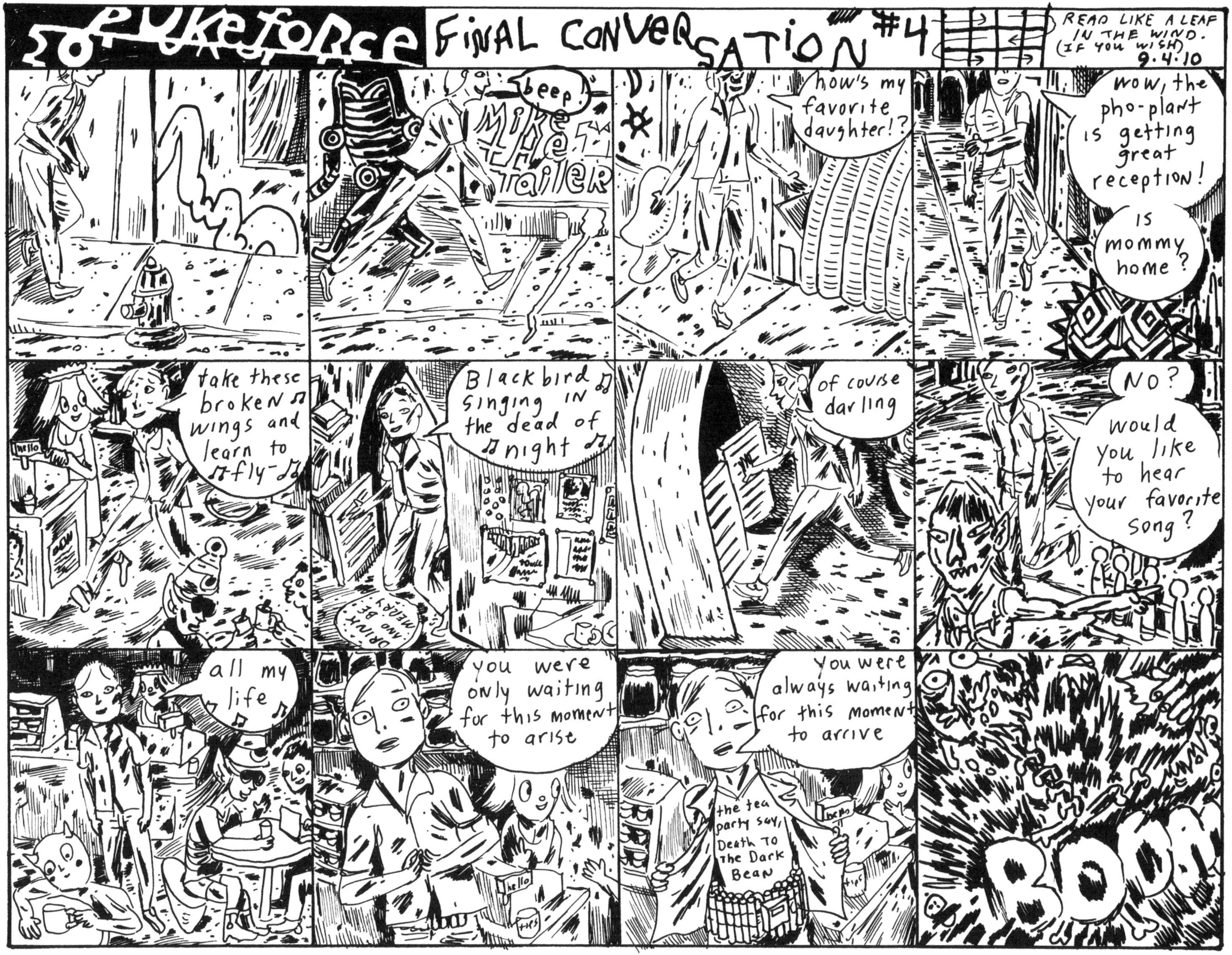
Pukeforce
Final Conversation #4
Read like a leaf in the wind. (if you wish)
9.4.10
beep!
Mike the Tailer
how's my favorite daughter!?
wow, the pho-plant is getting great reception!
is mommy home?
NO?
would you like to hear your favorite song?
of course darling
Blackbird singing in the dead of night
take these broken wings and learn to fly
hello
Drink and be merry
all my life
you were only waiting for this moment to arise
hello
tips
you were always waiting for this moment to arrive
the tea party say, Death to the Dark Bean
tips
BOOM

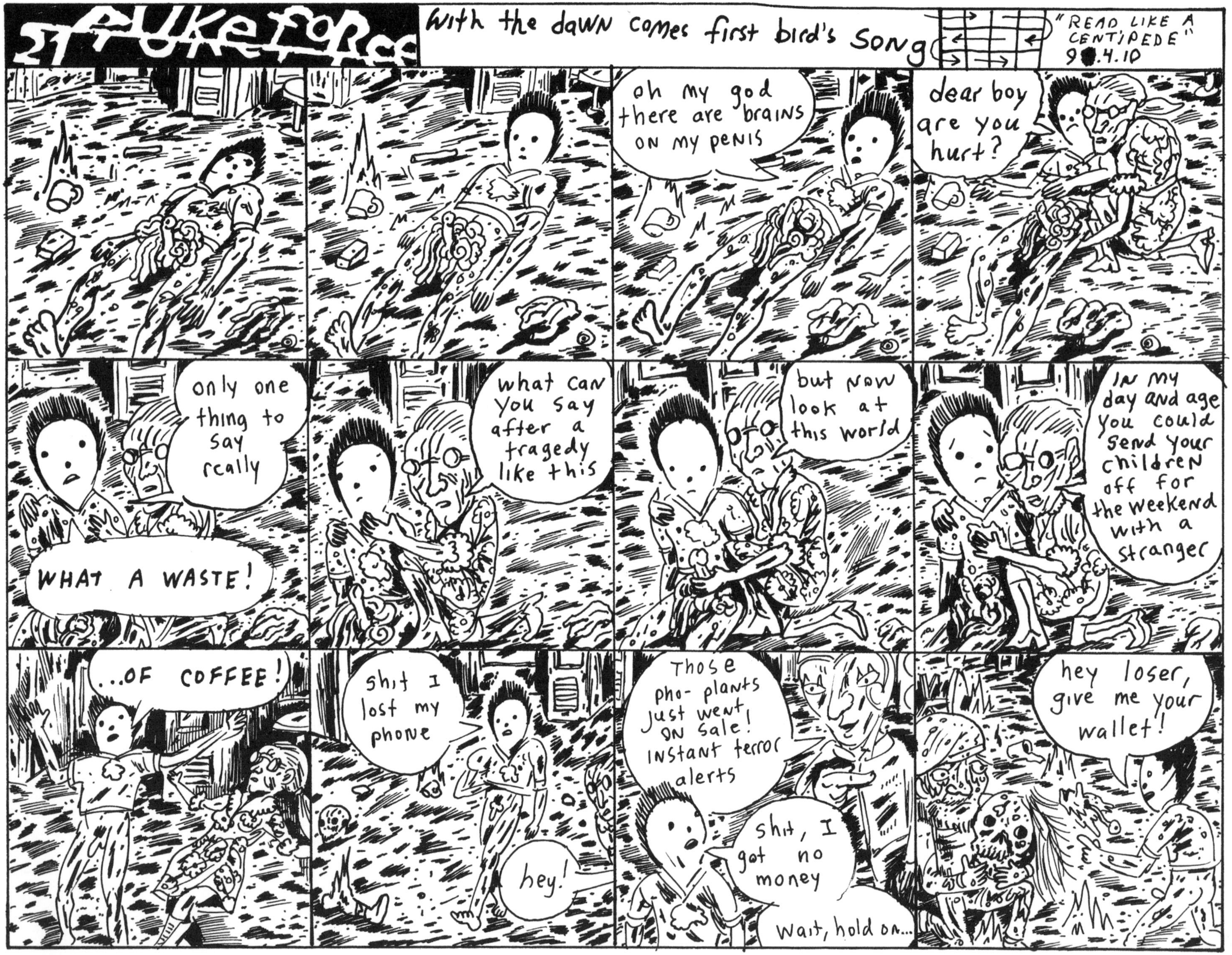
27
PUKE FORCE
With the dawn comes first bird's song
"READ LIKE A CENTIPEDE"
9.4.10
oh my god there are brains on my penis
dear boy are you hurt?
In my day and age you could send your children off for the weekend with a stranger
but now look at this world
what can you say after a tragedy like this
only one thing to say really
WHAT A WASTE!
...OF COFFEE!
shit I lost my phone
hey!
Those pho-plants just went on sale! INSTANT terror alerts
shit, I got no money
wait, hold on...
hey loser, give me your wallet!

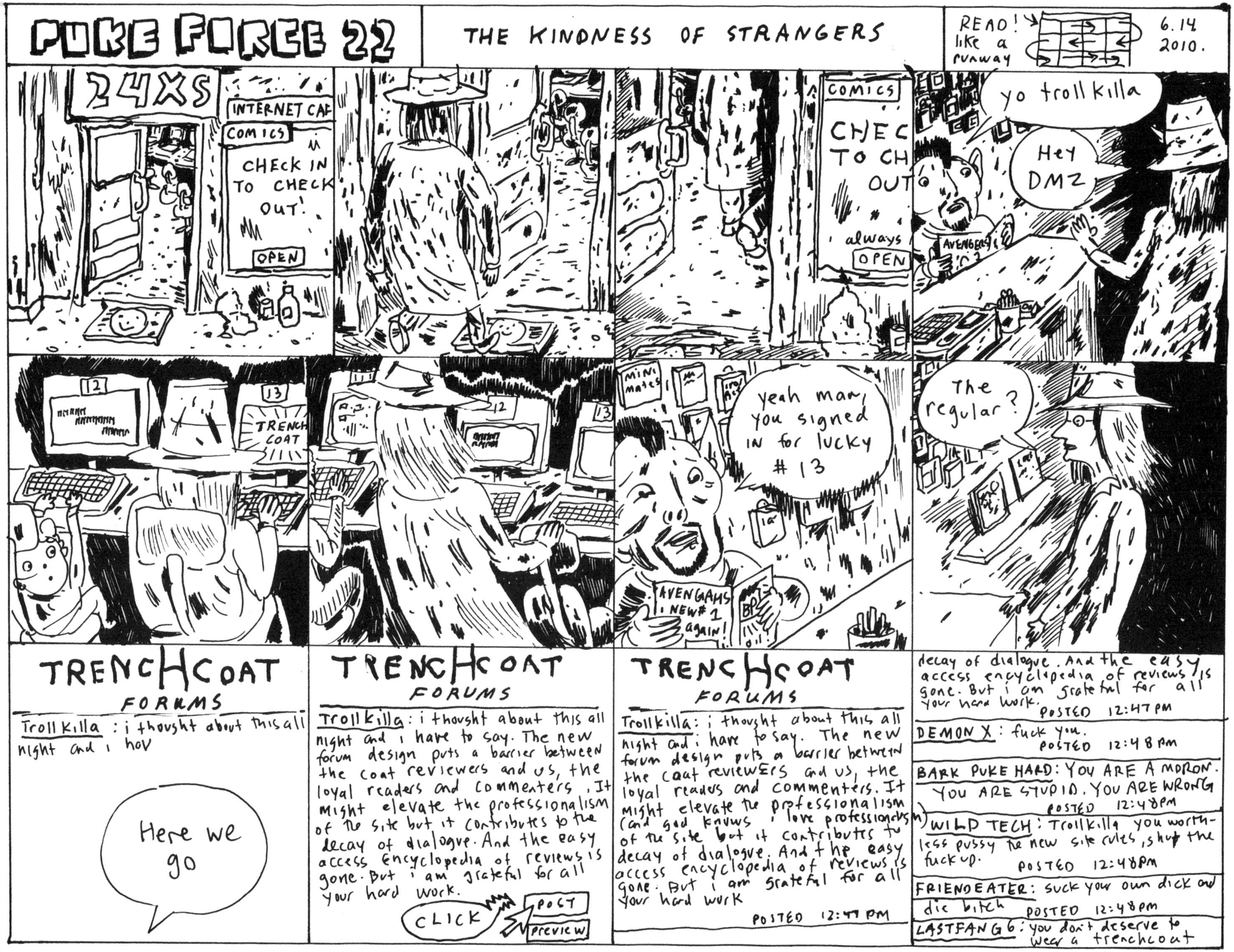
PUKE FORCE 22
THE KINDNESS OF STRANGERS
READ! like a runaway
6.14 2010.
24XS
INTERNET CAF
COMICS
CHECK IN TO CHECK OUT!
OPEN
COMICS
CHEC TO CH OUT
always OPEN
yo troll killa
Hey DMZ
AVENGERS
The regular?
yeah man you signed in for lucky #13
AVENGAMS NEW #1 again!
12
13
12
13
TRENCH COAT
TRENCHCOAT FORUMS
Trollkilla : i thought about this all night and i hav
Here we go
TRENCHCOAT FORUMS
Trollkilla: i thought about this all night and i have to say. The new forum design puts a barrier between the coat reviewers and us, the loyal readers and commenters. It might elevate the professionalism of the site but it contributes to the decay of dialogue. And the easy access encyclopedia of reviews is gone. But i am grateful for all your hard work.
CLICK
POST
PREVIEW
TRENCHCOAT FORUMS
Trollkilla: i thought about this all night and i have to say. The new forum design puts a barrier between the coat reviewers and us, the loyal readers and commenters. It might elevate the professionalism (and god knows i love professionalism) of the site but it contributes to decay of dialogue. And the easy access encyclopedia of reviews is gone. But i am grateful for all your hard work
POSTED 12:47 PM
decay of dialogue. And the easy access encyclopedia of reviews is gone. But i am grateful for all your hard work. POSTED 12:47 PM
DEMON X: fuck you. POSTED 12:48 PM
BARK PUKE HARD: YOU ARE A MORON. YOU ARE STUPID. YOU ARE WRONG POSTED 12:48 PM
WILD TECH: Trollkilla you worthless pussy the new site rules, shut the fuck up. POSTED 12:48 PM
FRIENDEATER: suck your own dick and die bitch POSTED 12:48 PM
LASTFANG6: you don't deserve to wear a trenchcoat

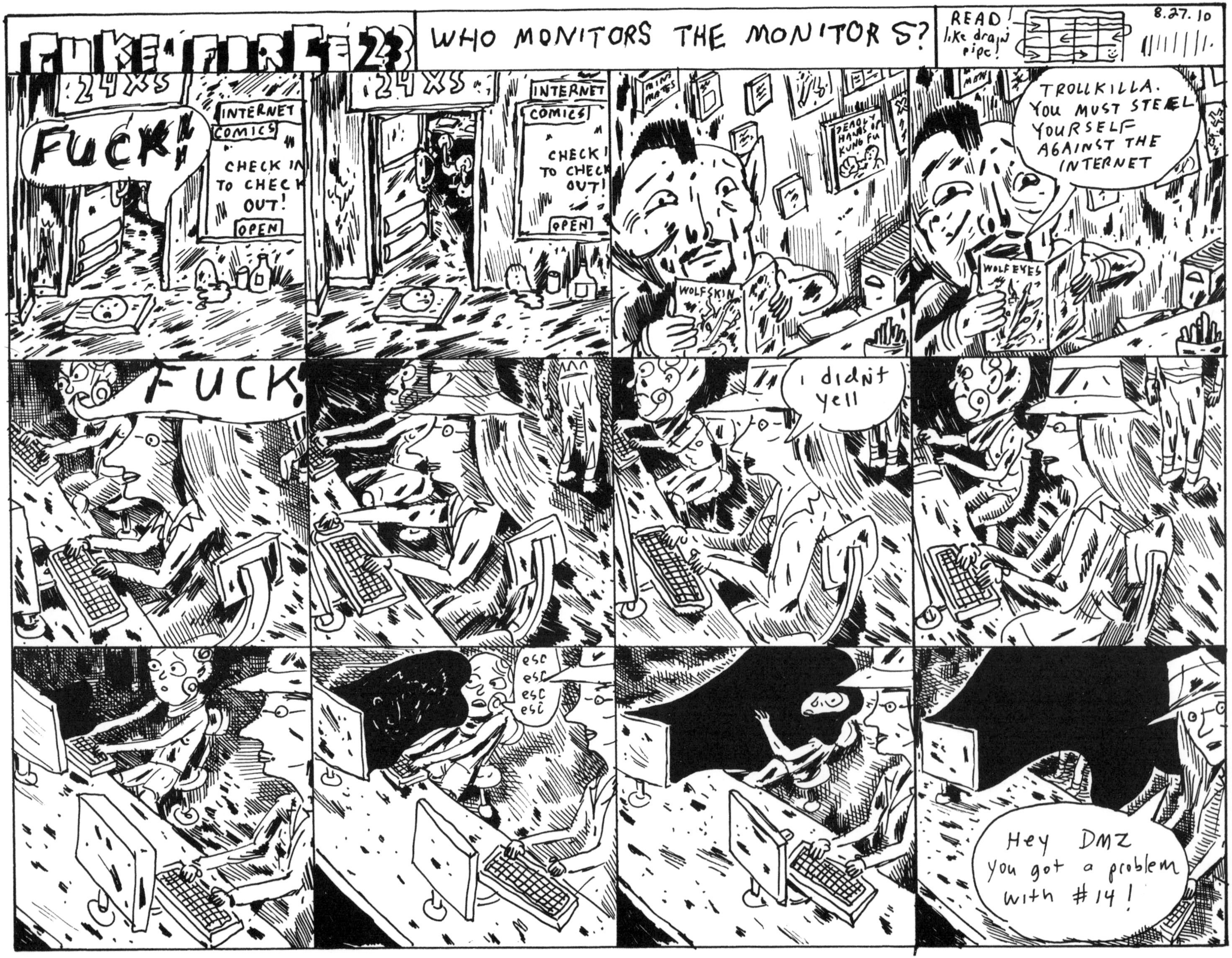

FUKE FORCE 23
WHO MONITORS THE MONITORS?
READ! like drain pipe!
8.27.10
24XS
FUCK!
INTERNET
COMICS
CHECK IN TO CHECK OUT!
OPEN
24XS
INTERNET
COMICS
CHECK IN TO CHECK OUT!
OPEN
MINI MATES
DEADLY HANDS OF KUNG FU
WOLFSKIN
WOLF EYES
TROLLKILLA. YOU MUST STEEL YOURSELF AGAINST THE INTERNET
i didnt yell
FUCK!
esc esc esc esc
Hey DMZ you got a problem with #14!

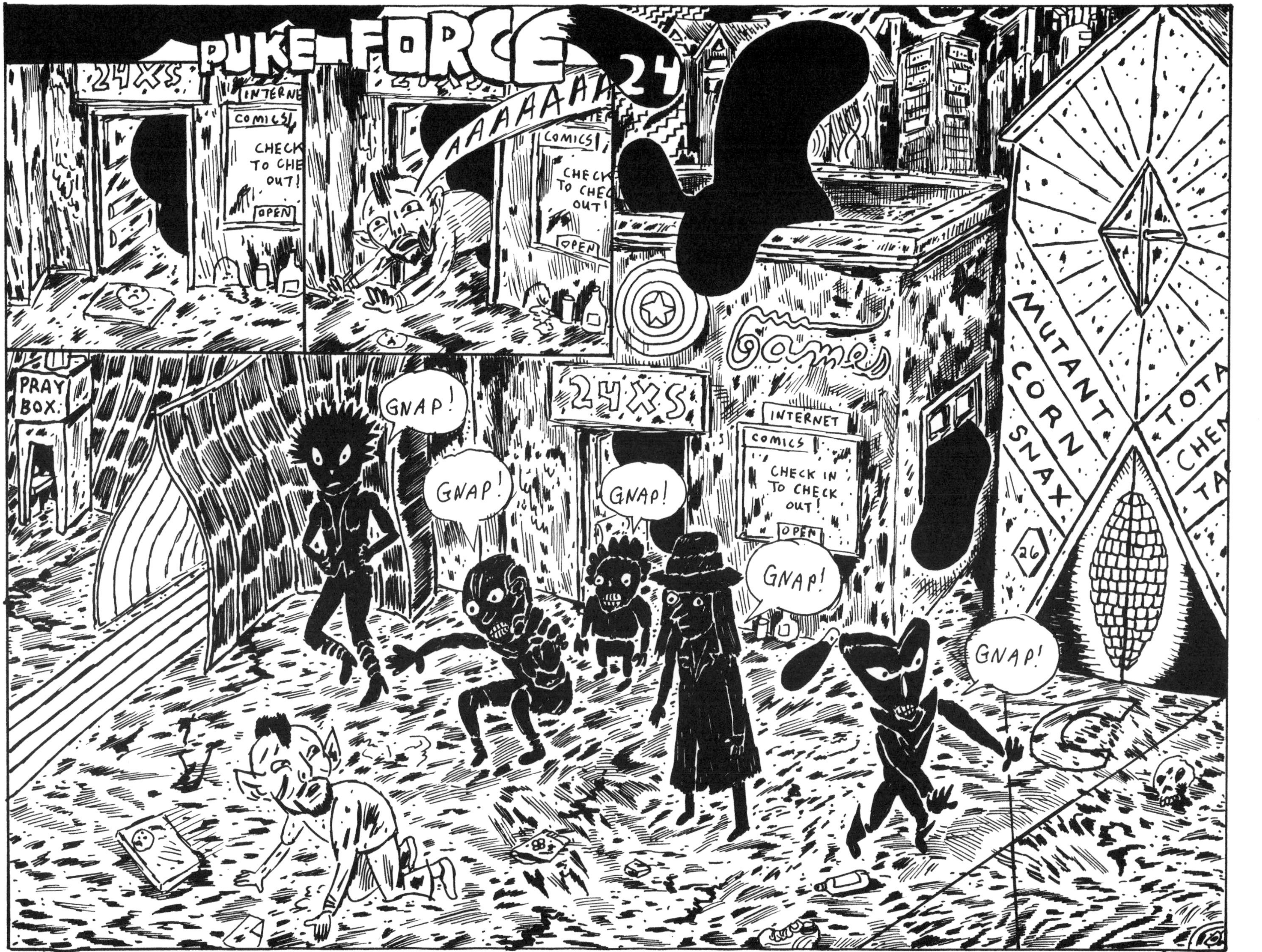
PUKE FORCE 24
24XS
INTERNET
COMICS
CHECK TO CHE OUT!
OPEN
AAAAAAAA
PRAY BOX
GNAP!
GNAP!
GNAP!
GNAP!
GNAP!
Games
24XS
INTERNET
COMICS
CHECK IN TO CHECK OUT!
OPEN
MUTANT CORN SNAX
26

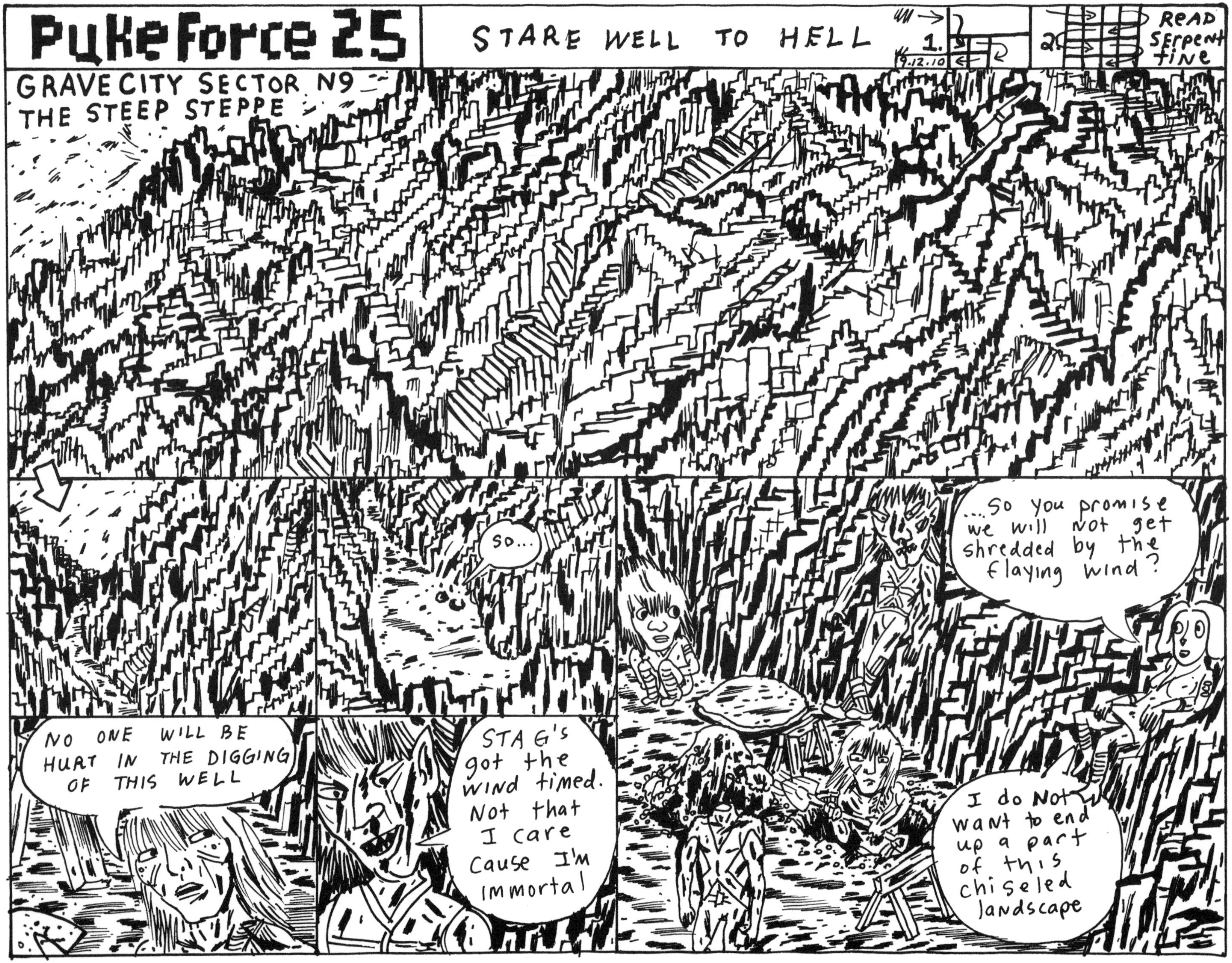
Puke Force 25
STARE WELL TO HELL
1.
2.
9.12.10
READ Serpentine
GRAVE CITY SECTOR N9
THE STEEP STEPPE
So...
...So you promise we will not get shredded by the flaying wind?
NO ONE WILL BE HURT IN THE DIGGING OF THIS WELL
STAG's got the wind timed. Not that I care cause I'm immortal
I do NOT want to end up a part of this chiseled landscape

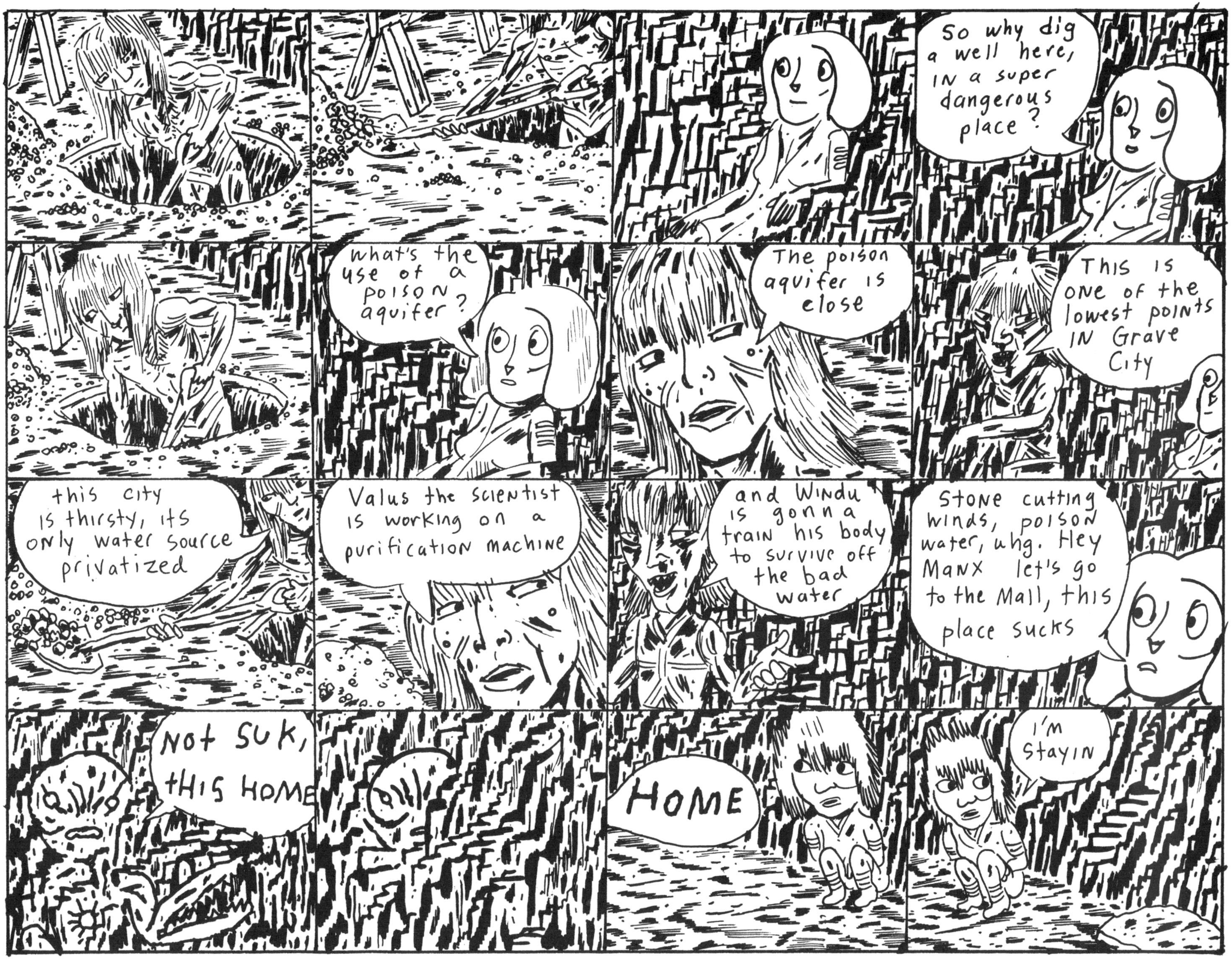
So why dig a well here, IN a super dangerous place?
what's the use of a poison aquifer?
The poison aquifer is close
This is one of the lowest points IN Grave City
this city is thirsty, its only water source privatized
Valus the scientist is working on a purification machine
and Windu is gonna train his body to survive off the bad water
Stone cutting winds, poison water, uhg. Hey Manx let's go to the Mall, this place sucks
Not SUK, tHIS HOME
HOME
I'm Stayin

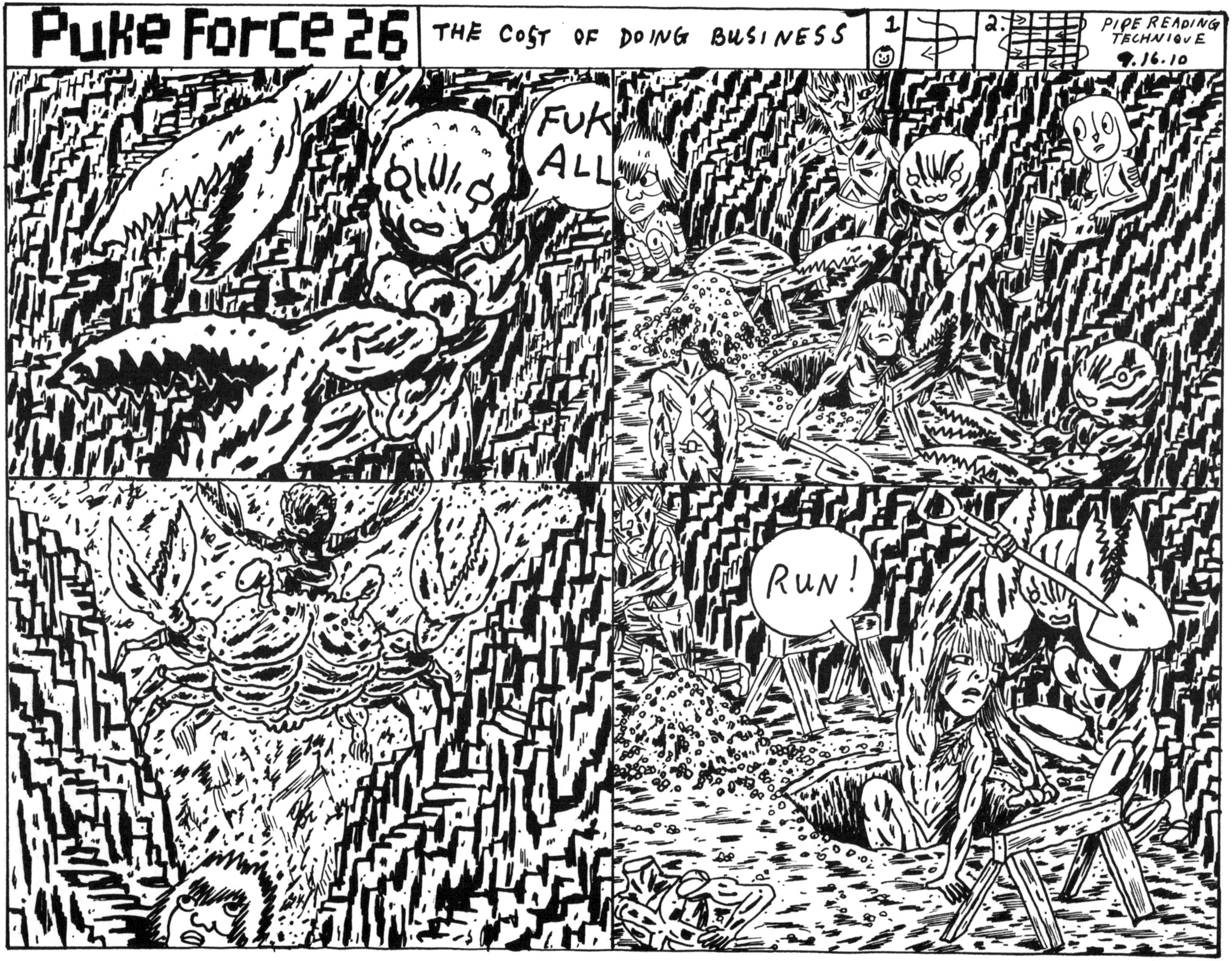
Puke Force 26
THE COST OF DOING BUSINESS
1
2.
PIPE READING TECHNIQUE
9.16.10
FUK ALL
RUN!

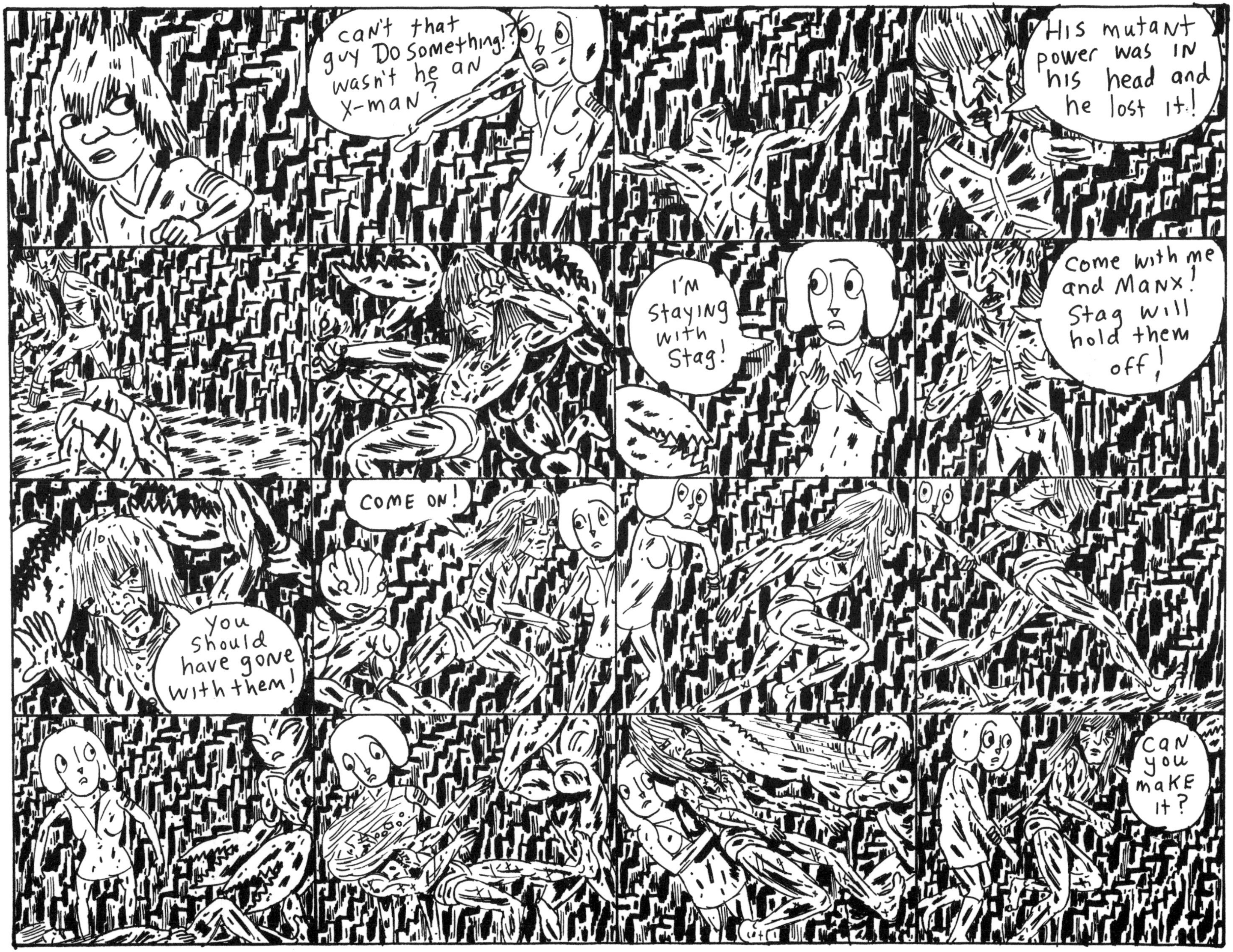

can't that guy Do something!? wasn't he an X-man?
His mutant power was IN his head and he lost it!
I'M Staying with Stag!
Come with me and Manx! Stag will hold them off!
You should have gone with them!
COME ON!
Can you make it?

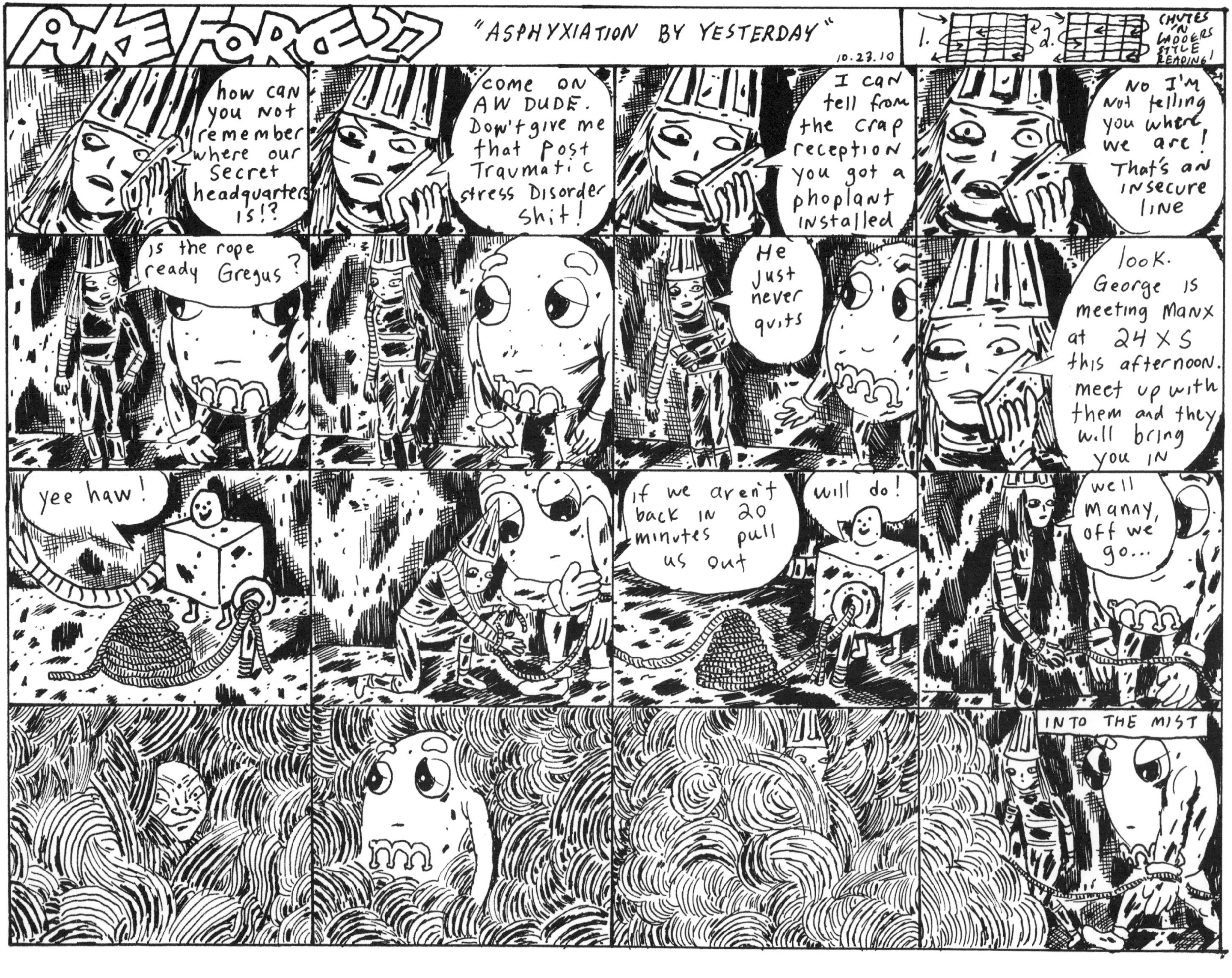
PUKE FORCE
"ASPHYXIATION BY YESTERDAY"
10.23.10
1.
2.
CHUTES 'N LADDERS STYLE READING!
how can you not remember where our secret headquarters is!?
come on AW DUDE. Don't give me that Post Traumatic stress Disorder shit!
I can tell from the crap reception you got a phoplant installed
No I'm not telling you where we are! That's an insecure line
look. George is meeting Manx at 24 X S this afternoon. meet up with them and they will bring you in
He just never quits
is the rope ready Gregus?
yee haw!
if we aren't back in 20 minutes pull us out
will do!
well Manny, off we go...
INTO THE MIST

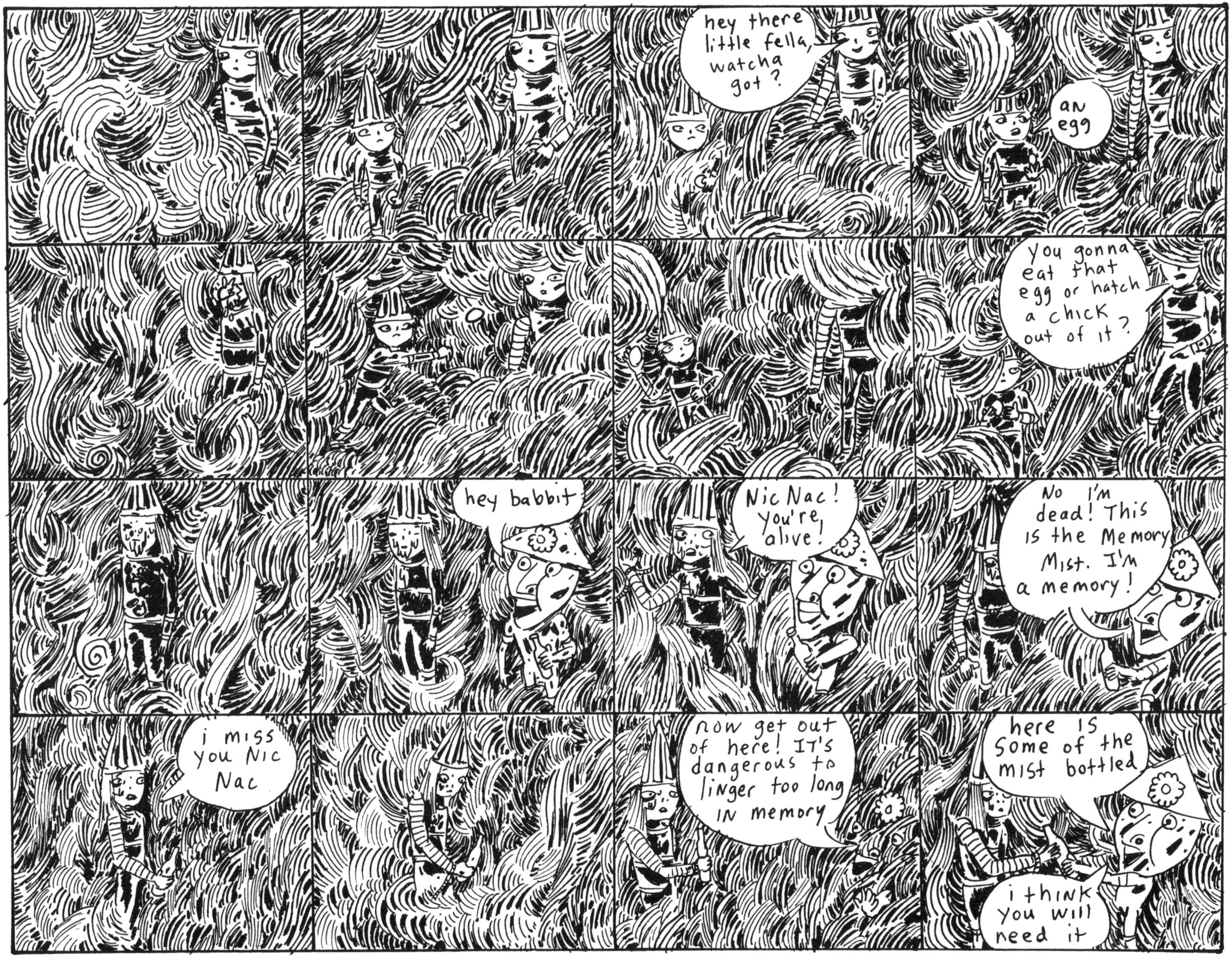
hey there little fella, watcha got?
an egg
you gonna eat that egg or hatch a chick out of it?
hey babbit
Nic Nac! you're alive!
No I'm dead! This is the Memory Mist. I'm a memory!
i miss you Nic Nac
now get out of here! IT'S dangerous to linger too long IN memory
here IS some of the mist bottled
i think you will need it

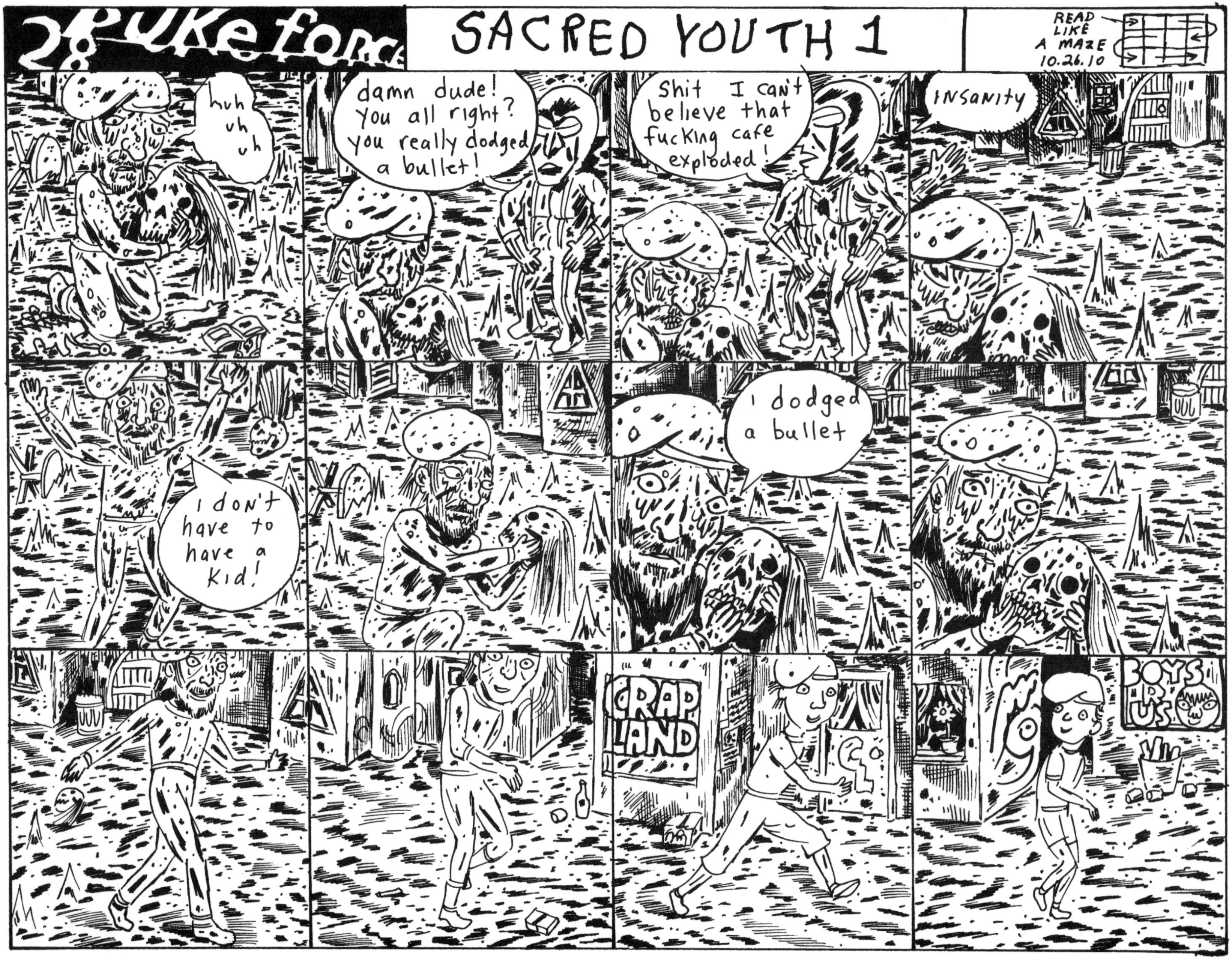
Puke Force
SACRED YOUTH 1
READ LIKE A MAZE 10.26.10
huh uh uh
damn dude! You all right? you really dodged a bullet!
Shit I can't believe that fucking cafe exploded!
INSANITY
I dodged a bullet
I don't have to have a kid!
CRAP LAND
BOYS R US

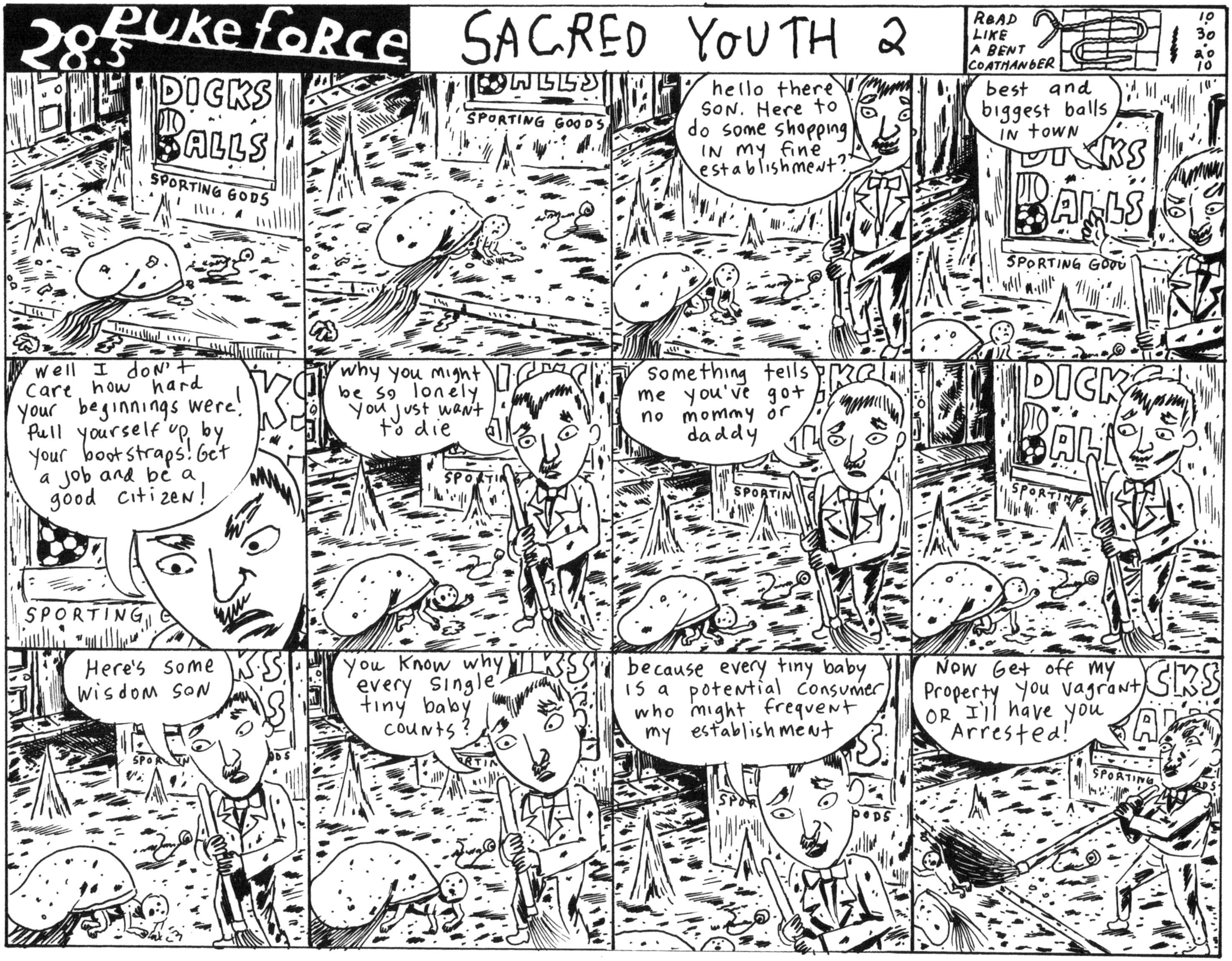
28.5 Puke Force
SACRED YOUTH 2
READ LIKE A BENT COATHANGER
10 30 20 10
DICKS BALLS
SPORTING GODS
SPORTING GOODS
hello there SON. Here to do some shopping IN my fine establishment?
best and biggest balls IN TOWN
DICKS BALLS
SPORTING GOOD
SOMething tells me you've got no mommy or daddy
why you might be so lonely you just want to die
well I don't care how hard your beginnings were! Pull yourself up by your bootstraps! Get a job and be a good citiZEN!
SPORTING
Here's some wisdom SON
You Know why every Single tiny baby counts?
because every tiny baby is a potential consumer who might frequent my establishment
Now Get off my Property you vagrant OR I'll have you Arrested!
SPORTING

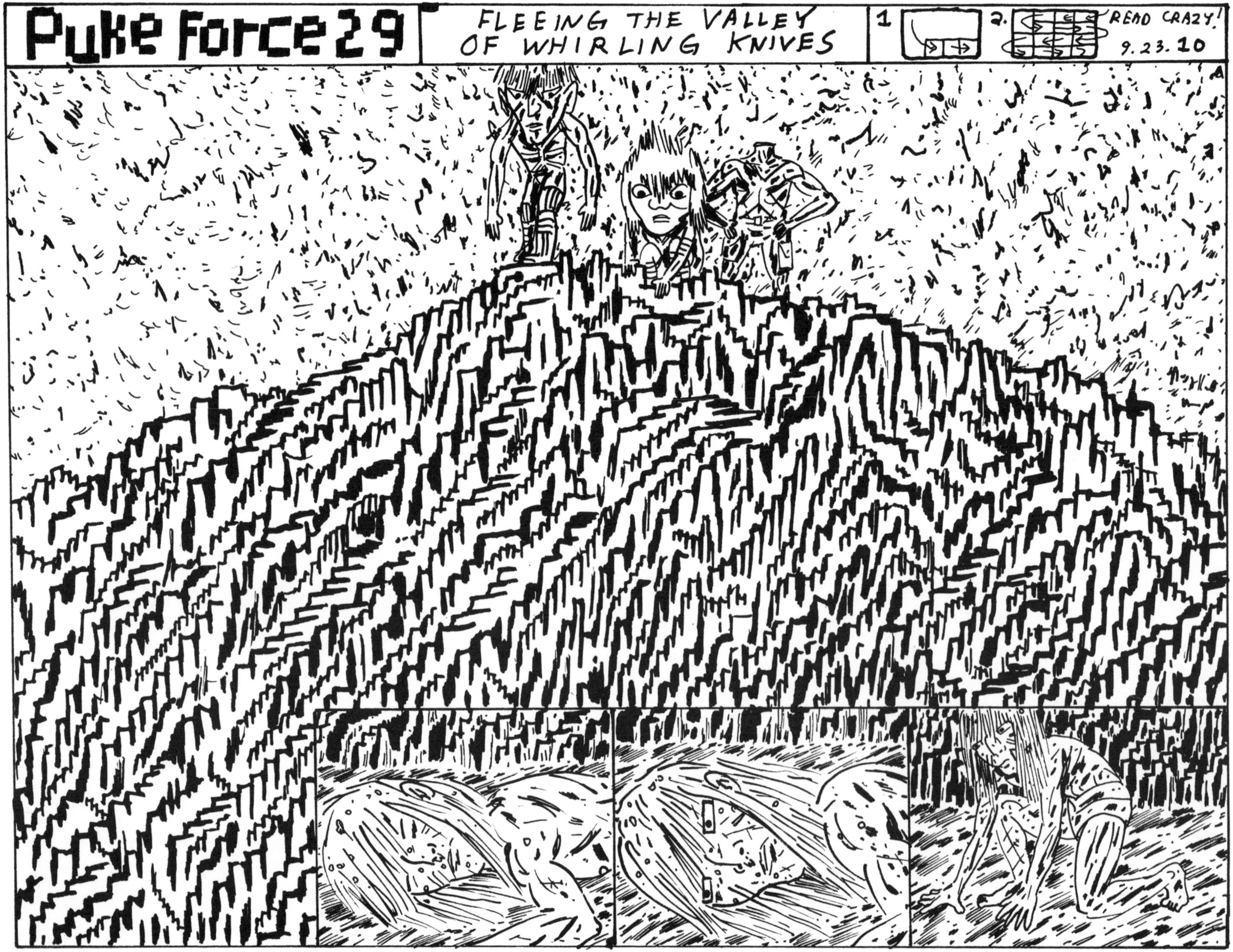

Puke Force 29
FLEEING THE VALLEY OF WHIRLING KNIVES
1
2.
READ CRAZY!
9.23.10

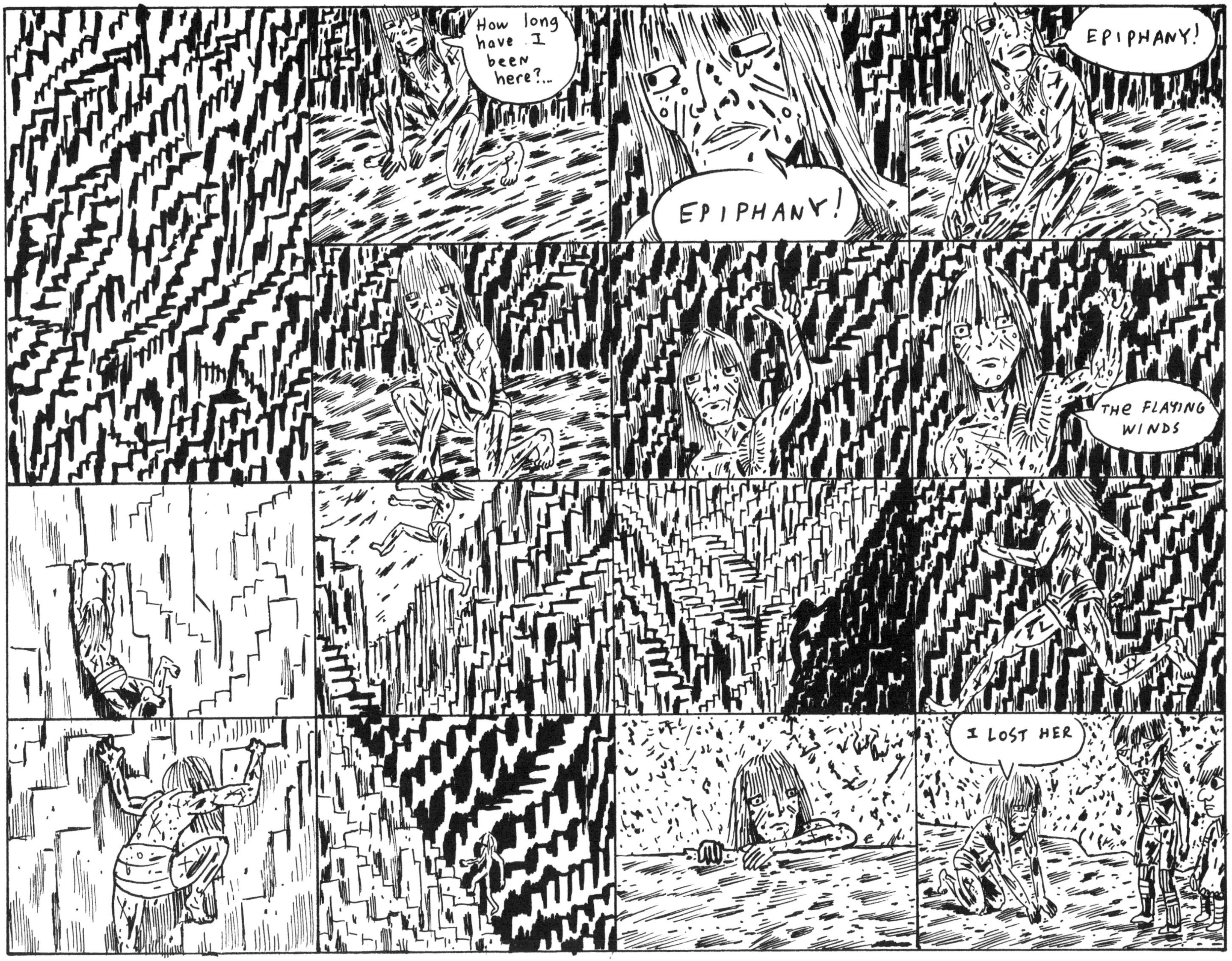
How long have I been here?...
EPIPHANY!
EPIPHANY!
THE FLAYING WINDS
I LOST HER

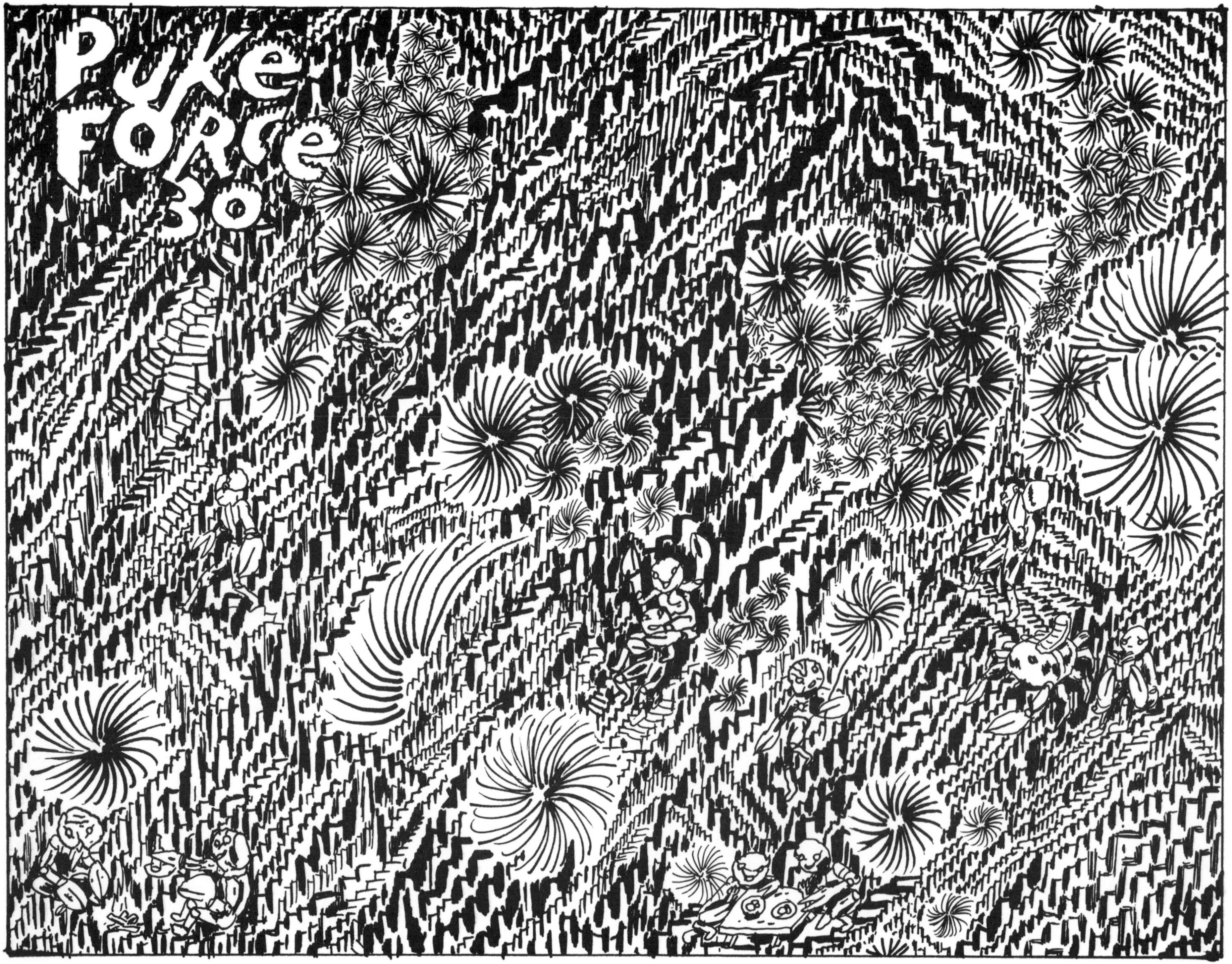
PUKE
FORCE
30

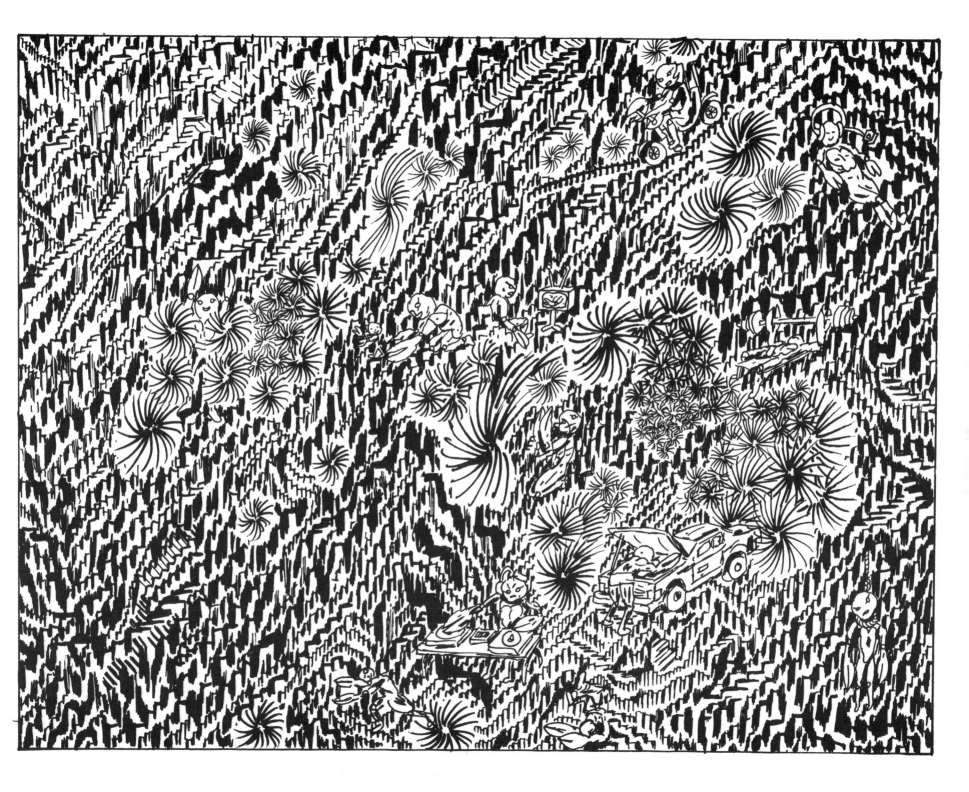

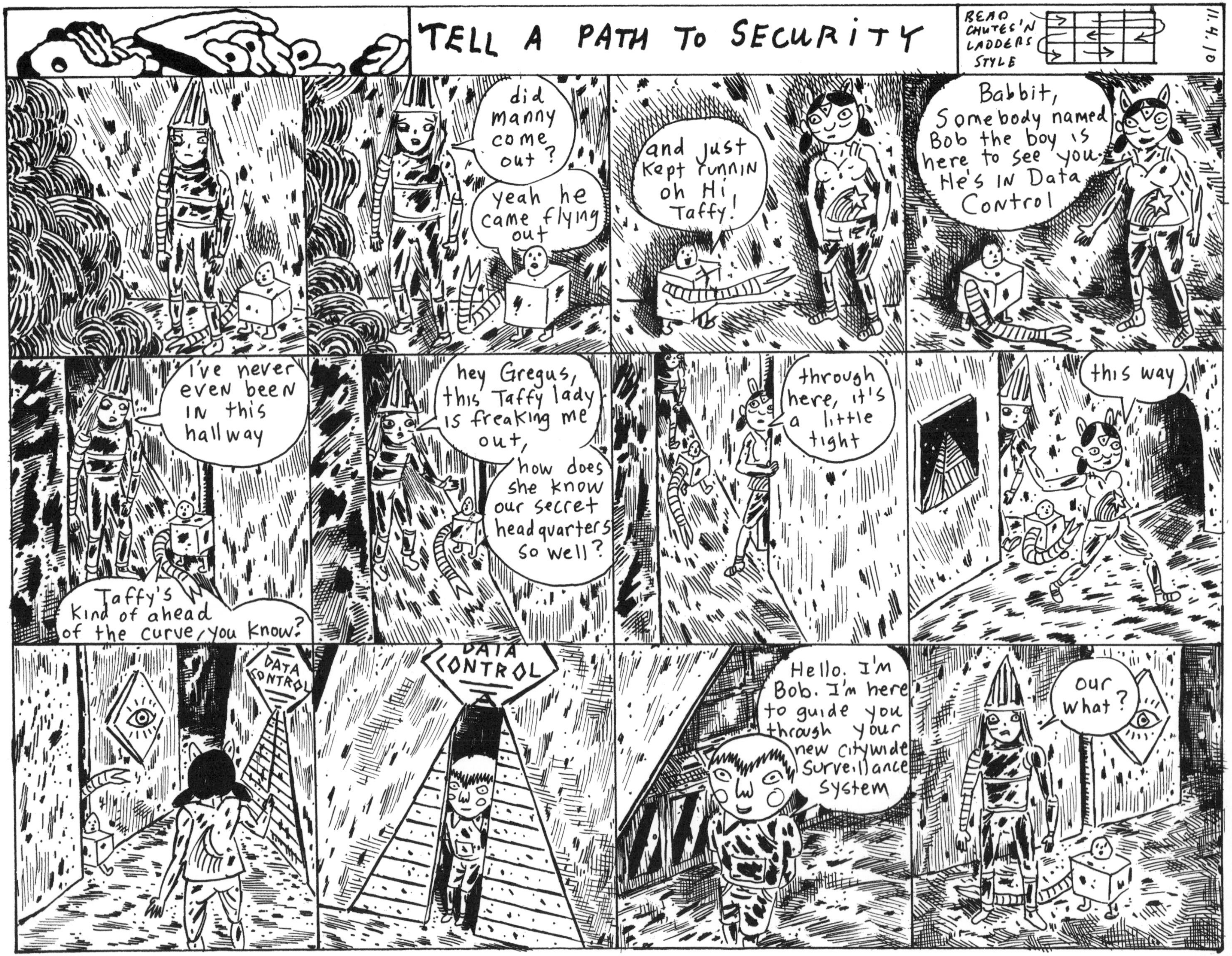
TELL A PATH TO SECURITY
READ CHUTES'N LADDERS STYLE
11.4.10
did manny come out?
yeah he came flying out
and just kept runnin oh Hi Taffy!
Babbit, Somebody named Bob the boy is here to see you. He's in Data Control
this way
through here, it's a little tight
hey Gregus, this Taffy lady is freaking me out,
how does she know our secret headquarters so well?
I've never even been in this hallway
Taffy's kind of ahead of the curve, you know?
DATA CONTROL
DATA CONTROL
Hello. I'm Bob. I'm here to guide you through your new citywide surveillance system
our what?

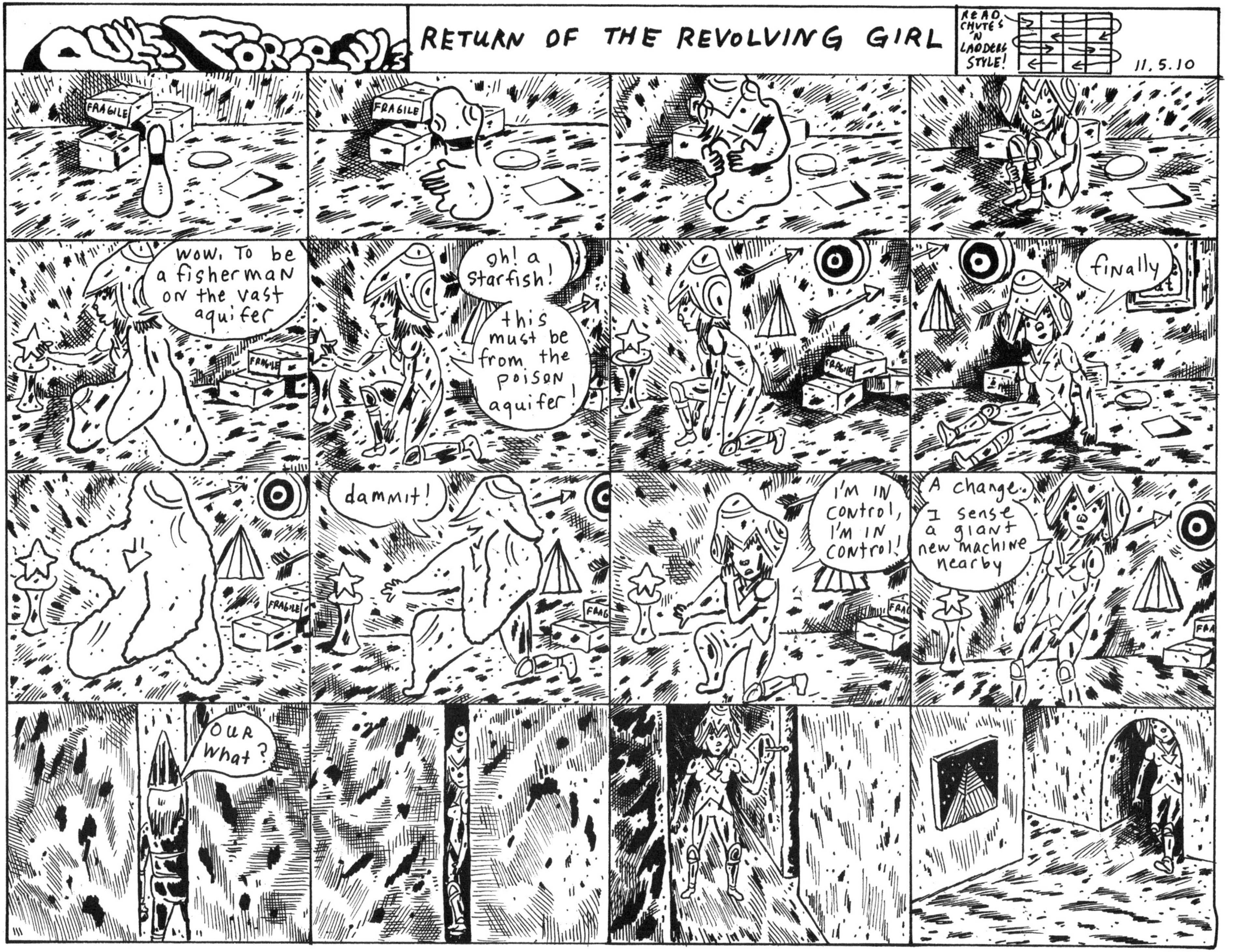
RETURN OF THE REVOLVING GIRL
READ CHUTES 'N LADDERS STYLE!
11.5.10
FRAGILE
FRAGILE
finally
oh! a starfish!
this must be from the poison aquifer!
WOW, TO be a fisherMAN on the vast aquifer
FRAGILE
FRAGILE
dammit!
I'M IN CONTROL, I'M IN CONTROL!
A change.. I sense a giant new machine nearby
OUR What?

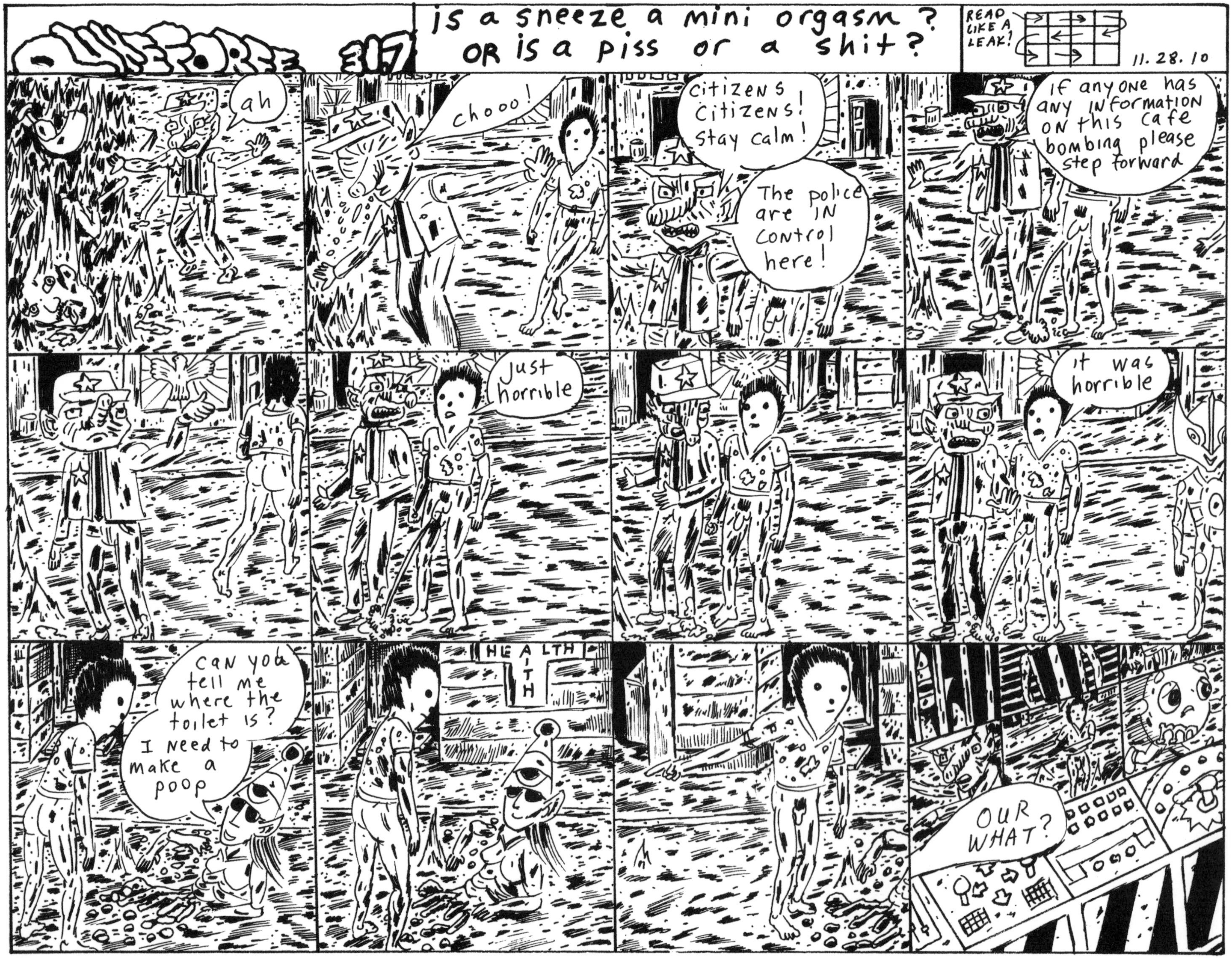
317
is a sneeze a mini orgasm? OR is a piss or a shit?
READ LIKE A LEAK!
11. 28. 10
ah
Chooo!
Citizens Citizens! Stay calm!
The police are IN control here!
If anyone has any information on this cafe bombing please step forward
Just horrible
It was horrible
Can you tell me where the toilet is? I need to make a poop
HEALTH
OUR WHAT?

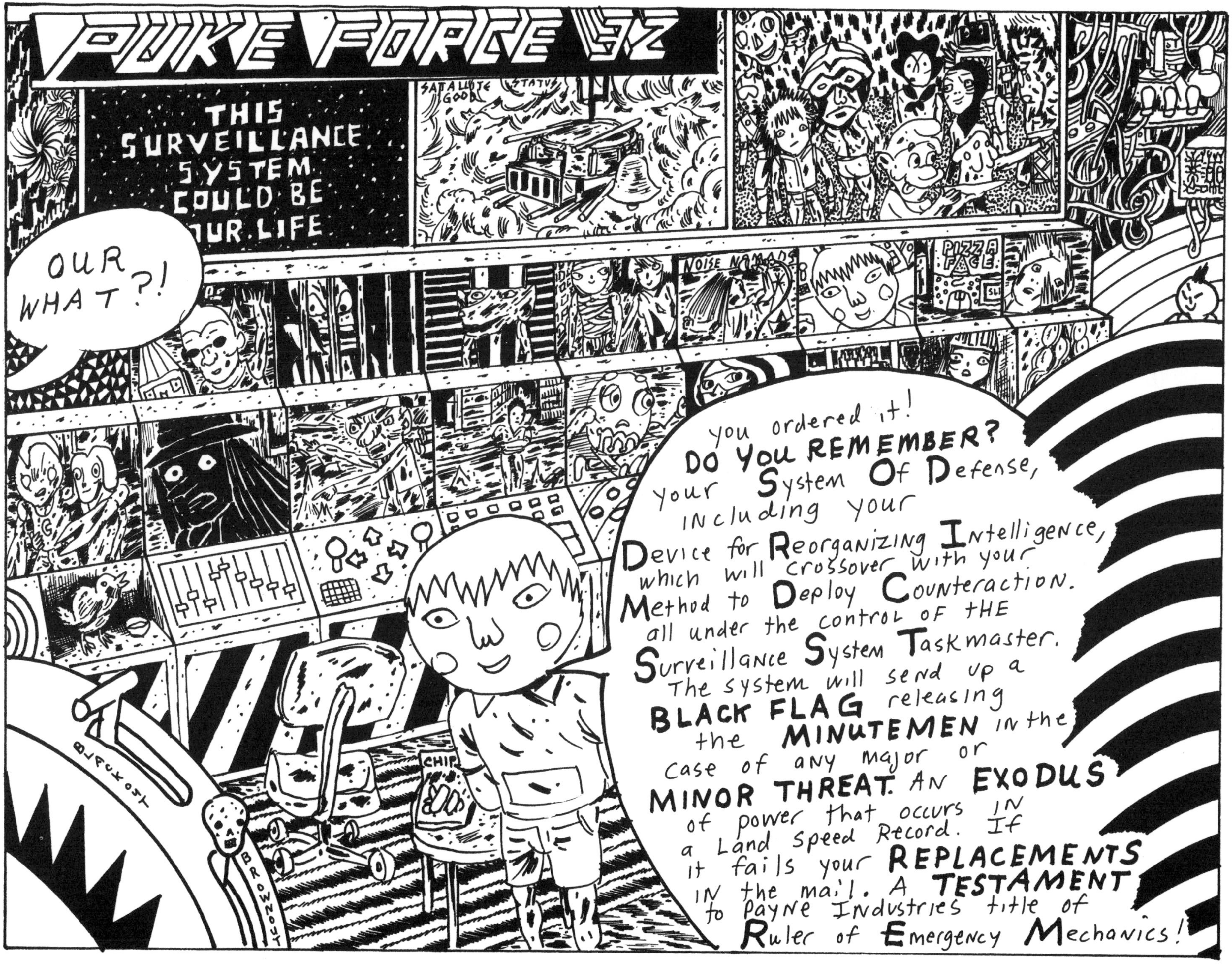
PUKE FORCE 92
THIS SURVEILLANCE SYSTEM COULD BE OUR LIFE
OUR WHAT?!
PIZZA FACE
you ordered it! DO YOU REMEMBER? your System Of Defense, including your Device for Reorganizing Intelligence, which will crossover with your Method to Deploy Counteraction. all under the control of the Surveillance System Taskmaster. The system will send up a BLACK FLAG releasing the MINUTEMEN in the case of any major or MINOR THREAT. AN EXODUS of power that occurs IN a Land Speed Record. If it fails your REPLACEMENTS IN the mail. A TESTAMENT to Payne Industries title of Ruler of Emergency Mechanics!
CHIP
BROWNOUT

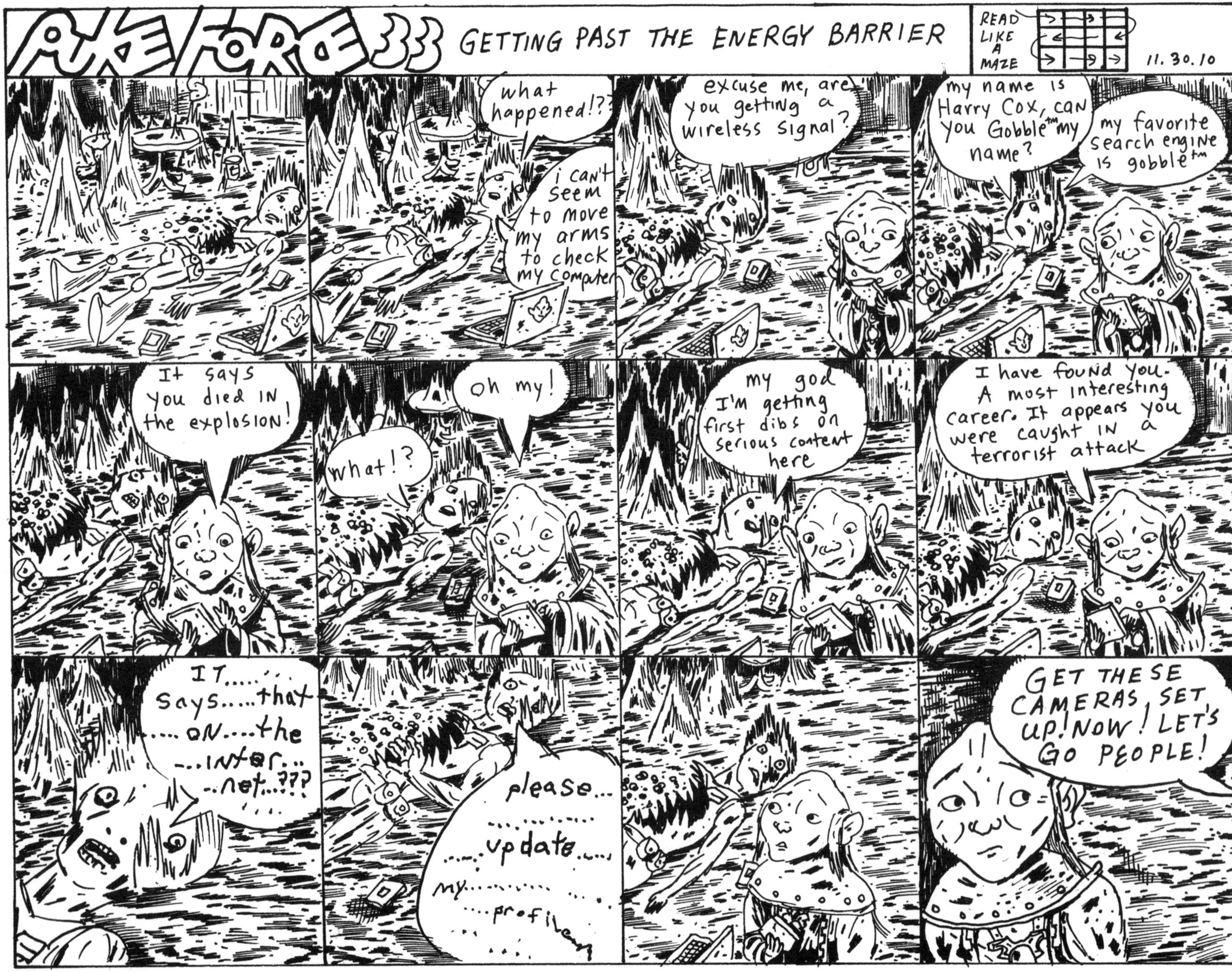
PUKE FORCE 333
GETTING PAST THE ENERGY BARRIER
READ LIKE A MAZE
11.30.10
what happened!??
i can't seem to move my arms to check my computer
excuse me, are you getting a wireless signal?
my name is Harry Cox, can you Gobble™ my name?
my favorite search engine is gobble™
I have found you. A most interesting career. It appears you were caught in a terrorist attack
my god I'm getting first dibs on serious content here
oh my!
what!?
It says you died in the explosion!
IT...... says.....that ....ON....the ...inter... ..net...???
please... .... update..... my........ ....profile...
GET THESE CAMERAS SET UP! NOW! LET'S GO PEOPLE!

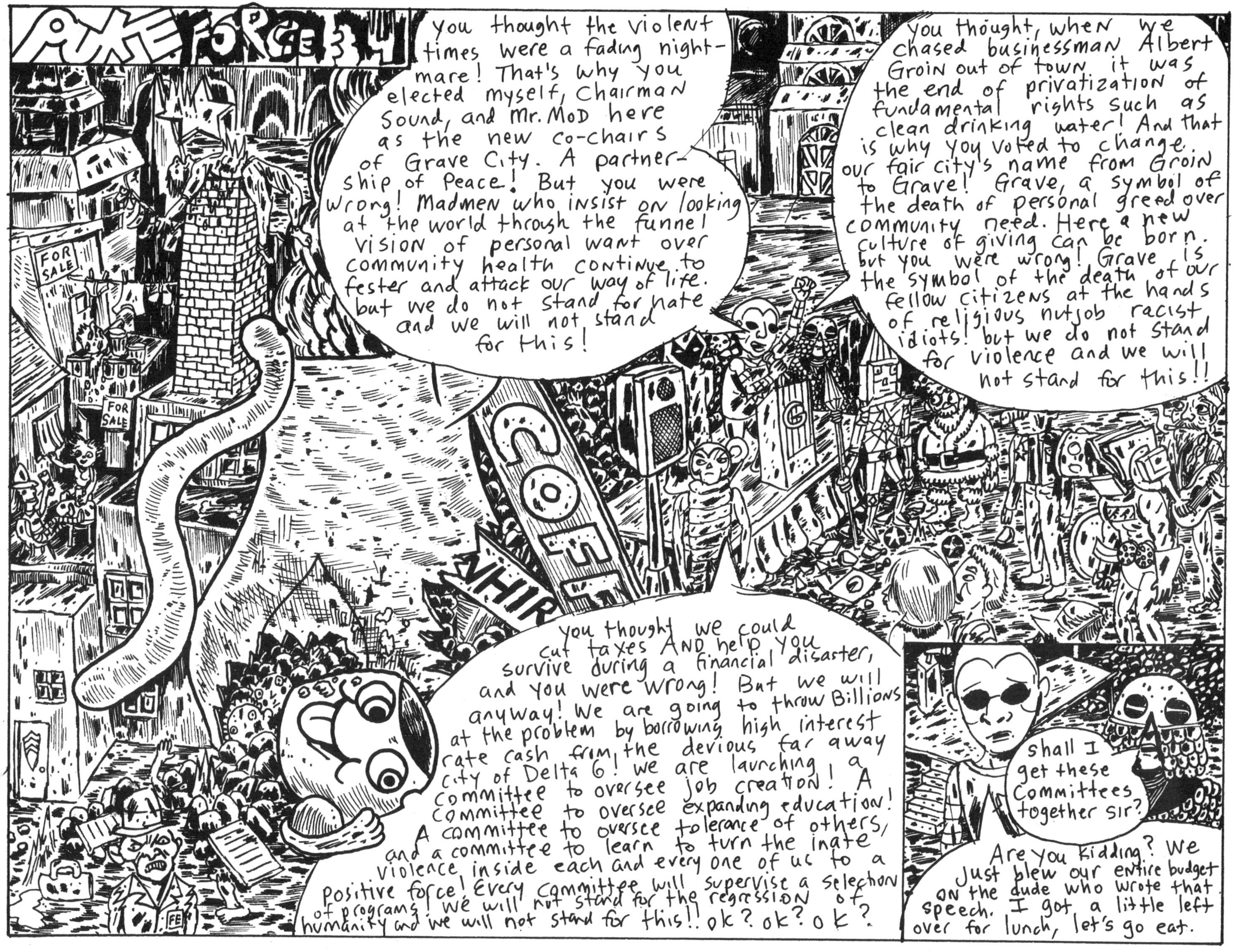
PUKE FORCE 34
you thought the violent times were a fading nightmare! That's why you elected myself, Chairman Sound, and Mr. MoD here as the new co-chairs of Grave City. A partnership of Peace! But you were wrong! Madmen who insist on looking at the world through the funnel vision of personal want over community health continue to fester and attack our way of life. but we do not stand for hate and we will not stand for this!
You thought, when we chased businessman Albert Groin out of town it was the end of privatization of fundamental rights such as clean drinking water! And that is why you voted to change our fair city's name from Groin to Grave! Grave, a symbol of the death of personal greed over community need. Here a new culture of giving can be born. but you were wrong! Grave is the symbol of the death of our fellow citizens at the hands of religious nutjob racist idiots! but we do not stand for violence and we will not stand for this!!
FOR SALE
FOR SALE
you thought we could cut taxes AND help you survive during a financial disaster, and you were wrong! But we will anyway! We are going to throw Billions at the problem by borrowing high interest rate cash from the devious far away city of Delta 6! We are launching a committee to oversee job creation! A committee to oversee expanding education! A committee to oversee tolerance of others, and a committee to learn to turn the inate violence inside each and every one of us to a positive force! Every committee will supervise a selection of programs! We will not stand for the regression of humanity and we will not stand for this!! ok? ok? ok?
Shall I get these Committees together sir?
Are you kidding? We just blew our entire budget on the dude who wrote that speech. I got a little left over for lunch, let's go eat.

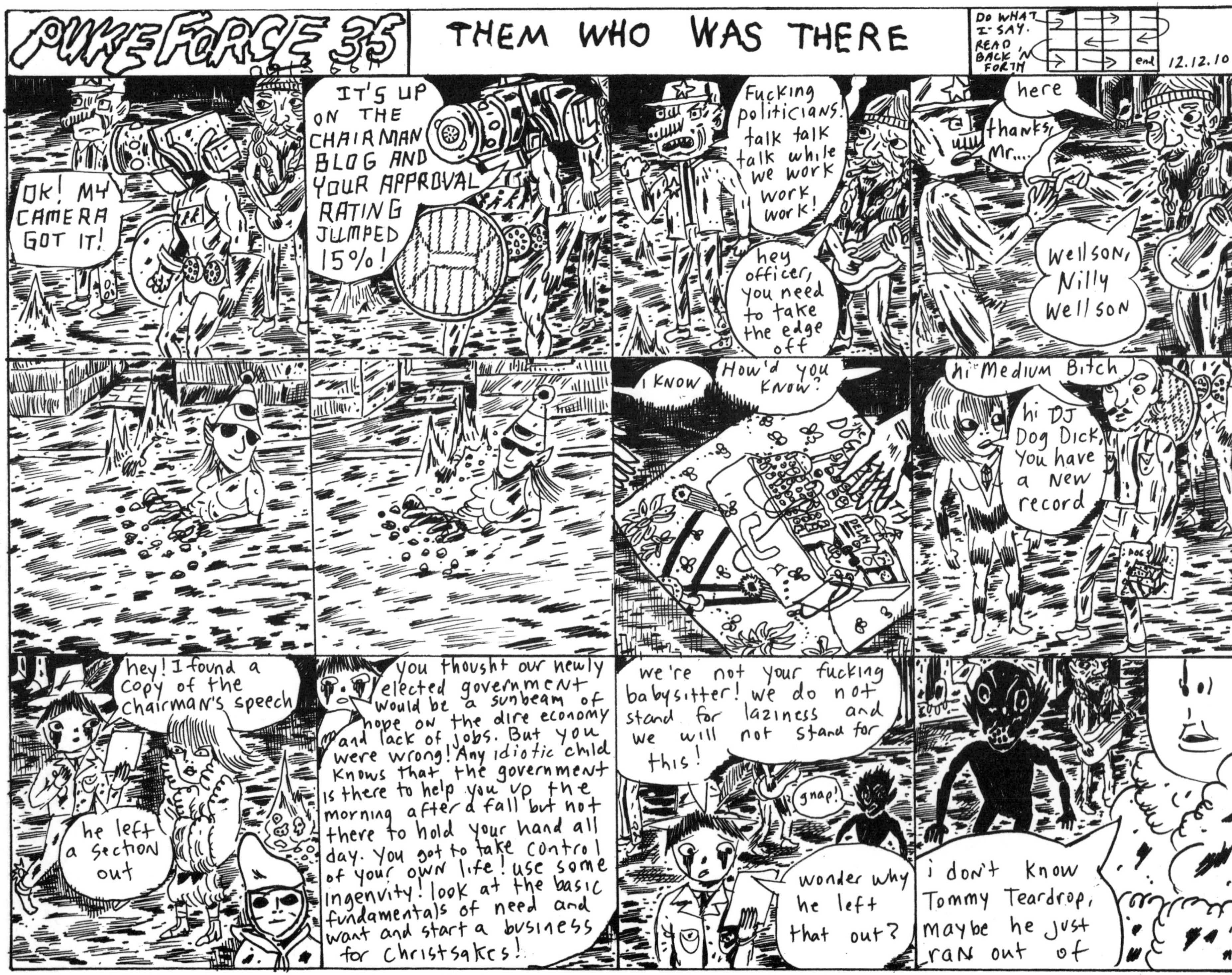
PUKE FORCE 35
THEM WHO WAS THERE
DO WHAT I SAY. READ BACK 'N FORTH
end
12.12.10
OK! MY CAMERA GOT IT!
IT'S UP ON THE CHAIRMAN BLOG AND YOUR APPROVAL RATING JUMPED 15%!
Fucking politicians! talk talk talk while we work work work!
hey officer, you need to take the edge off
here
thanks, Mr....
Wellson, Nilly Wellson
hi Medium Bitch
hi DJ Dog Dick, You have a New record
How'd you know?
i know
hey! I found a copy of the chairman's speech
he left a section out
you thought our newly elected government would be a sunbeam of hope on the dire economy and lack of jobs. But you were wrong! Any idiotic child knows that the government is there to help you up the morning after a fall but not there to hold your hand all day. You got to take control of your own life! use some ingenvity! look at the basic fundamentals of need and want and start a business for christsakes!
we're not your fucking babysitter! we do not stand for laziness and we will not stand for this!
gnap!
wonder why he left that out?
i don't know Tommy Teardrop, maybe he just ran out of

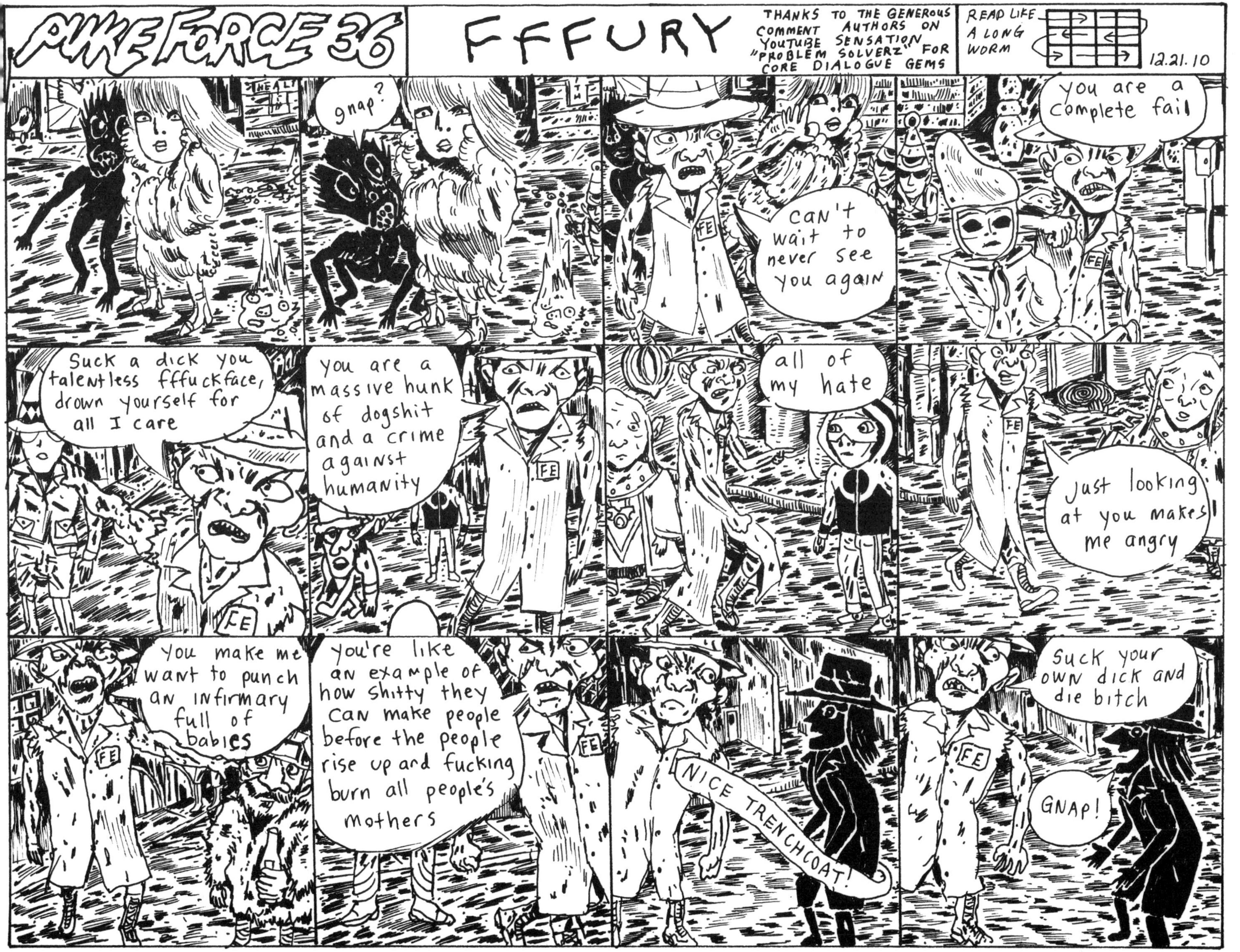
PUKE FORCE 36
FFFURY
THANKS TO THE GENEROUS COMMENT AUTHORS ON YOUTUBE SENSATION "PROBLEM SOLVERZ" FOR CORE DIALOGUE GEMS
READ LIKE A LONG WORM
12.21.10
gnap?
can't wait to never see you again
you are a complete fail
Just looking at you makes me angry
all of my hate
you are a massive hunk of dogshit and a crime against humanity
Suck a dick you talentless fffuckface, drown yourself for all I care
You make me want to punch an infirmary full of babies
you're like an example of how shitty they can make people before the people rise up and fucking burn all people's mothers
NICE TRENCHCOAT!
Suck your own dick and die bitch
GNAP!

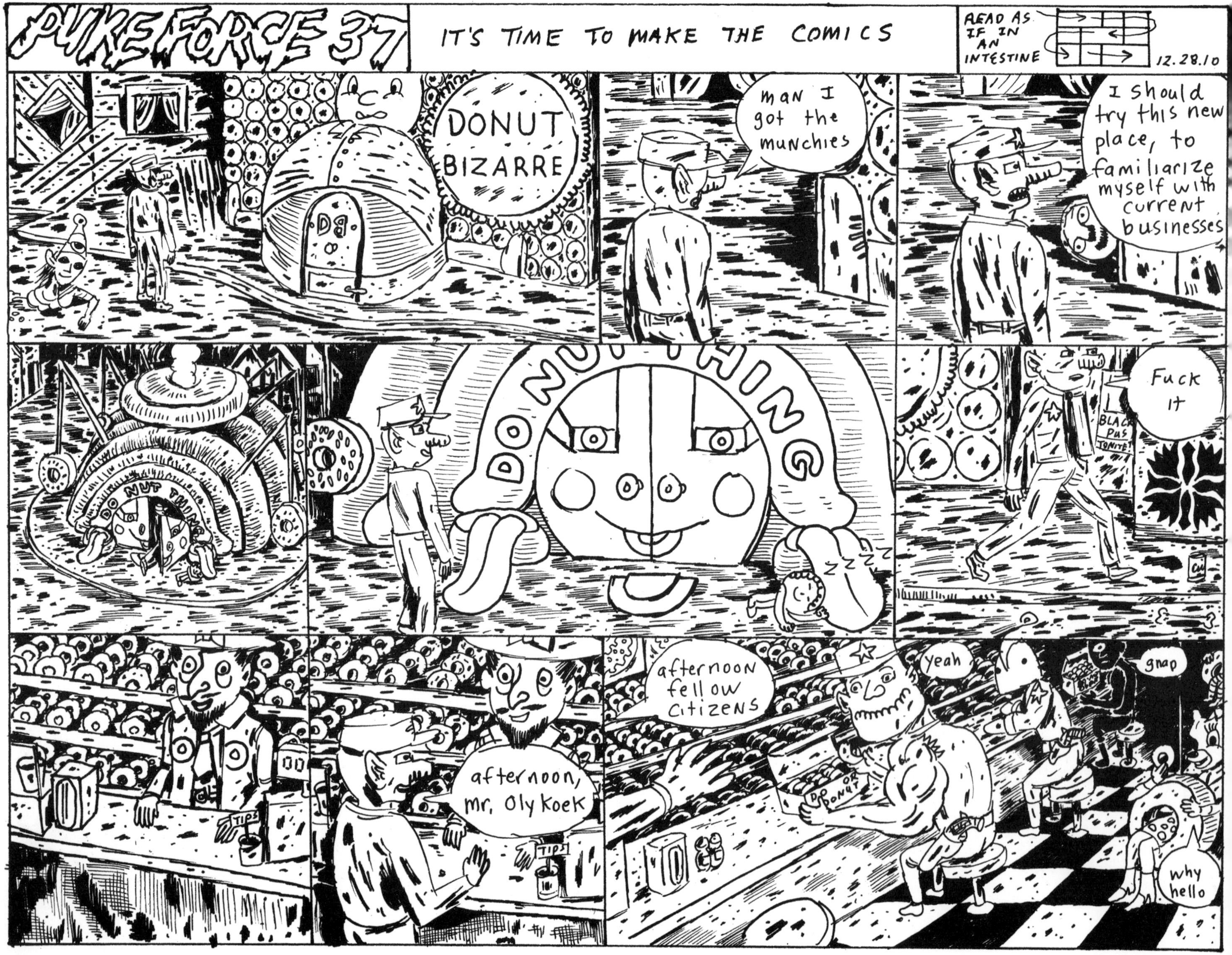
PUKE FORCE 37
IT'S TIME TO MAKE THE COMICS
READ AS IF IN AN INTESTINE
12.28.10
DONUT BIZARRE
DB
man I got the munchies
I should try this new place, to familiarize myself with current businesses
Fuck it
BLAC PUS TONITE
DO NUT THING
DO NUT THING
TIPS
afternoon, mr. Oly Koek
TIPS
afternoon fellow citizens
yeah
gnap
DO OR DONUT
why hello

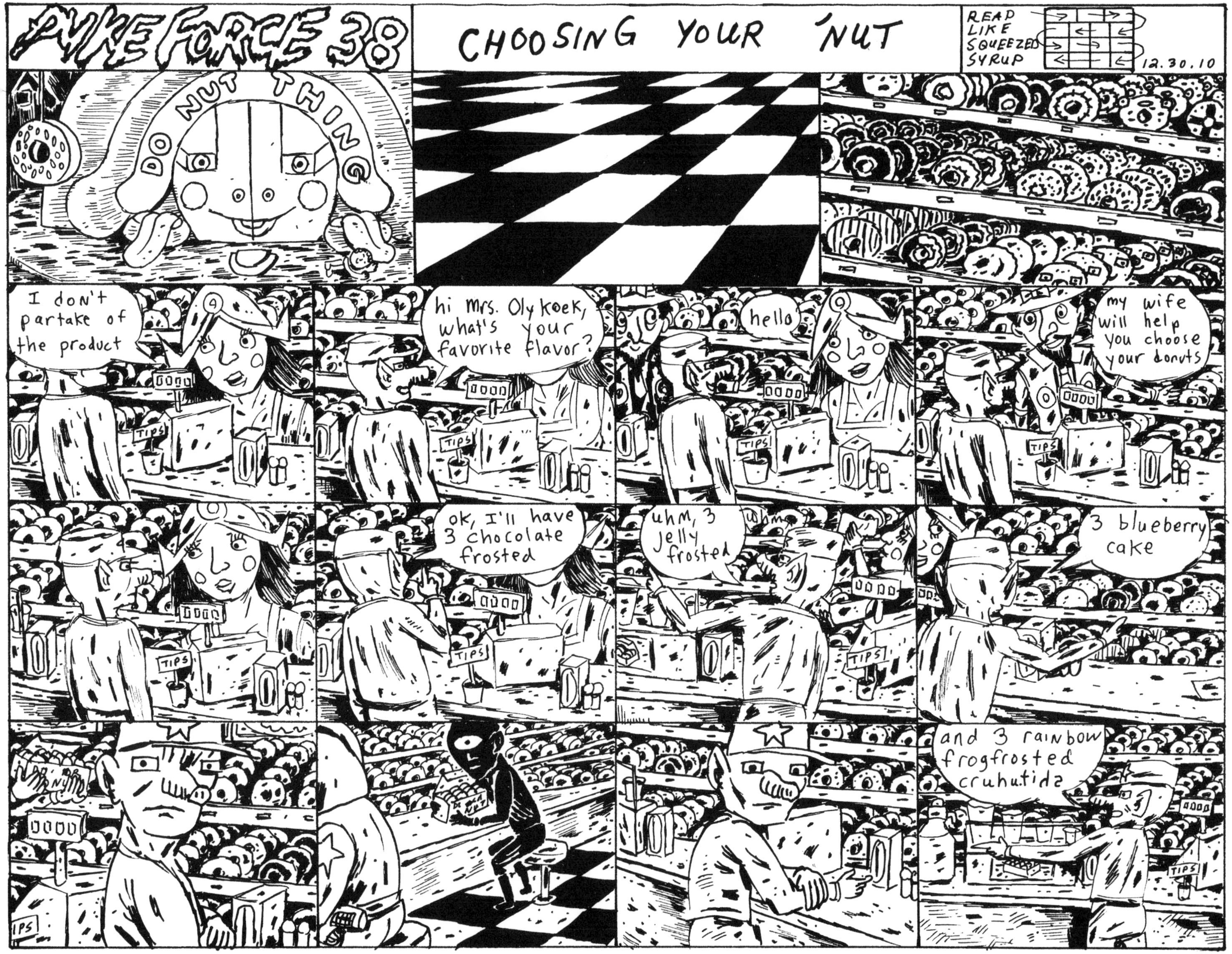
PUKE FORCE 38
CHOOSING YOUR 'NUT
READ LIKE SQUEEZED SYRUP
12.30.10
DO NUT THING
my wife will help you choose your donuts
hello
hi mrs. Oly koek, what's your favorite flavor?
I don't partake of the product
TIPS
ok, I'll have 3 chocolate frosted
uhm, 3 jelly frosted
uhm
3 blueberry cake
and 3 rainbow frogfrosted cruhutida

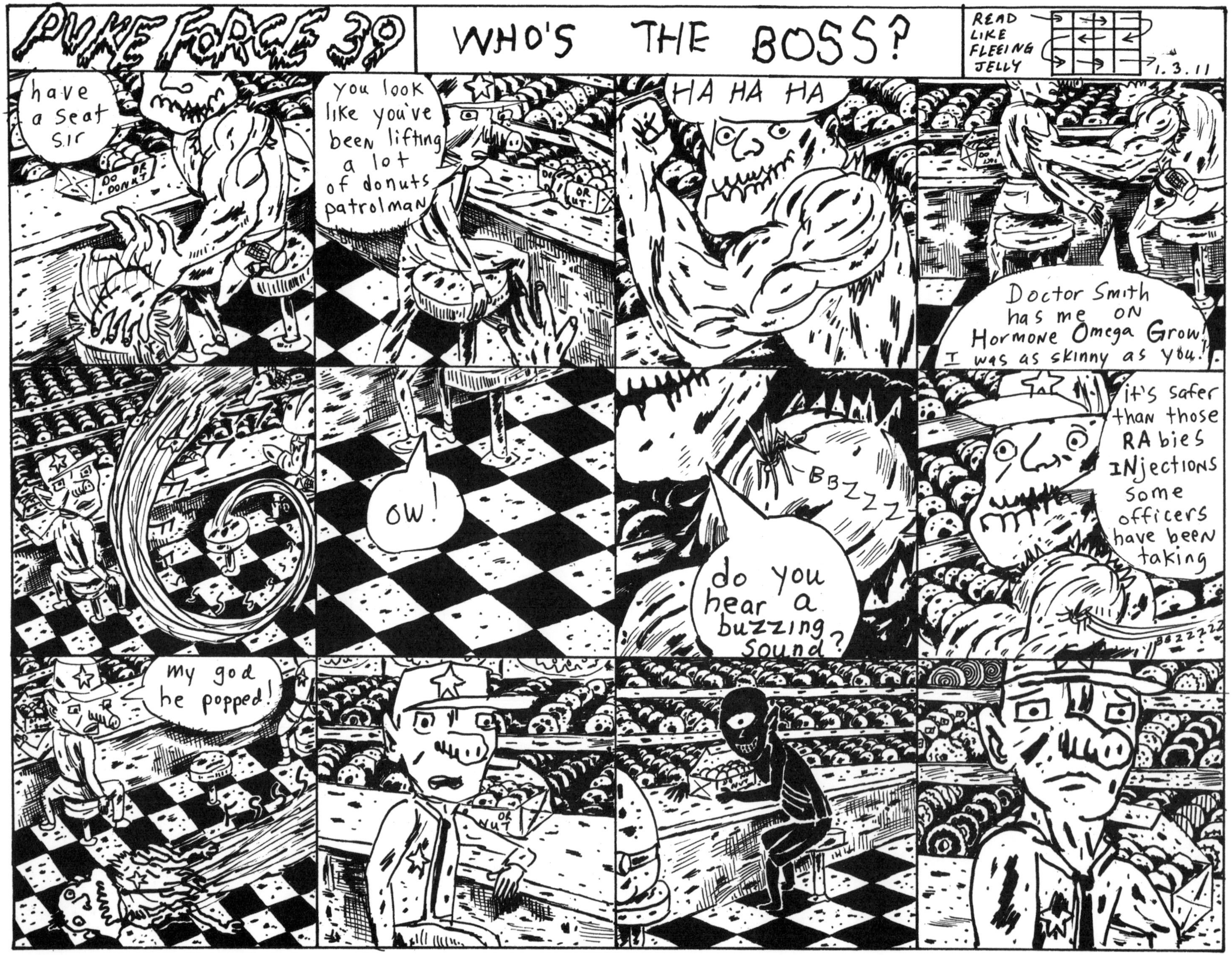
PUKE FORCE 39
WHO'S THE BOSS?
READ LIKE FLEEING JELLY
1.3.11
have a Seat Sir
DO OR DONUT
you look like you've been lifting a lot of donuts patrolman
HA HA HA
Doctor Smith has me ON Hormone Omega Grow! I was as skinny as you!
it's safer than those RAbies INjections some officers have been taking
do you hear a buzzing sound?
BBZZZZ
OW!
My god he popped!
OR NUT

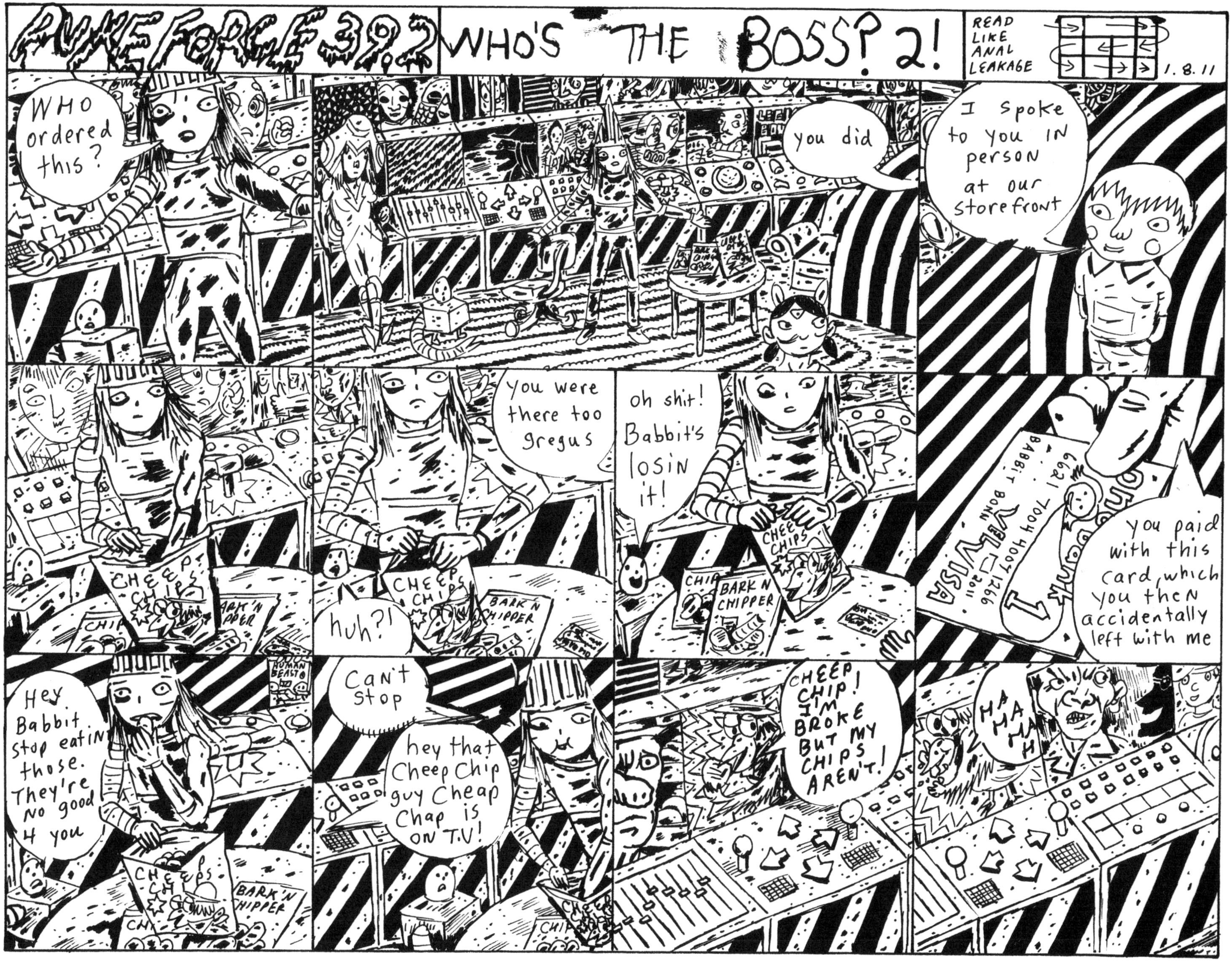
PUKE FORCE 39.2
WHO'S THE BOSS? 2!
READ LIKE ANAL LEAKAGE
1.8.11
WHO ordered this?
you did
I spoke to you IN person at our storefront
You paid with this card, which you then accidentally left with me
oh shit! Babbit's losin it!
CHEEP CHIPS
You were there too gregus
huh?!
CHEEP CHIPS
BARK 'N CHIPPER
Hey Babbit stop eatin those. They're no good 4 you
HUMAN BEAST
Can't stop
hey that Cheep Chip guy Cheap Chap is ON T.V!
CHEEP CHIP! I'M BROKE BUT MY CHIPS AREN'T!
HA HA HA H

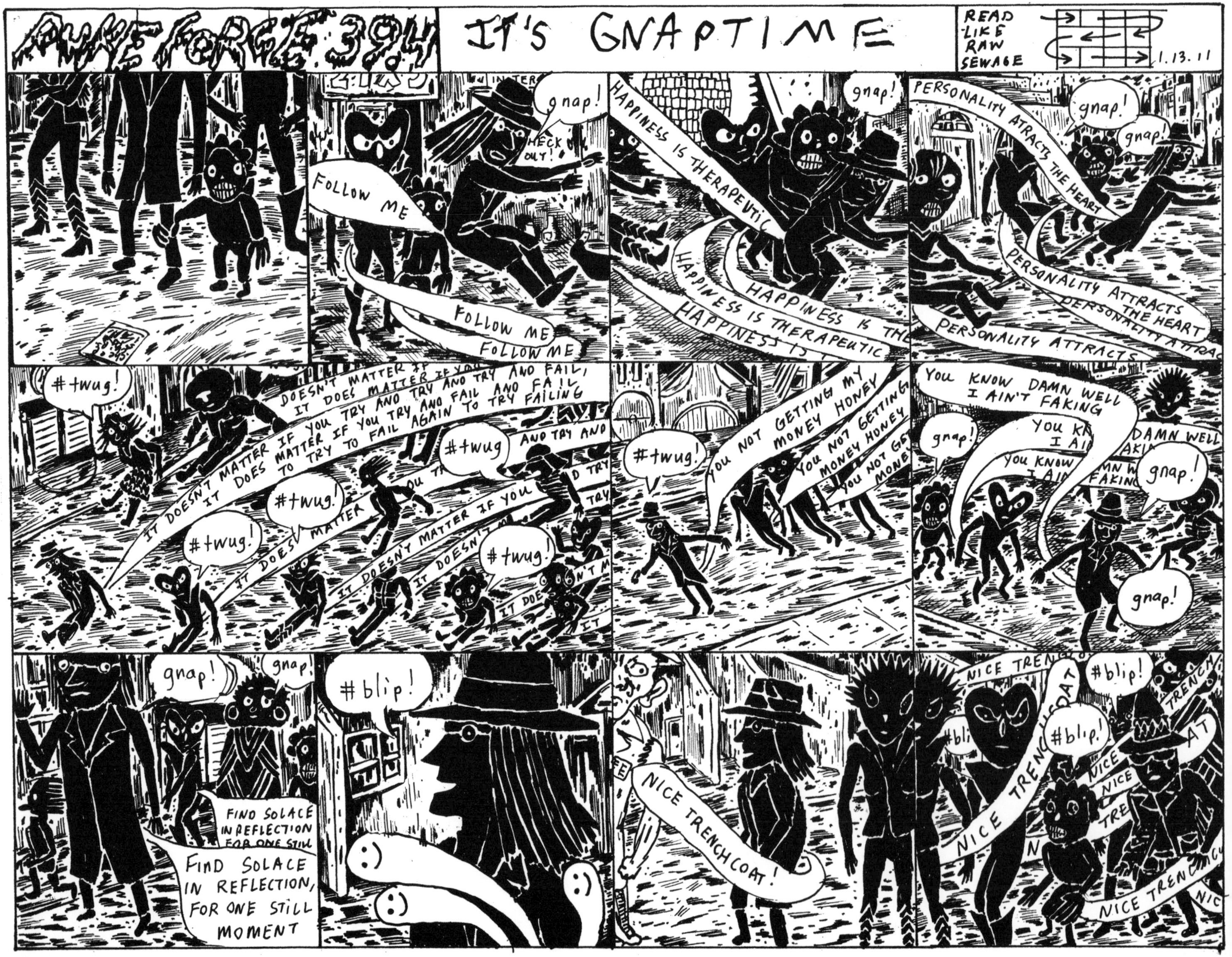
AWE FORCE 394
IT'S GNAPTIME
READ LIKE RAW SEWAGE
1.13.11
gnap!
CHECK OUT!
FOLLOW ME
FOLLOW ME
FOLLOW ME
gnap!
HAPPINESS IS THERAPEUTIC
HAPPINESS IS THE
HAPPINESS IS THERAPEUTIC
HAPPINESS IS
PERSONALITY ATTRACTS THE HEART
gnap!
gnap!
PERSONALITY ATTRACTS THE HEART
PERSONALITY ATTRAC
PERSONALITY ATTRACTS
YOU KNOW DAMN WELL I AIN'T FAKING
gnap!
YOU KNOW DAMN WELL I AIN'T FAKING
YOU KNOW DAMN WELL I AIN'T FAKING
gnap!
gnap!
#twug!
YOU NOT GETTING MY MONEY HONEY
YOU NOT GETTING MY MONEY HONEY
YOU NOT GET MONEY
#twug!
IT DOESN'T MATTER IF YOU TRY AND TRY AND TRY AND FAIL, IT DOES MATTER IF YOU TRY AND FAIL AND FAIL TO TRY TO FAIL AGAIN TO TRY FAILING
#twug
AND TRY AND
#twug!
#twug!
IT DOESN'T MATTER IF YOU
IT DOES MATTER
IT DOESN'T MATTER IF YOU
#twug!
IT DOESN'T M
IT DOE
gnap!
gnap
FIND SOLACE IN REFLECTION FOR ONE STILL
FIND SOLACE IN REFLECTION, FOR ONE STILL MOMENT
#blip!
NICE TRENCHCOAT!
NICE TRENCHCOAT
#blip!
#blip!
NICE TRENCHCOAT
NICE
NICE
NICE TRENCHCOAT

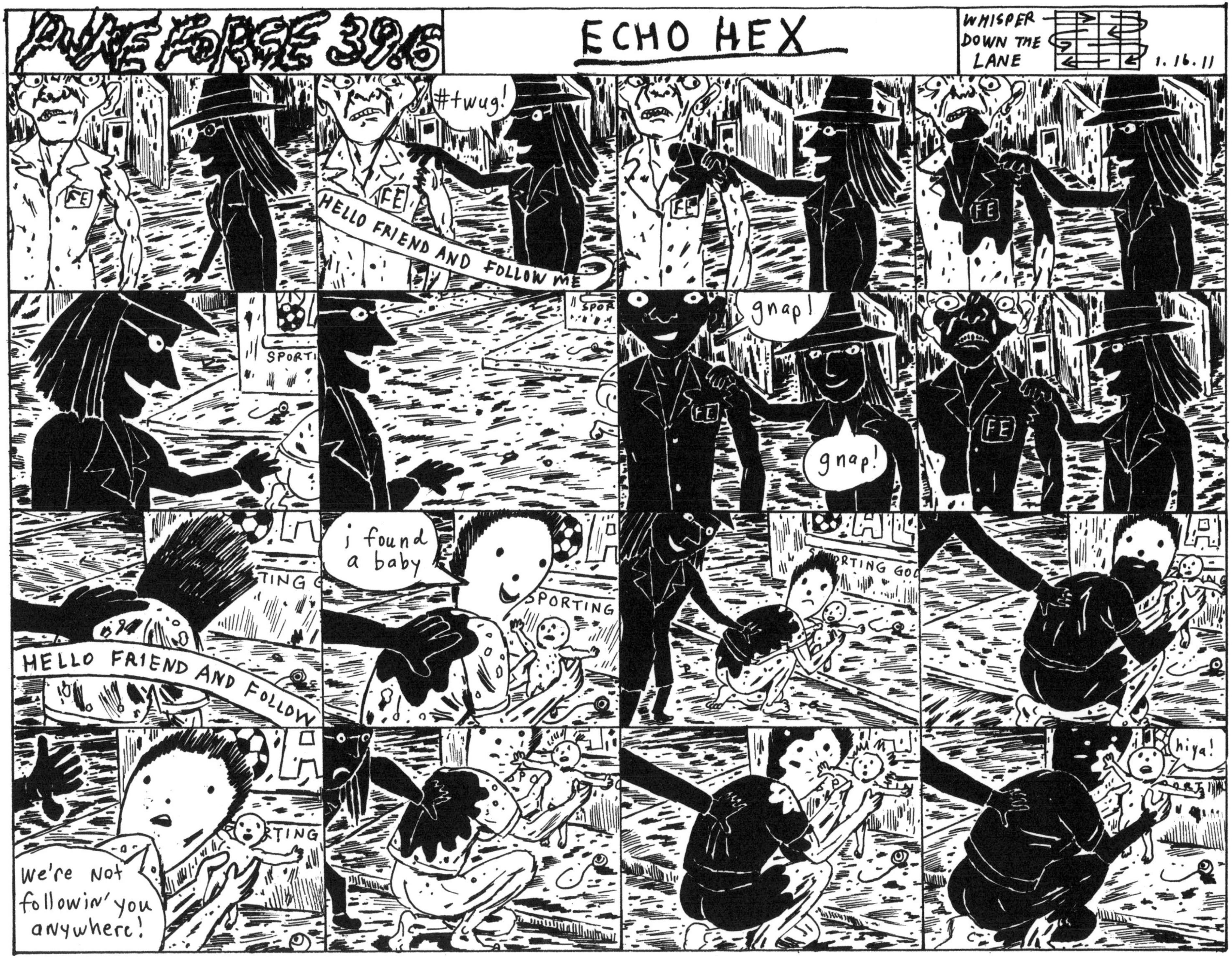

ECHO HEX
WHISPER DOWN THE LANE
1.16.11
#twug!
HELLO FRIEND AND FOLLOW ME
gnap!
gnap!
HELLO FRIEND AND FOLLOW
i found a baby
We're not followin' you anywhere!
hiya!

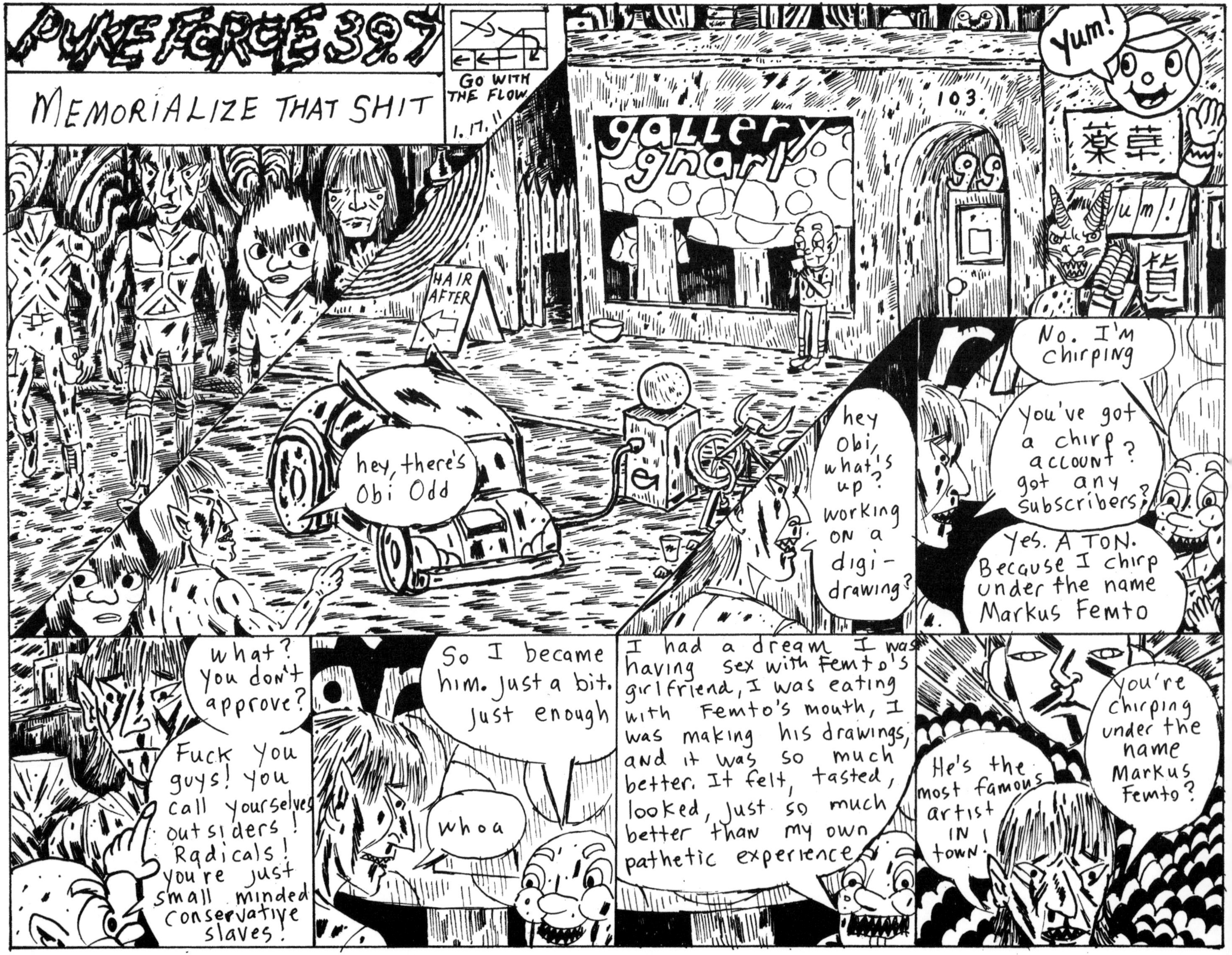
PUKE FORCE 39.7
MEMORIALIZE THAT SHIT
GO WITH THE FLOW
1.17.11
103
gallery gnarl
99
Yum!
薬草
yum!
貨
HAIR AFTER
hey, there's Obi Odd
hey Obi, what's up? working on a digi-drawing?
No. I'm chirping
You've got a chirp account? got any subscribers?
Yes. A TON. Because I chirp under the name Markus Femto
what? you don't approve?
Fuck you guys! you call yourselves outsiders! Radicals! you're just small minded conservative slaves!
So I became him. just a bit. just enough
whoa
I had a dream I was having sex with Femto's girlfriend, I was eating with Femto's mouth, I was making his drawings, and it was so much better. It felt, tasted, looked, just so much better than my own pathetic experience
You're chirping under the name Markus Femto?
He's the most famous artist in town!

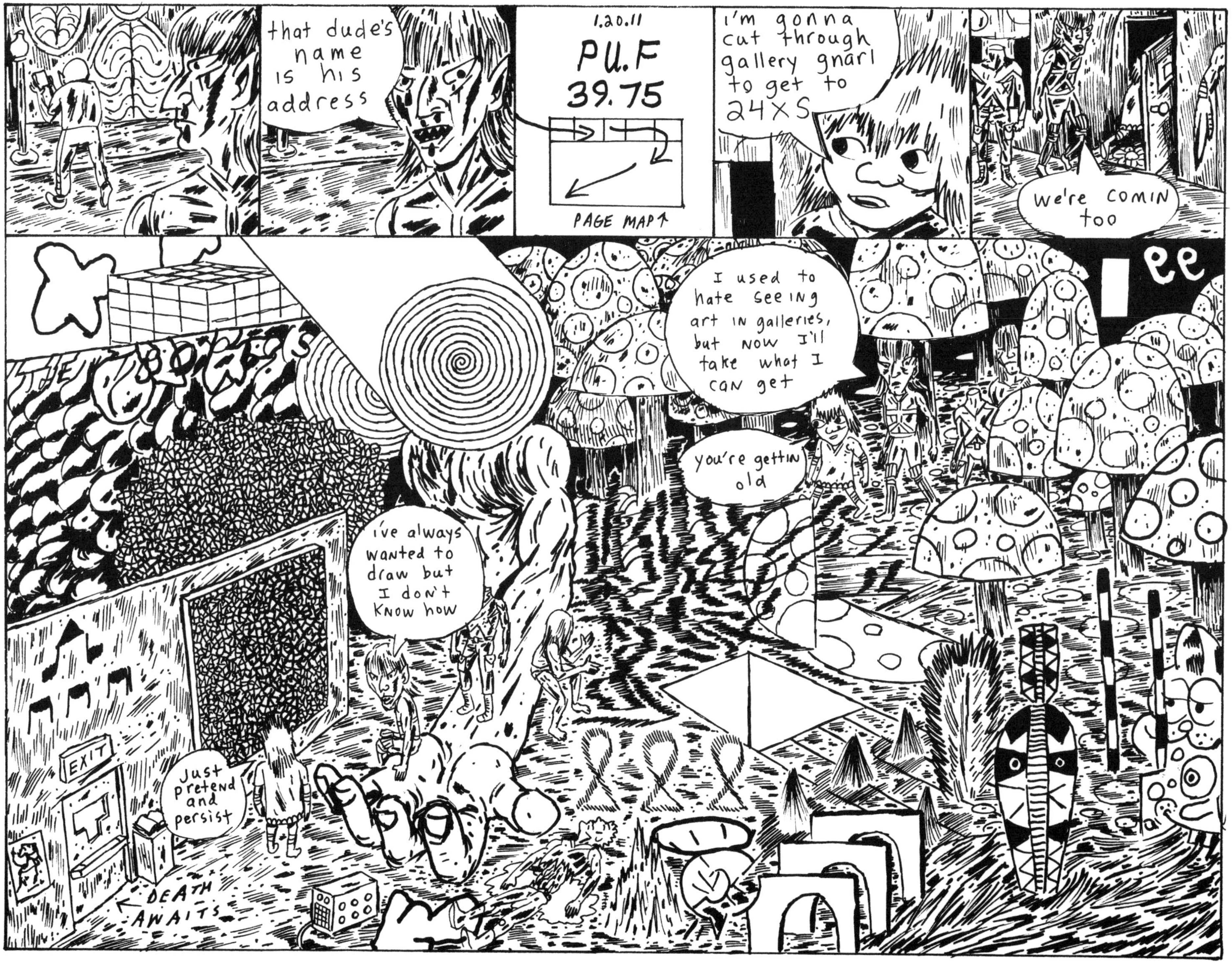
that dude's name is his address
1.20.11
PU.F 39.75
PAGE MAP↑
i'm gonna cut through gallery gnarl to get to 24XS
we're COMIN too
THE
I used to hate seeing art in galleries, but now I'll take what I can get
you're gettin old
i've always wanted to draw but I don't know how
EXIT
Just pretend and persist
DEATH AWAITS

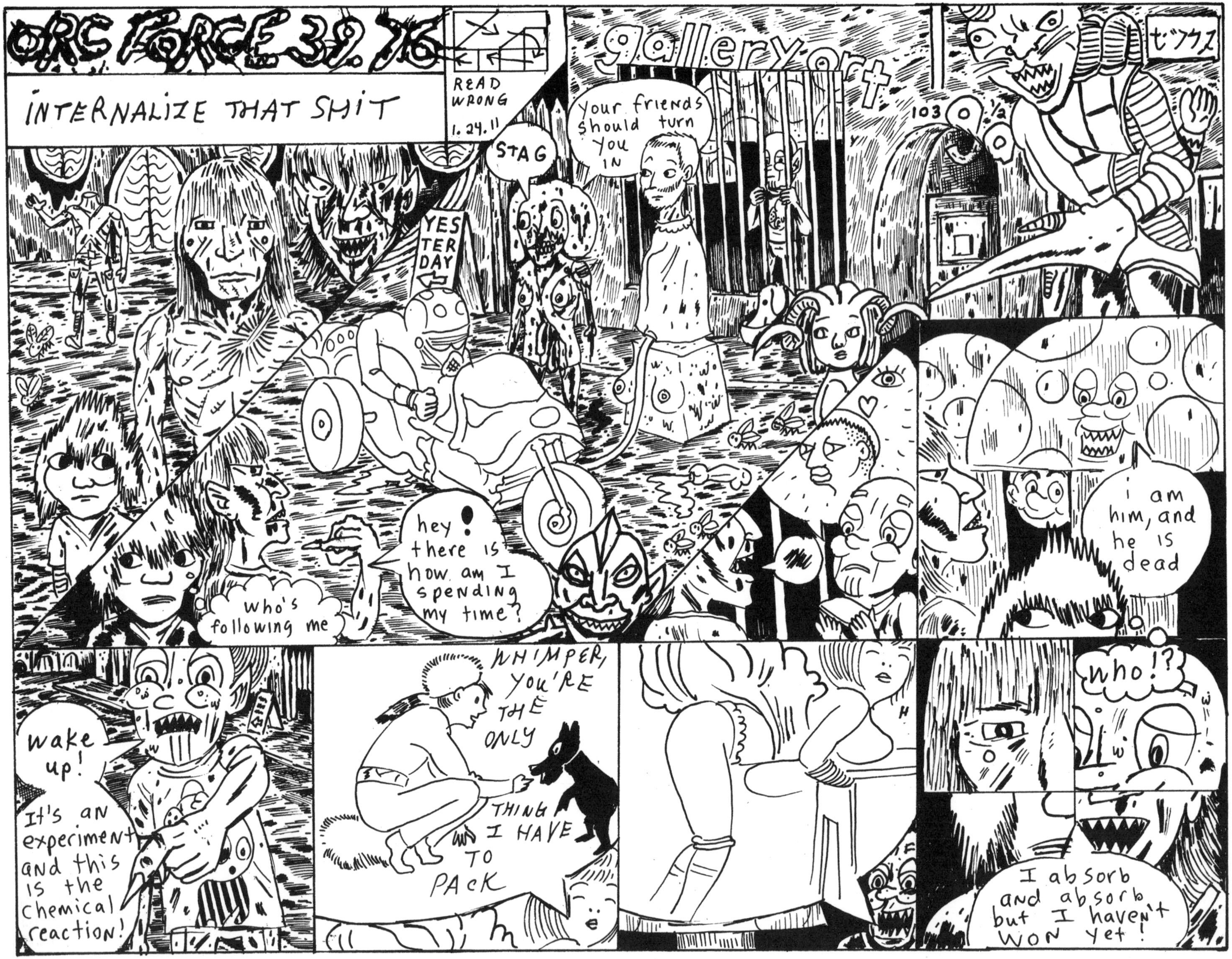

ORC FORCE 39.76
INTERNALIZE THAT SHIT
READ WRONG
1.24.11
gallery art
ゼツクス
103 1/2
YESTERDAY
STAG
your friends should turn you in
hey! there is how am I spending my time?
who's following me
i am him, and he is dead
wake up!
It's an experiment and this is the chemical reaction!
WHIMPER, YOU'RE THE ONLY THING I HAVE TO PACK
who!?
I absorb and absorb but I haven't won yet!

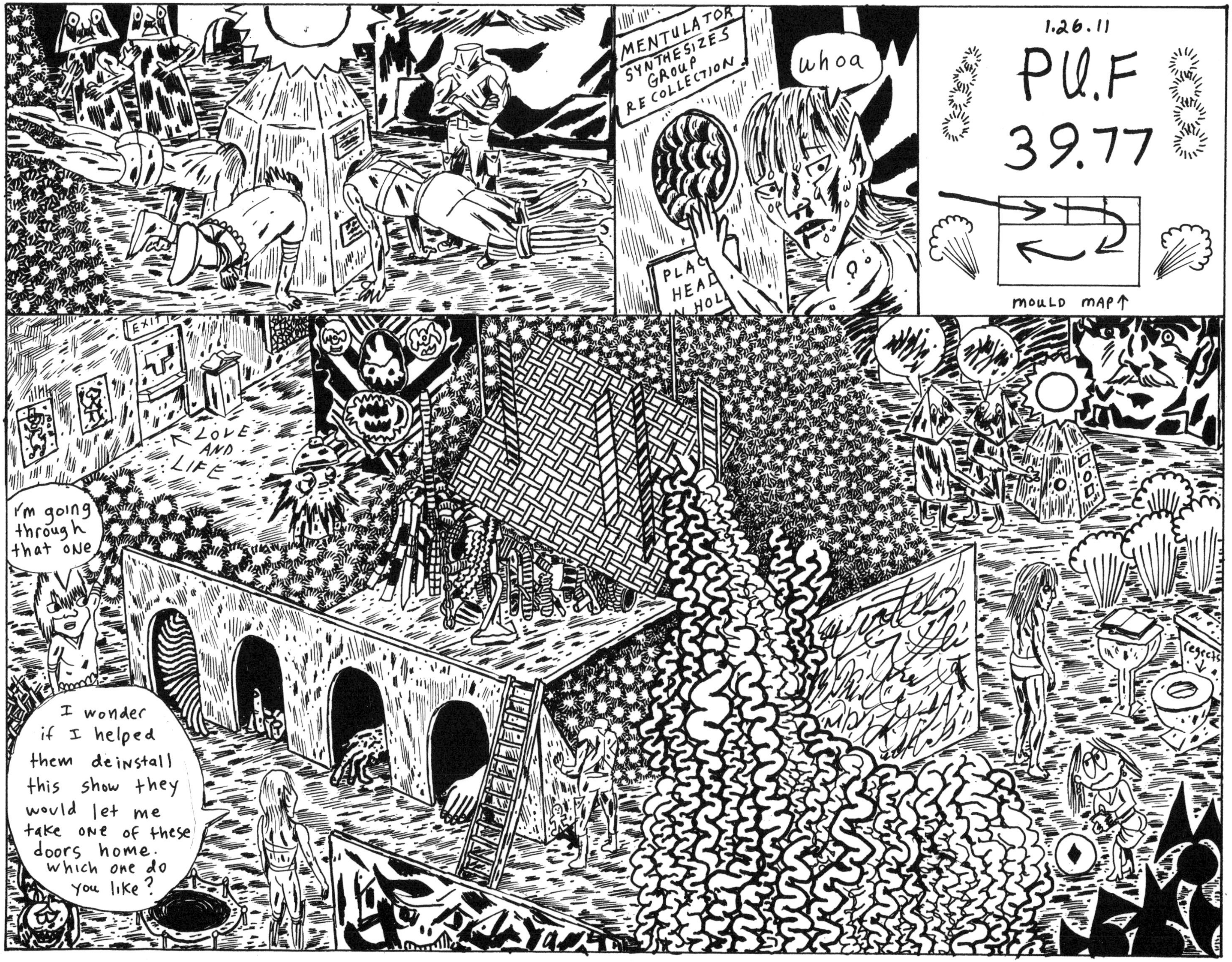
MENTULATOR SYNTHESIZES GROUP RECOLLECTION
whoa
PLAC HEAD HOL
1.26.11
PU.F
39.77
MOULD MAP↑
EXIT
LOVE AND LIFE
I'm going through that one
I wonder if I helped them deinstall this show they would let me take one of these doors home. Which one do you like?
rejects

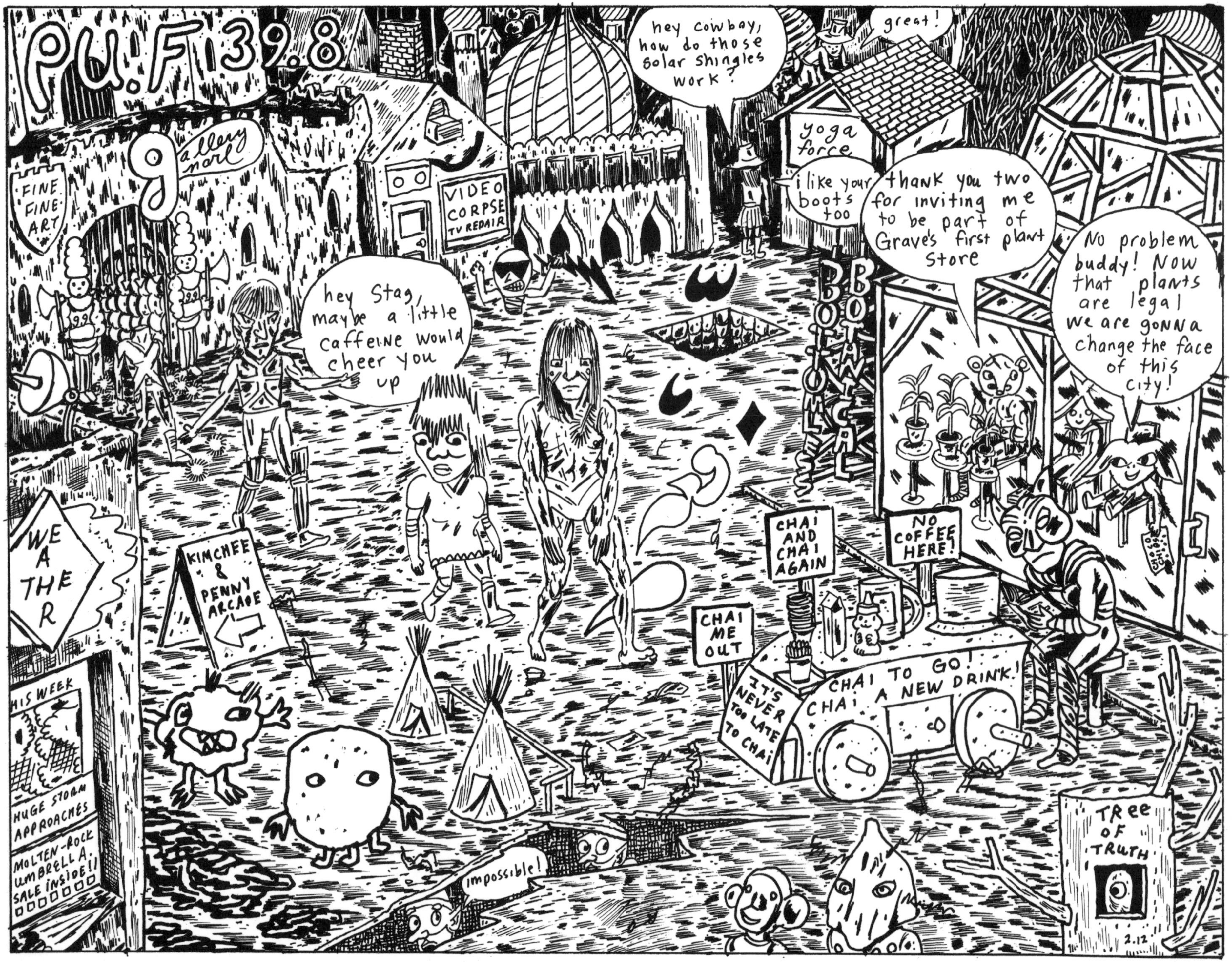

PU.F 39.8
gallery narl
FINE FINE ART
VIDEO CORPSE TV REPAIR
hey cowboy, how do those solar shingles work?
great!
yoga force
i like your boots too
thank you two for inviting me to be part of Grave's first plant store
No problem buddy! Now that plants are legal we are gonna change the face of this city!
hey Stag, maybe a little caffeine would cheer you up
BOTANICAL
WEATHER
KIMCHEE & PENNY ARCADE
CHAI AND CHAI AGAIN
NO COFFEE HERE!
CHAI ME OUT
IT'S NEVER TOO LATE TO CHAI
CHAI TO GO! CHAI A NEW DRINK!
HIS WEEK
HUGE STORM APPROACHES
MOLTEN-ROCK UMBRELLA SALE INSIDE!!
impossible!
TREE OF TRUTH
2.12

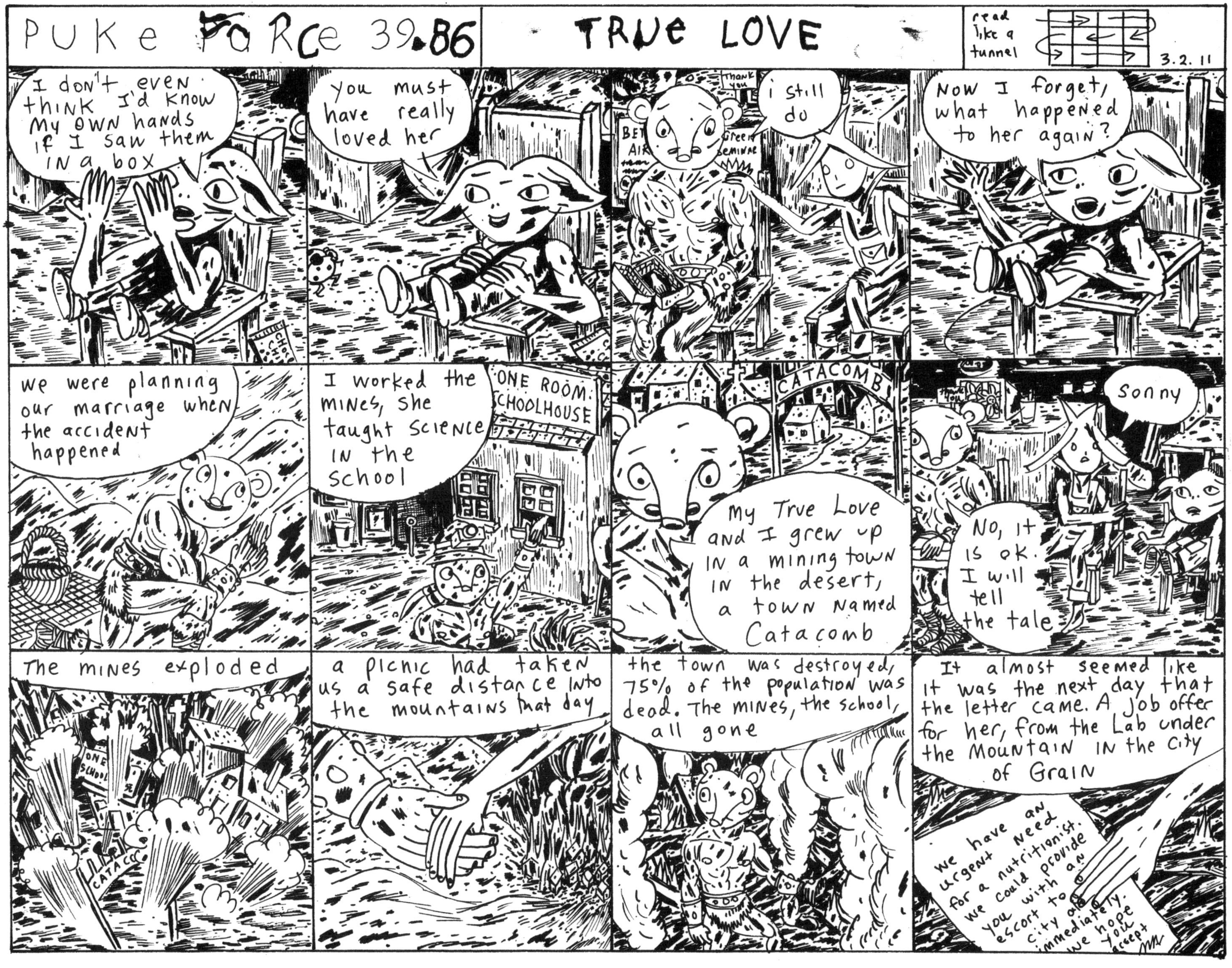
PUKE FORCE 39.86
TRUE LOVE
read like a tunnel
3.2.11
I don't even think I'd know my own hands if I saw them in a box
you must have really loved her
i still do
THANK YOU
Now I forget, what happened to her again?
Sonny
No, it is ok. I will tell the tale
CATACOMB
My True Love and I grew up in a mining town in the desert, a town named Catacomb
ONE ROOM SCHOOLHOUSE
I worked the mines, she taught science in the school
we were planning our marriage when the accident happened
The mines exploded
a picnic had taken us a safe distance into the mountains that day
the town was destroyed, 75% of the population was dead. The mines, the school, all gone
It almost seemed like it was the next day that the letter came. A job offer for her, from the Lab under the Mountain in the City of Grain
we have an urgent need for a nutritionist. we could provide you with an escort to city immediately. we hope you accept

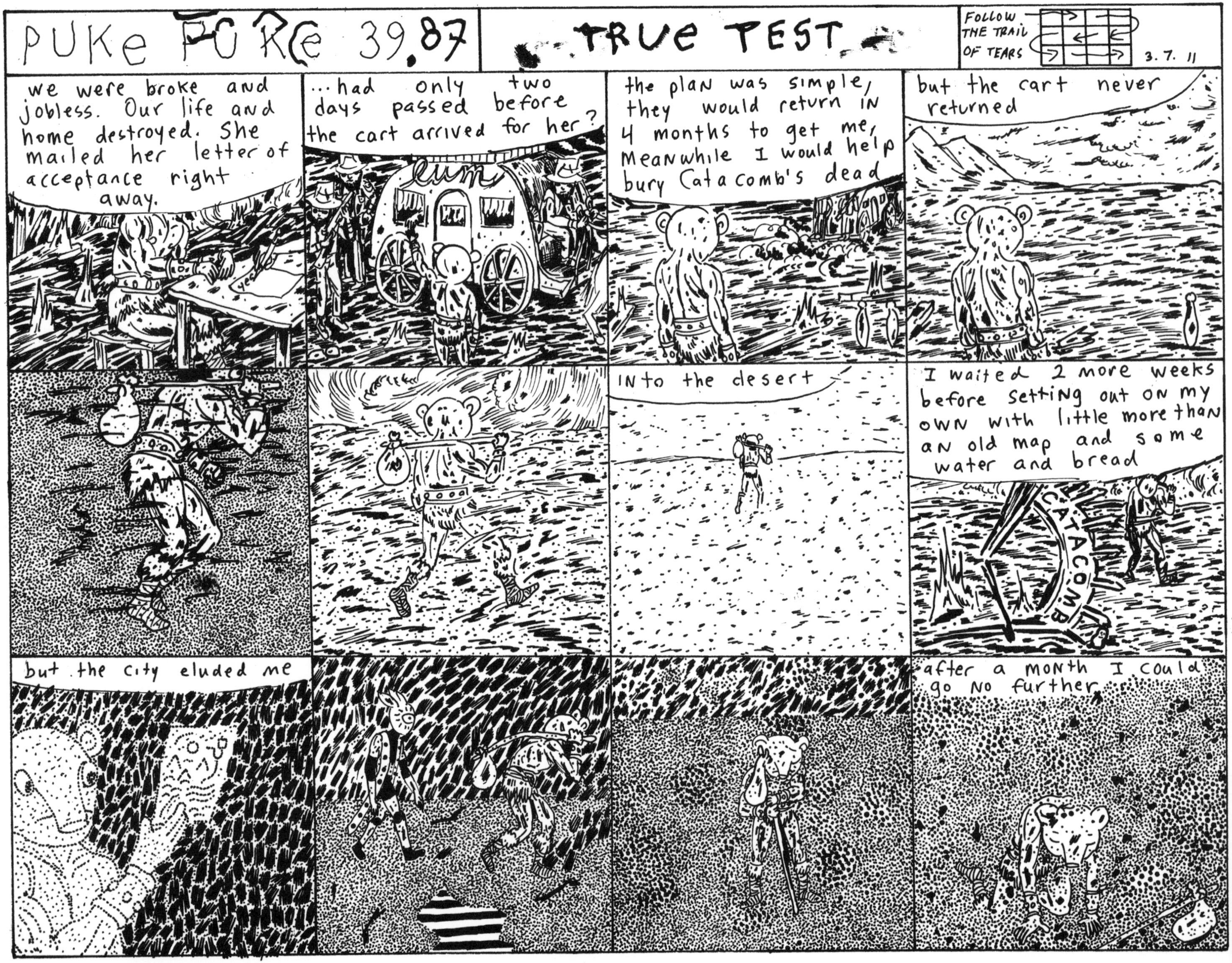
PUKE FORCE 39.87
TRUE TEST
FOLLOW THE TRAIL OF TEARS
3. 7. 11
we were broke and jobless. Our life and home destroyed. She mailed her letter of acceptance right away.
...had only two days passed before the cart arrived for her?
the plan was simple, they would return in 4 months to get me, Meanwhile I would help bury Catacomb's dead
but the cart never returned
Into the desert
I waited 2 more weeks before setting out on my own with little more than an old map and some water and bread
CATACOMB
but the city eluded me
after a month I could go no further

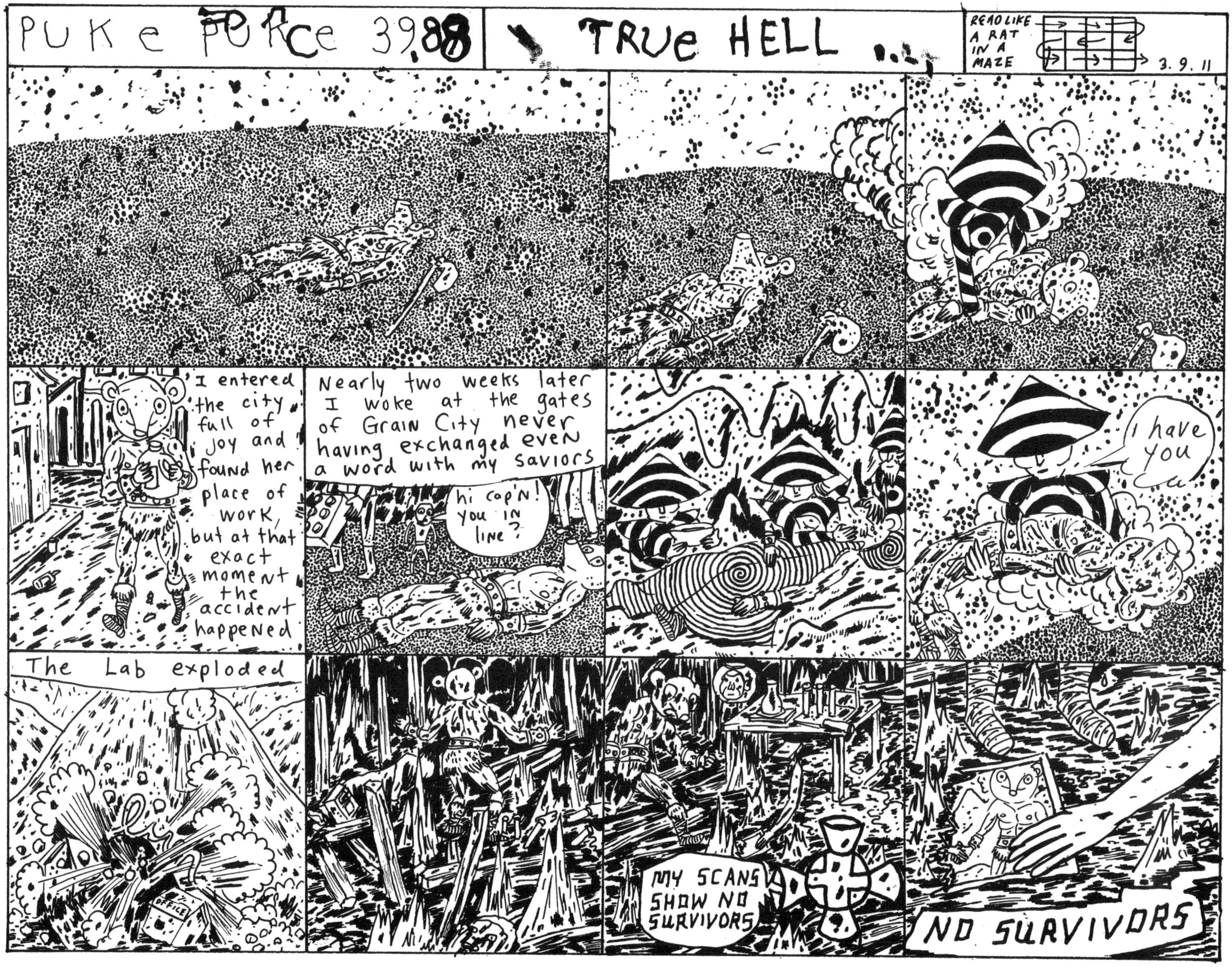

PUKE FORCE 39.8
TRUE HELL
READ LIKE A RAT IN A MAZE
3.9.11
I have you
Nearly two weeks later I woke at the gates of Grain City never having exchanged even a word with my saviors
hi cop'N! you in line?
I entered the city full of joy and found her place of work, but at that exact moment the accident happened
The Lab exploded
OFFICE
MY SCANS SHOW NO SURVIVORS
NO SURVIVORS

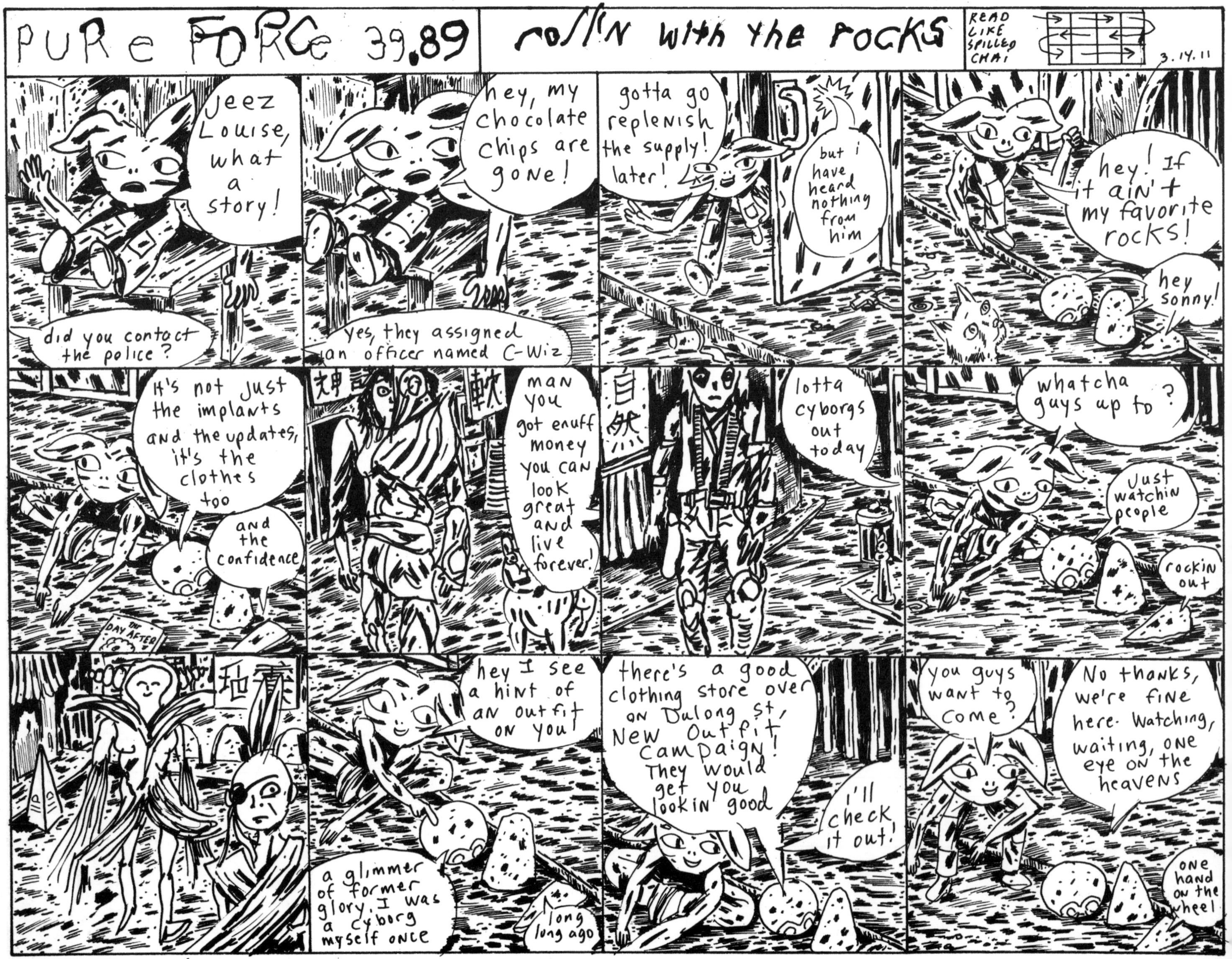
PURe FORCe 39.89
rollin with the rocks
READ LIKE SPILLED CHAI
3.14.11
Jeez Louise, what a story!
did you contact the police?
hey, my chocolate chips are gone!
yes, they assigned an officer named C-Wiz
gotta go replenish the supply! later!
but i have heard nothing from him
hey! If it ain't my favorite rocks!
hey sonny!
whatcha guys up to?
Just watchin people
rockin out
lotta cyborgs out today
man you got enuff money you can look great and live forever!
it's not just the implants and the updates, it's the clothes too
and the confidence
DAY AFTER
hey I see a hint of an outfit on you!
a glimmer of former glory. I was a cyborg myself once
long long ago
there's a good clothing store over on Dulong St, New Outfit Campaign! They would get you lookin good
I'll check it out!
you guys want to come?
No thanks, we're fine here. Watching, waiting, one eye on the heavens
one hand on the wheel

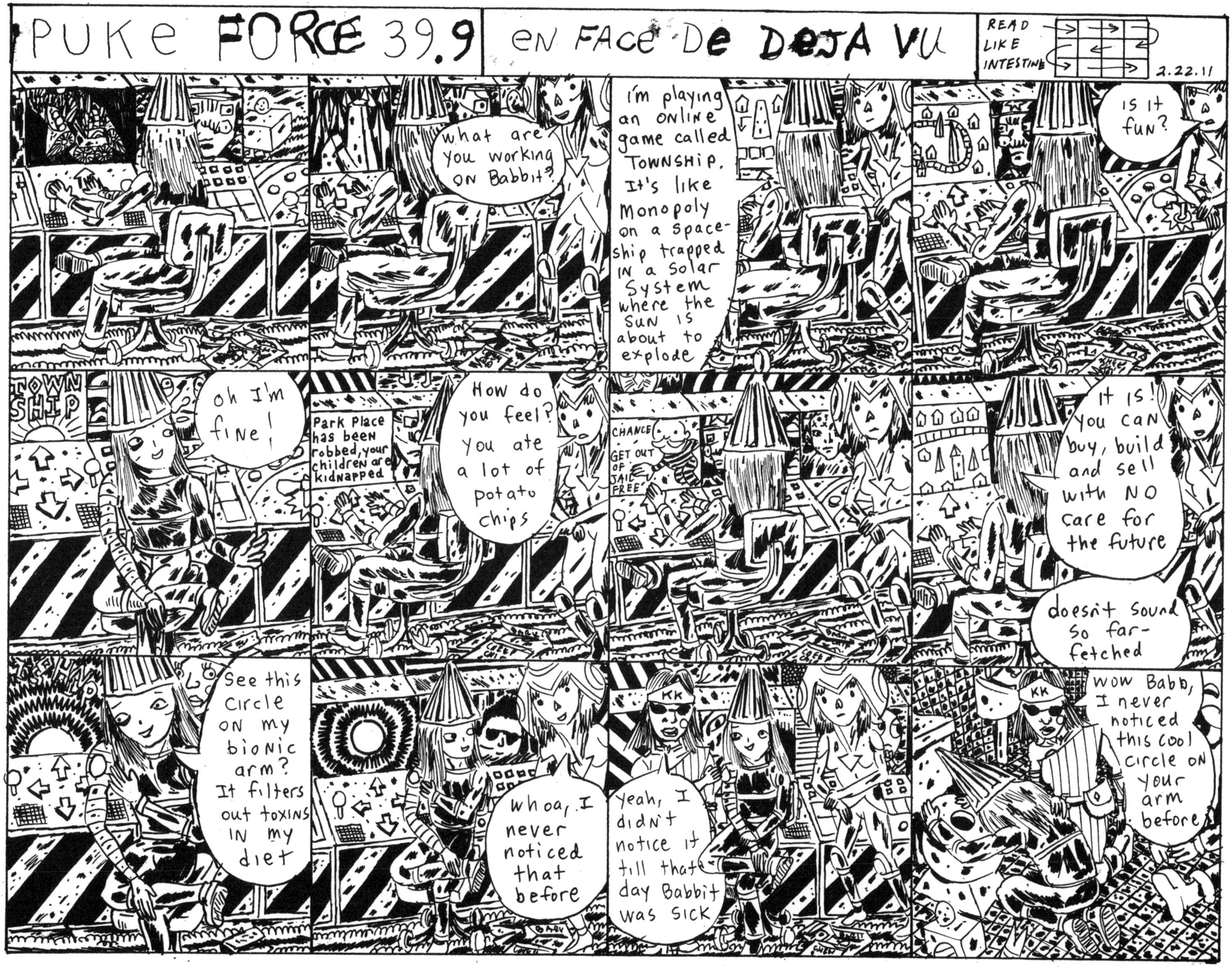
PUKE FORCE 39.9
en FACE De DeJA VU
READ LIKE INTESTINE
2.22.11
what are you working on Babbit?
I'm playing an online game called TOWNSHIP. It's like Monopoly on a spaceship trapped in a Solar System where the sun is about to explode
is it fun?
It is! You can buy, build and sell with NO care for the future
doesn't sound so far-fetched
CHANCE
GET OUT OF JAIL FREE
Park Place has been robbed, your children are kidnapped
How do you feel? You ate a lot of potato chips
TOWN SHIP
oh I'm fine!
See this circle on my bionic arm? It filters out toxins in my diet
whoa, I never noticed that before
KK
Yeah, I didn't notice it till that day Babbit was sick
KK
wow Babb, I never noticed this cool circle on your arm before

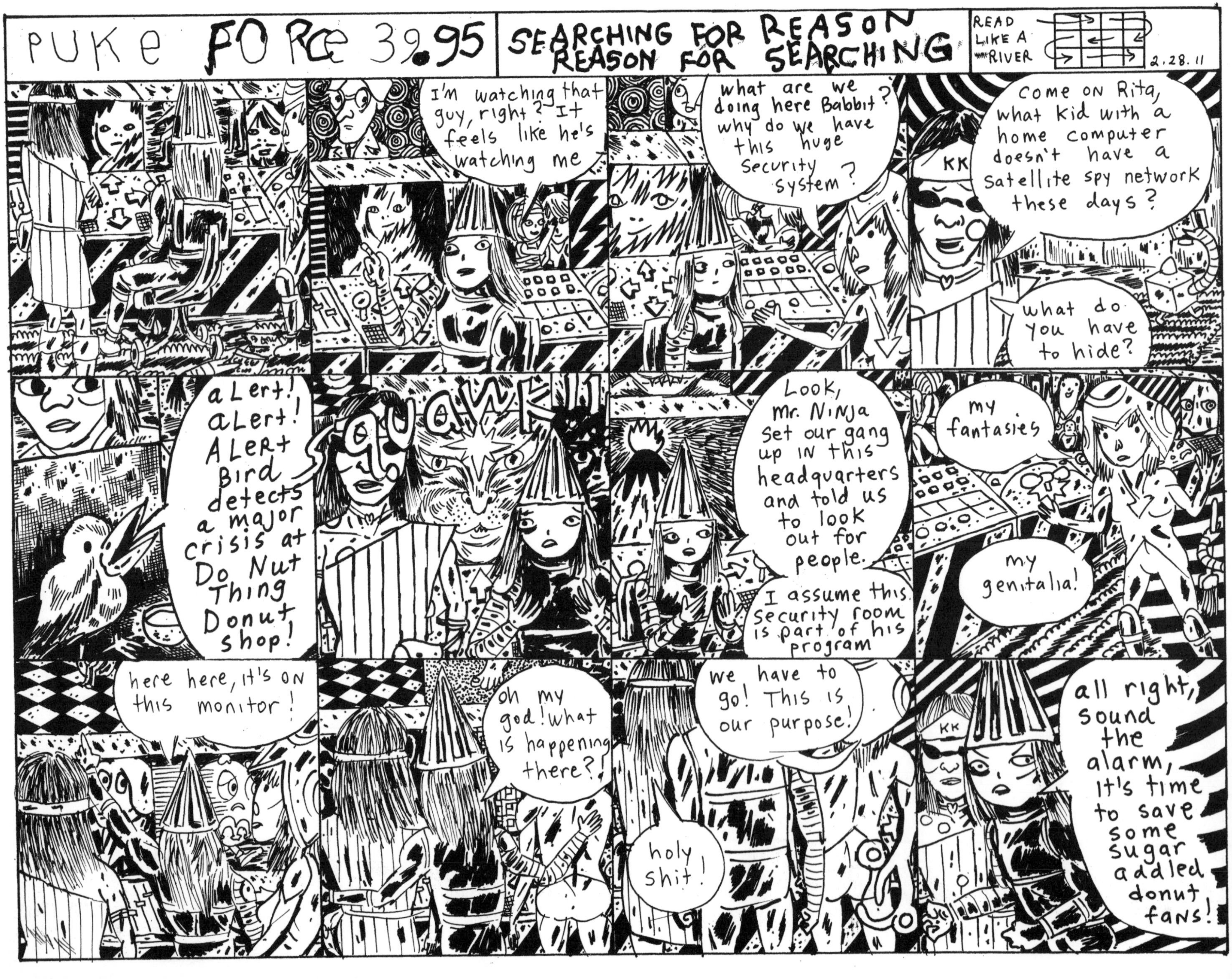
PUKE FORCE 39.95
SEARCHING FOR REASON REASON FOR SEARCHING
READ LIKE A RIVER
2.28.11
I'm watching that guy, right? It feels like he's watching me
what are we doing here Babbit? why do we have this huge security system?
come on Rita, what kid with a home computer doesn't have a satellite spy network these days?
KK
what do you have to hide?
my fantasies
my genitalia!
Look, Mr. Ninja set our gang up in this headquarters and told us to look out for people.
I assume this security room is part of his program
SQUAWK!!!
aLert! aLert! ALert Bird detects a major crisis at Do Nut Thing Donut shop!
here here, it's on this monitor!
oh my god! what is happening there?!
we have to go! This is our purpose!
holy shit!
KK
all right, sound the alarm, it's time to save some sugar addled donut fans!

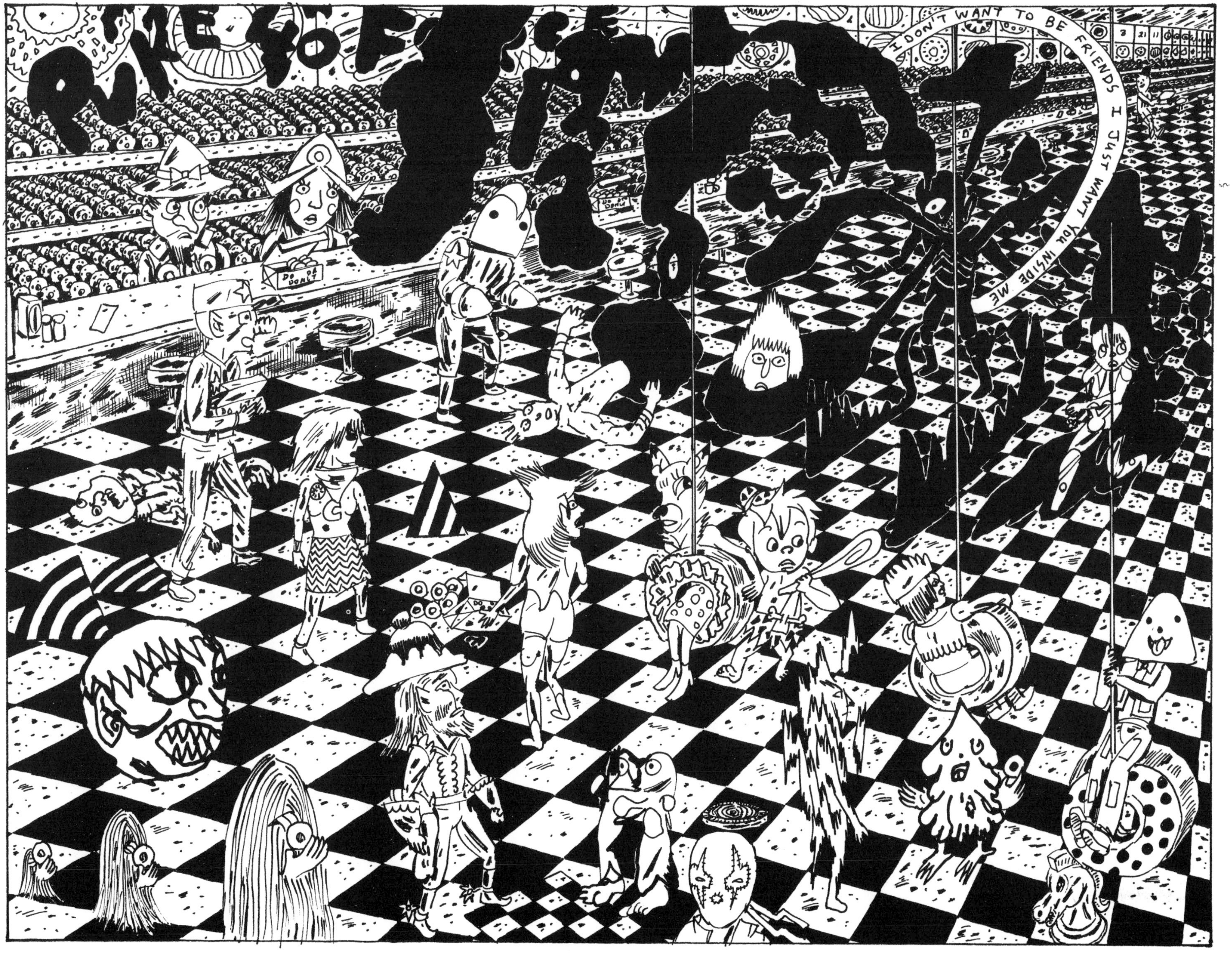
I DON'T WANT TO BE FRIENDS I JUST WANT YOU INSIDE ME

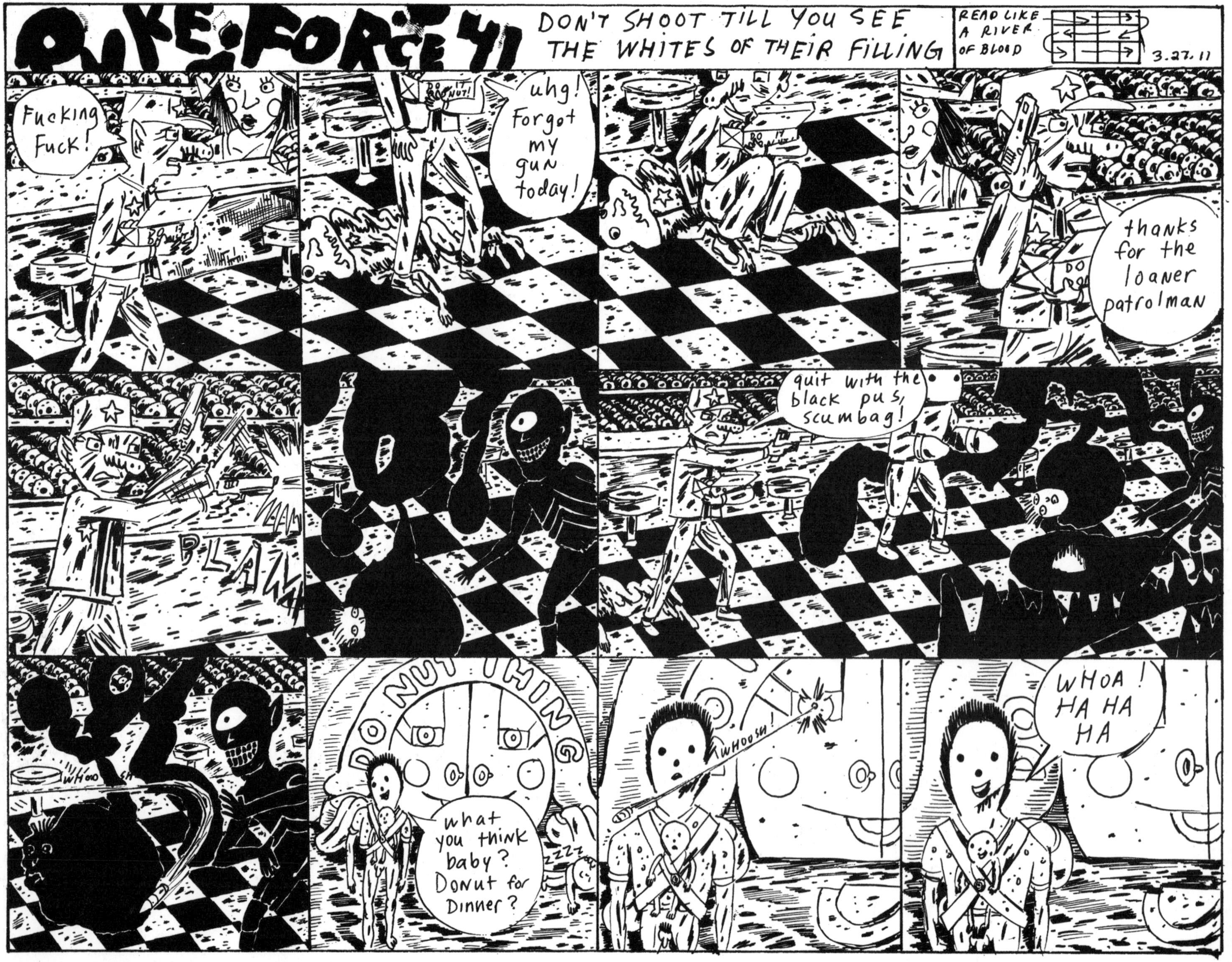

DON'T SHOOT TILL YOU SEE THE WHITES OF THEIR FILLING
READ LIKE A RIVER OF BLOOD
3.27.11
Fucking Fuck!
uhg! Forgot my gun today!
thanks for the loaner patrolman
quit with the black pus, scumbag!
BLAM
DO NUT THING
what you think baby? Donut for Dinner?
zzzz
WHOOSH!
WHOA! HA HA HA

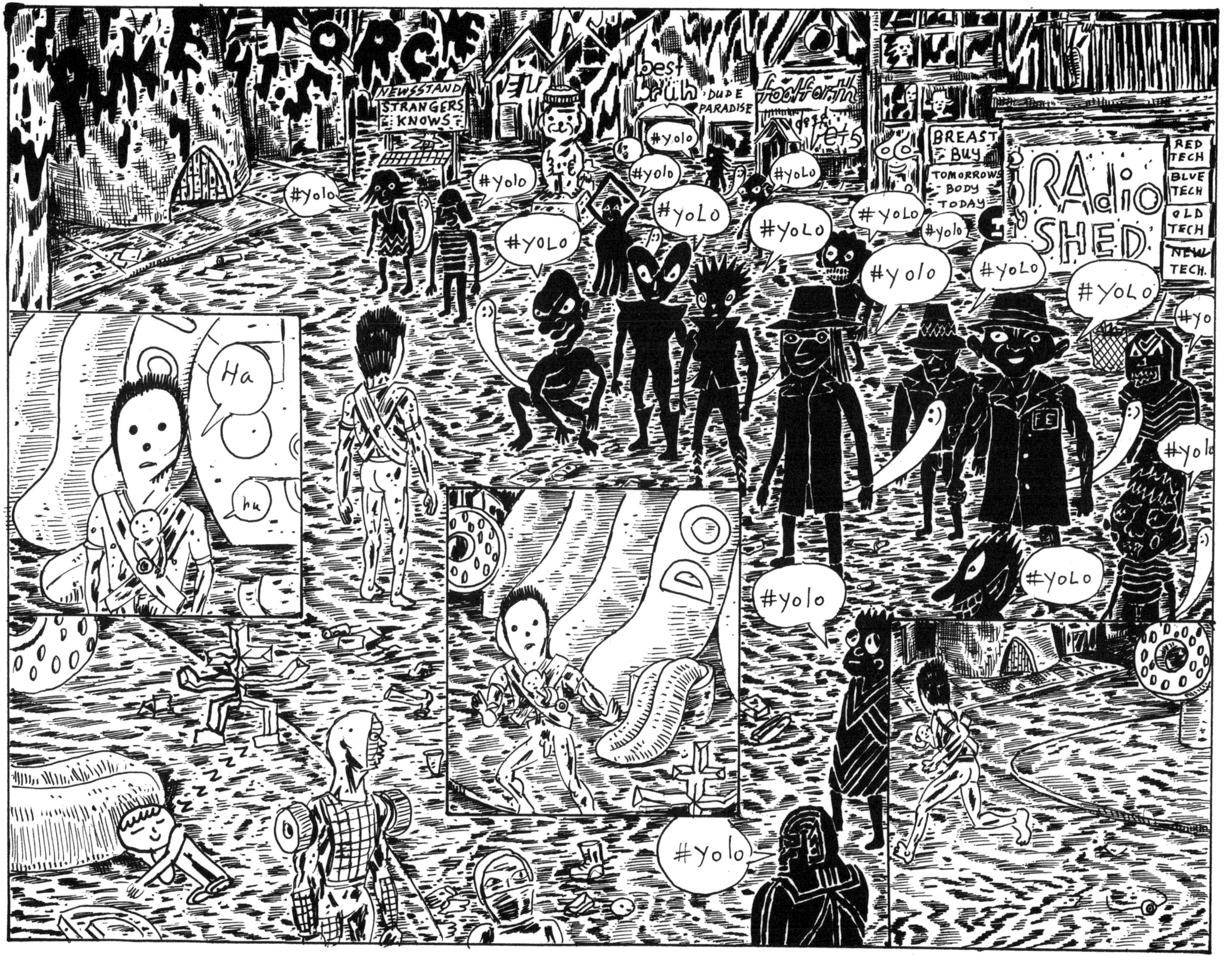

NEWSSTAND
STRANGERS KNOWS
best bruh
DUDE PARADISE
BREAST BUY
TOMORROWS BODY TODAY
RAdio SHED
RED TECH
BLUE TECH
OLD TECH
NEW TECH.
#yolo
#yolo
#yolo
#yolo
#yoLo
#yoLo
#yoLo
#yoLo
#yolo
#yolo
#yolo
#yoLo
#yoLo
Ha
hu
#yolo
#yoLo
#yolo

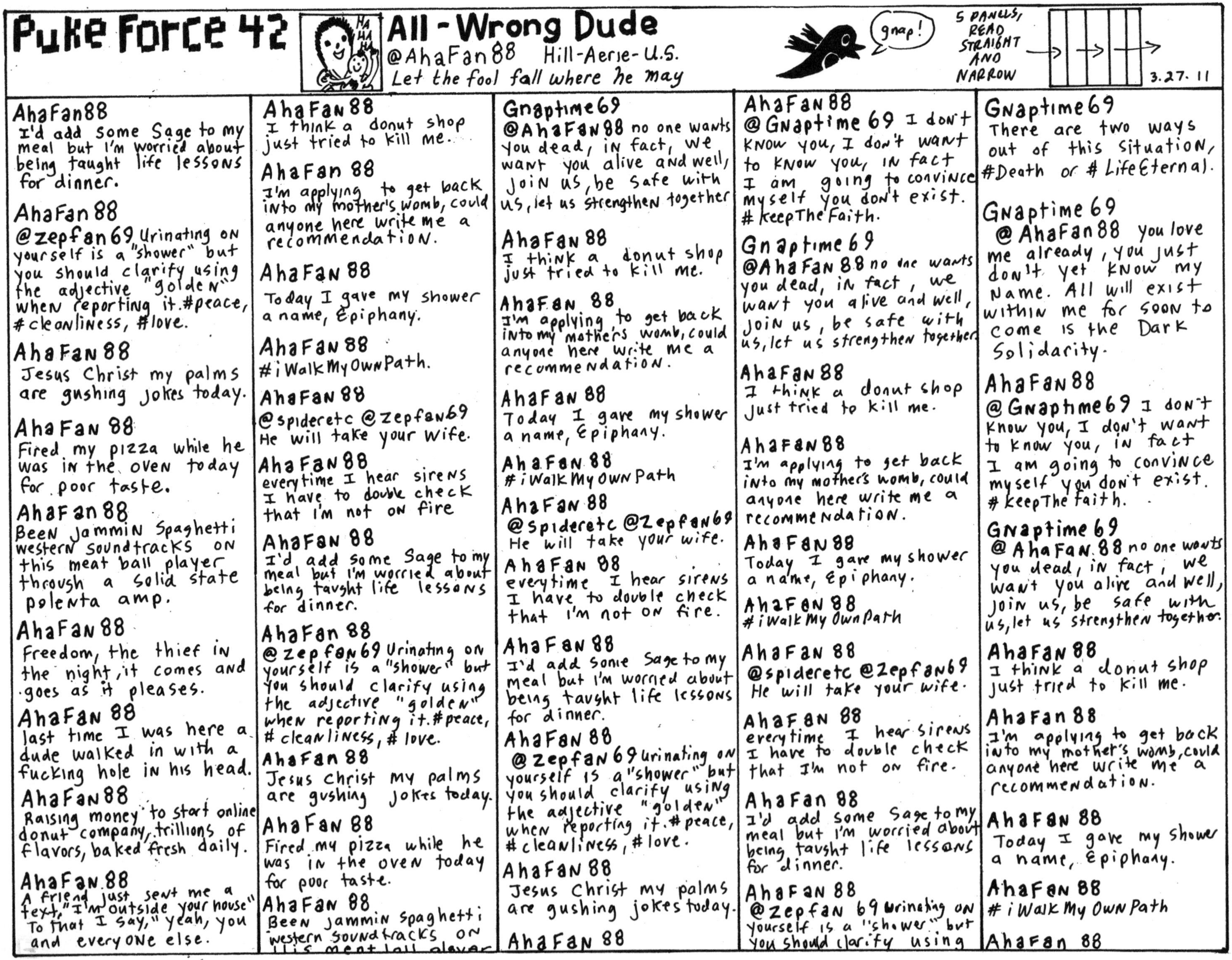
Puke Force 42
HA HA HA
All-Wrong Dude
@AhaFan88 Hill-Aerie-U.S.
Let the fool fall where he may
gnap!
5 PANELS, READ STRAIGHT AND NARROW
3.27.11
AhaFan88
I'd add some Sage to my meal but I'm worried about being taught life lessons for dinner.
AhaFan88
@zepfan69 Urinating on yourself is a "shower" but you should clarify using the adjective "golden" when reporting it. #peace, #cleanliness, #love.
AhaFan88
Jesus Christ my palms are gushing jokes today.
AhaFan 88
Fired my pizza while he was in the oven today for poor taste.
AhaFan88
Been jammin Spaghetti western soundtracks on this meat ball player through a solid state polenta amp.
AhaFan88
Freedom, the thief in the night, it comes and goes as it pleases.
AhaFan 88
last time I was here a dude walked in with a fucking hole in his head.
AhaFan88
Raising money to start online donut company, trillions of flavors, baked fresh daily.
AhaFan88
A friend just sent me a text, "I'm outside your house" To that I say, "yeah, you and everyone else.
AhaFan88
I think a donut shop just tried to kill me.
AhaFan 88
I'm applying to get back into my mother's womb, could anyone here write me a recommendation.
AhaFan88
Today I gave my shower a name, Epiphany.
AhaFan88
#iWalkMyOwnPath.
AhaFan88
@spideretc @zepfan69 He will take your wife.
AhaFan88
everytime I hear sirens I have to double check that I'm not on fire
AhaFan 88
I'd add some Sage to my meal but I'm worried about being taught life lessons for dinner.
AhaFan 88
@zepfan69 Urinating on yourself is a "shower" but you should clarify using the adjective "golden" when reporting it. #peace, #cleanliness, #love.
AhaFan88
Jesus christ my palms are gushing jokes today.
AhaFan 88
Fired my pizza while he was in the oven today for poor taste.
AhaFan 88
Been jammin spaghetti western soundtracks on
Gnaptime69
@AhaFan88 no one wants you dead, in fact, we want you alive and well, join us, be safe with us, let us strengthen together
AhaFan88
I think a donut shop just tried to kill me.
AhaFan 88
I'm applying to get back into my mother's womb, could anyone here write me a recommendation.
AhaFan88
Today I gave my shower a name, Epiphany.
AhaFan 88
#iWalkMyOwnPath
AhaFan 88
@spideretc @Zepfan69 He will take your wife.
AhaFan 88
everytime I hear sirens I have to double check that I'm not on fire.
AhaFan 88
I'd add some Sage to my meal but I'm worried about being taught life lessons for dinner.
AhaFan 88
@zepfan69 Urinating on yourself is a "shower" but you should clarify using the adjective "golden" when reporting it. #peace, #cleanliness, #love.
AhaFan 88
Jesus Christ my palms are gushing jokes today.
AhaFan 88
AhaFan88
@Gnaptime69 I don't know you, I don't want to know you, in fact I am going to convince myself you don't exist. #keepTheFaith.
Gnaptime69
@AhaFan88 no one wants you dead, in fact, we want you alive and well, join us, be safe with us, let us strengthen together
AhaFan88
I think a donut shop just tried to kill me.
AhaFan88
I'm applying to get back into my mother's womb, could anyone here write me a recommendation.
AhaFan88
Today I gave my shower a name, Epiphany.
AhaFan 88
#iWalkMyOwnPath
AhaFan 88
@spideretc @Zepfan69 He will take your wife.
AhaFan 88
everytime I hear sirens I have to double check that I'm not on fire.
AhaFan 88
I'd add some Sage to my meal but I'm worried about being taught life lessons for dinner.
AhaFan 88
@zepfan 69 Urinating on yourself is a "shower" but you should clarify using
Gnaptime69
There are two ways out of this situation, #Death or #LifeEternal.
Gnaptime 69
@AhaFan88 you love me already, you just don't yet know my name. All will exist within me for soon to come is the Dark Solidarity.
AhaFan88
@Gnaptime69 I don't know you, I don't want to know you, in fact I am going to convince myself you don't exist. #keepTheFaith.
Gnaptime69
@AhaFan88 no one wants you dead, in fact, we want you alive and well, join us, be safe with us, let us strengthen together.
AhaFan88
I think a donut shop just tried to kill me.
AhaFan88
I'm applying to get back into my mother's womb, could anyone here write me a recommendation.
AhaFan 88
Today I gave my shower a name, Epiphany.
AhaFan 88
#iWalkMyOwnPath
AhaFan 88

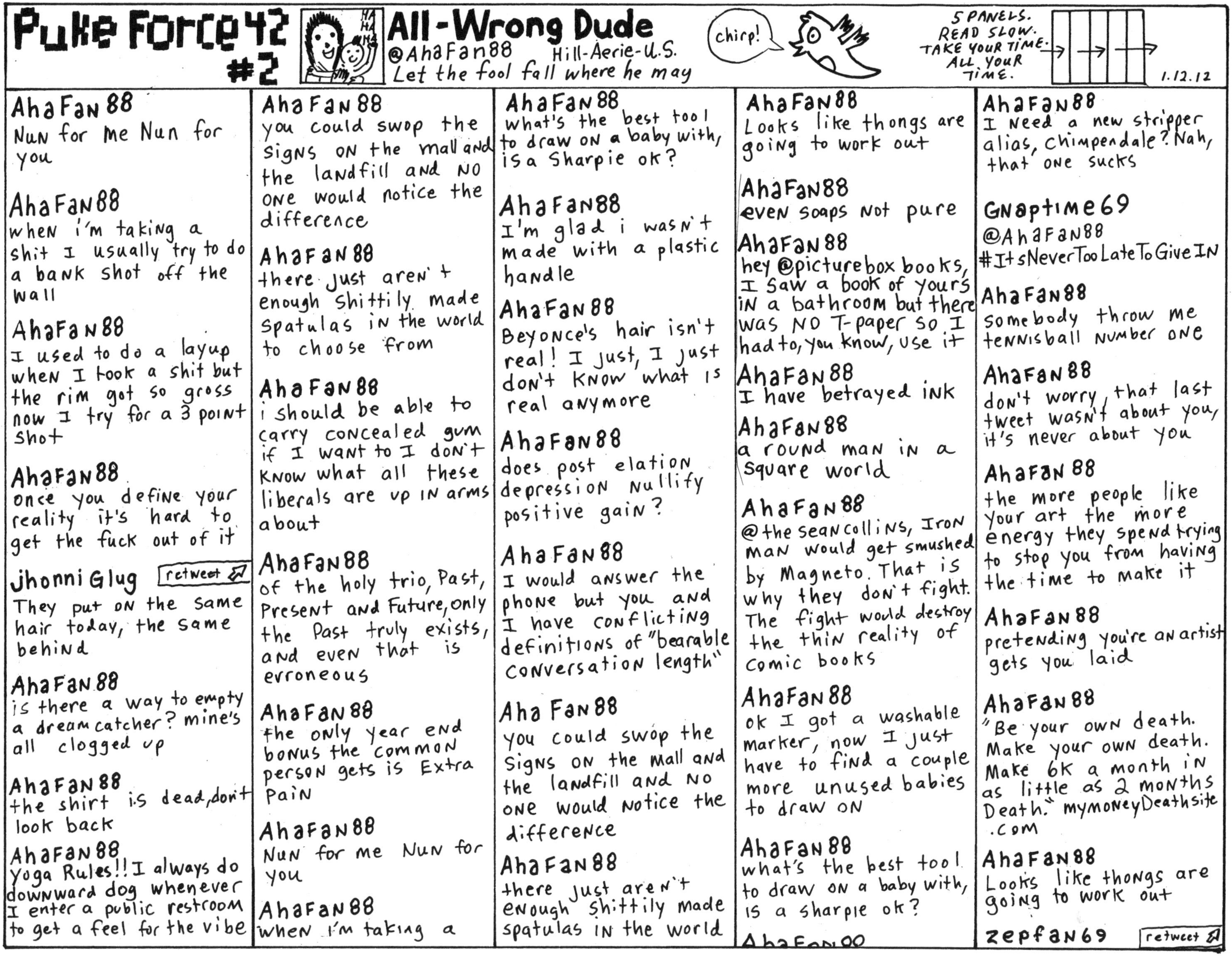
Puke Force 42
#2
HA HA HA
All-Wrong Dude
@AhaFan88 Hill-Aerie-U.S.
Let the fool fall where he may
chirp!
5 PANELS. READ SLOW. TAKE YOUR TIME. ALL YOUR TIME.
1.12.12
AhaFan88
Nun for me Nun for you
AhaFan88
when i'm taking a shit I usually try to do a bank shot off the wall
AhaFan88
I used to do a layup when I took a shit but the rim got so gross now I try for a 3 point shot
AhaFan88
once you define your reality it's hard to get the fuck out of it
jhonniGlug
retweet
They put on the same hair today, the same behind
AhaFan88
is there a way to empty a dream catcher? mine's all clogged up
AhaFan88
the shirt is dead, don't look back
AhaFan88
Yoga Rules!! I always do downward dog whenever I enter a public restroom to get a feel for the vibe
AhaFan88
you could swop the signs on the mall and the landfill and no one would notice the difference
AhaFan88
there just aren't enough shittily made spatulas in the world to choose from
AhaFan88
i should be able to carry concealed gum if I want to I don't know what all these liberals are up in arms about
AhaFan88
of the holy trio, Past, Present and Future, only the Past truly exists, and even that is erroneous
AhaFan88
the only year end bonus the common person gets is Extra Pain
AhaFan88
Nun for me Nun for you
AhaFan88
when i'm taking a
AhaFan88
what's the best tool to draw on a baby with, is a Sharpie ok?
AhaFan88
I'm glad i wasn't made with a plastic handle
AhaFan88
Beyonce's hair isn't real! I just, I just don't know what is real anymore
AhaFan88
does post elation depression nullify positive gain?
AhaFan88
I would answer the phone but you and I have conflicting definitions of "bearable conversation length"
AhaFan88
you could swop the signs on the mall and the landfill and no one would notice the difference
AhaFan88
there just aren't enough shittily made spatulas in the world
AhaFan88
Looks like thongs are going to work out
AhaFan88
even soaps not pure
AhaFan88
hey @pictureboxbooks, I saw a book of yours in a bathroom but there was no T-paper so I had to, you know, use it
AhaFan88
I have betrayed ink
AhaFan88
a round man in a square world
AhaFan88
@theseancollins, Iron man would get smushed by Magneto. That is why they don't fight. The fight would destroy the thin reality of comic books
AhaFan88
ok I got a washable marker, now I just have to find a couple more unused babies to draw on
AhaFan88
what's the best tool to draw on a baby with, is a sharpie ok?
AhaFan88
I need a new stripper alias, Chimpendale? Nah, that one sucks
Gnaptime69
@AhaFan88
#ItsNeverTooLateToGiveIn
AhaFan88
somebody throw me tennisball number one
AhaFan88
don't worry, that last tweet wasn't about you, it's never about you
AhaFan88
the more people like your art the more energy they spend trying to stop you from having the time to make it
AhaFan88
pretending you're an artist gets you laid
AhaFan88
"Be your own death. Make your own death. Make 6K a month in as little as 2 months Death." mymoneyDeathsite.com
AhaFan88
Looks like thongs are going to work out
zepfan69
retweet

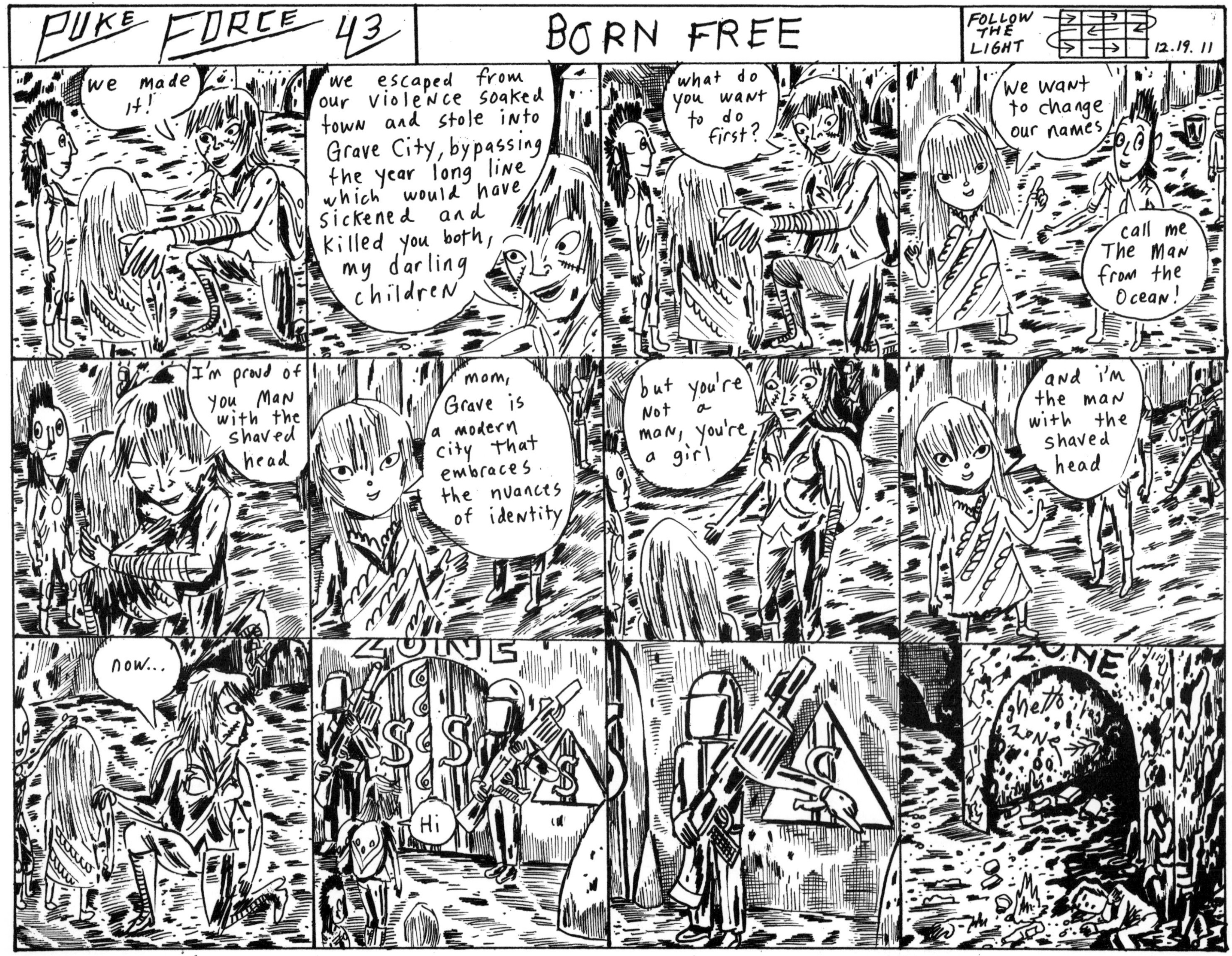
PUKE FORCE 43
BORN FREE
FOLLOW THE LIGHT
12.19.11
we made it!
we escaped from our violence soaked town and stole into Grave City, bypassing the year long line which would have sickened and killed you both, my darling children
what do you want to do first?
We want to change our names
call me The Man from the Ocean!
and i'm the man with the shaved head
but you're not a man, you're a girl
mom, Grave is a modern city that embraces the nuances of identity
I'm proud of you Man with the shaved head
now...
ZONE
Hi
ZONE
ghetto zone

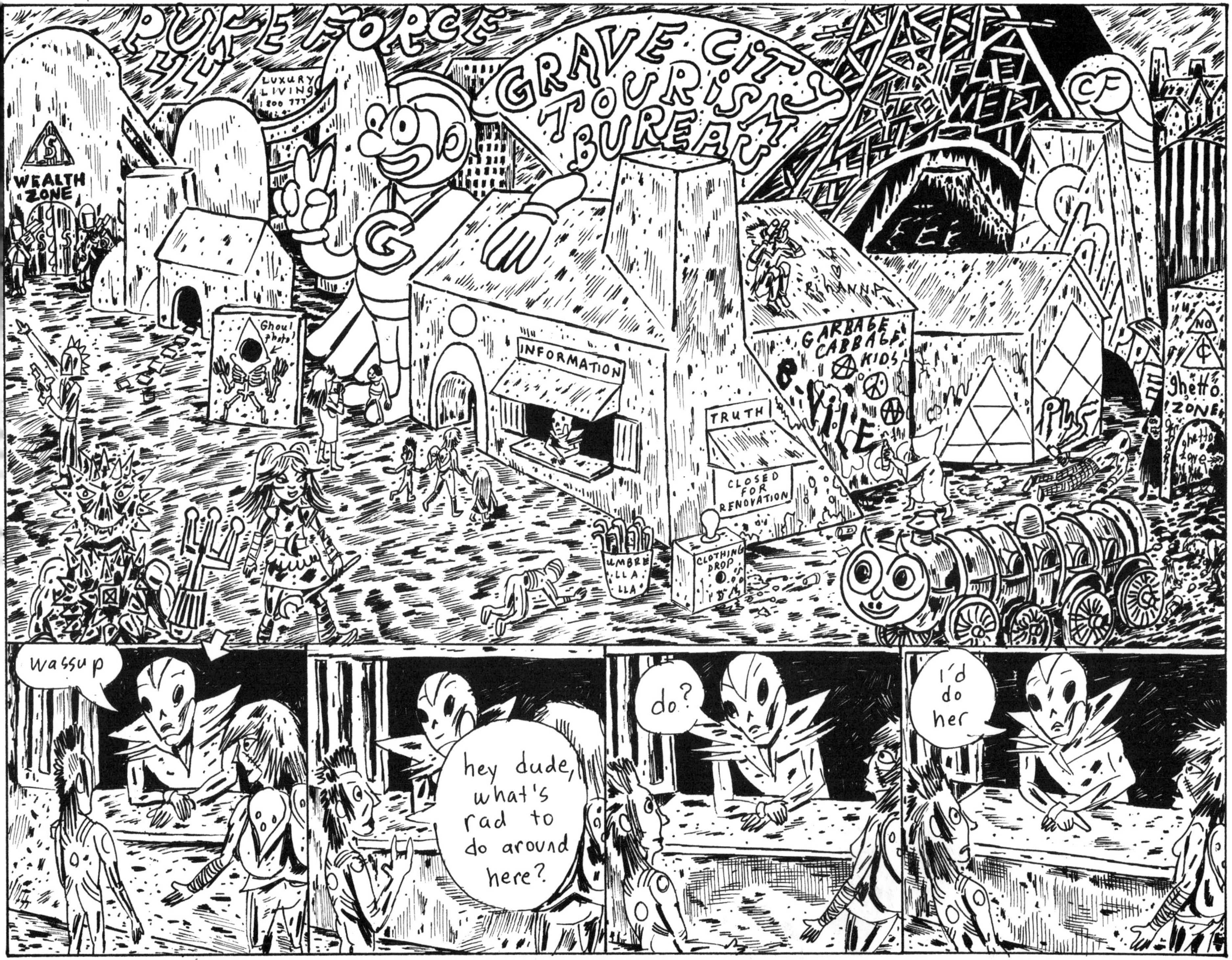
PURE FORCE
LUXURY LIVING 800 777
GRAVE CITY TOURISM BUREAU
EIFFLE TOWER
WEALTH ZONE
Ghoul photo
INFORMATION
TRUTH
CLOSED FOR RENOVATION
GARBAGE CABBAGE KIDS
B-VILE
RIHANNA
NO ¢
ghetto ZONE
ghetto zone
UMBRELLA LLA
CLOTHING DROP
wassup
hey dude, what's rad to do around here?
do?
I'd do her

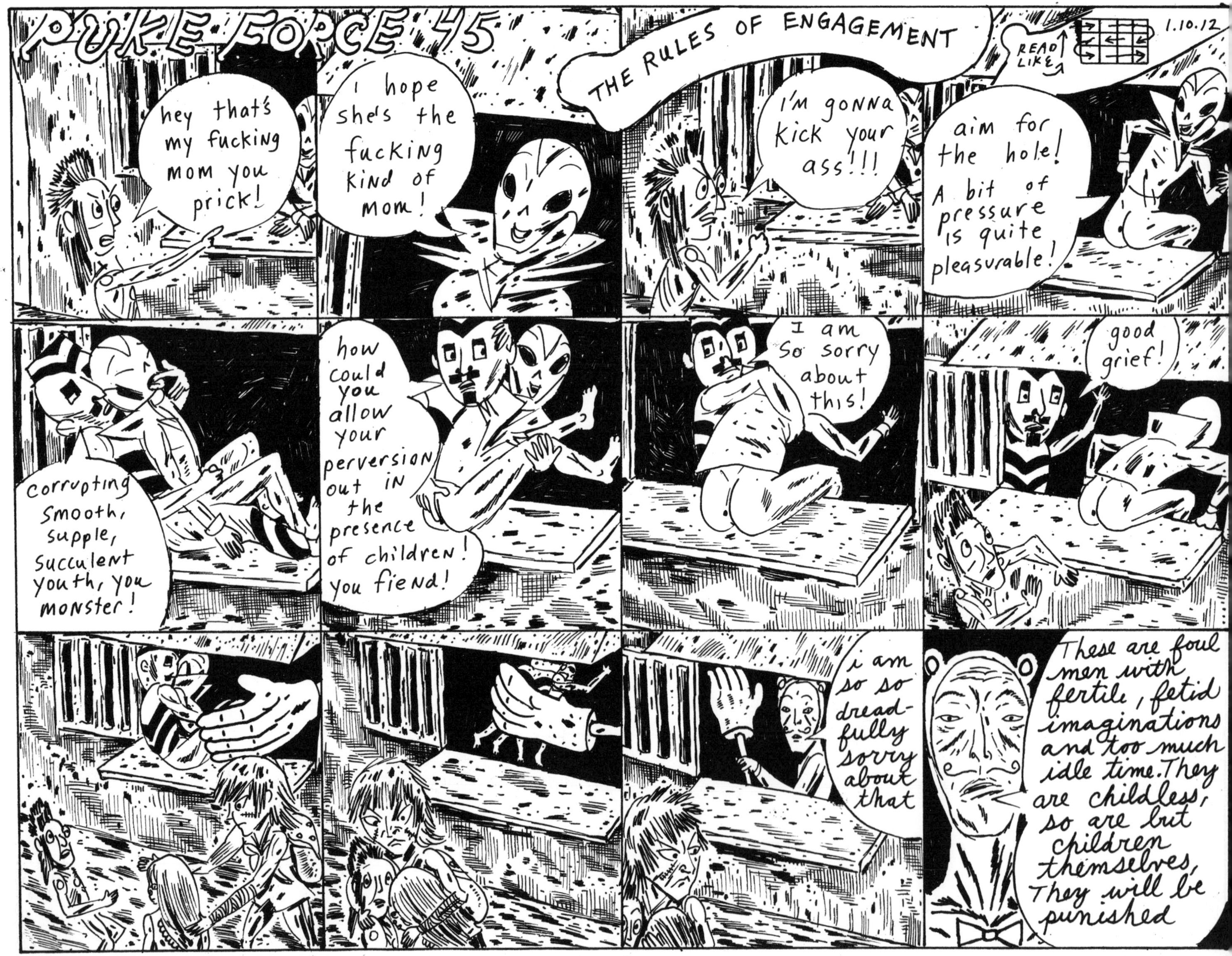

PUKE FORCE 45
THE RULES OF ENGAGEMENT
READ LIKE
1.10.12
hey that's my fucking mom you prick!
i hope she's the fucking kind of mom!
I'M GONNA KICK YOUR ASS!!!
aim for the hole! A bit of pressure is quite pleasurable!
good grief!
I am so sorry about this!
how could you allow your perversion out in the presence of children! you fiend!
corrupting smooth, supple, succulent youth, you monster!
i am so so dreadfully sorry about that
These are foul men with fertile, fetid imaginations and too much idle time. They are childless, so are but children themselves, They will be punished

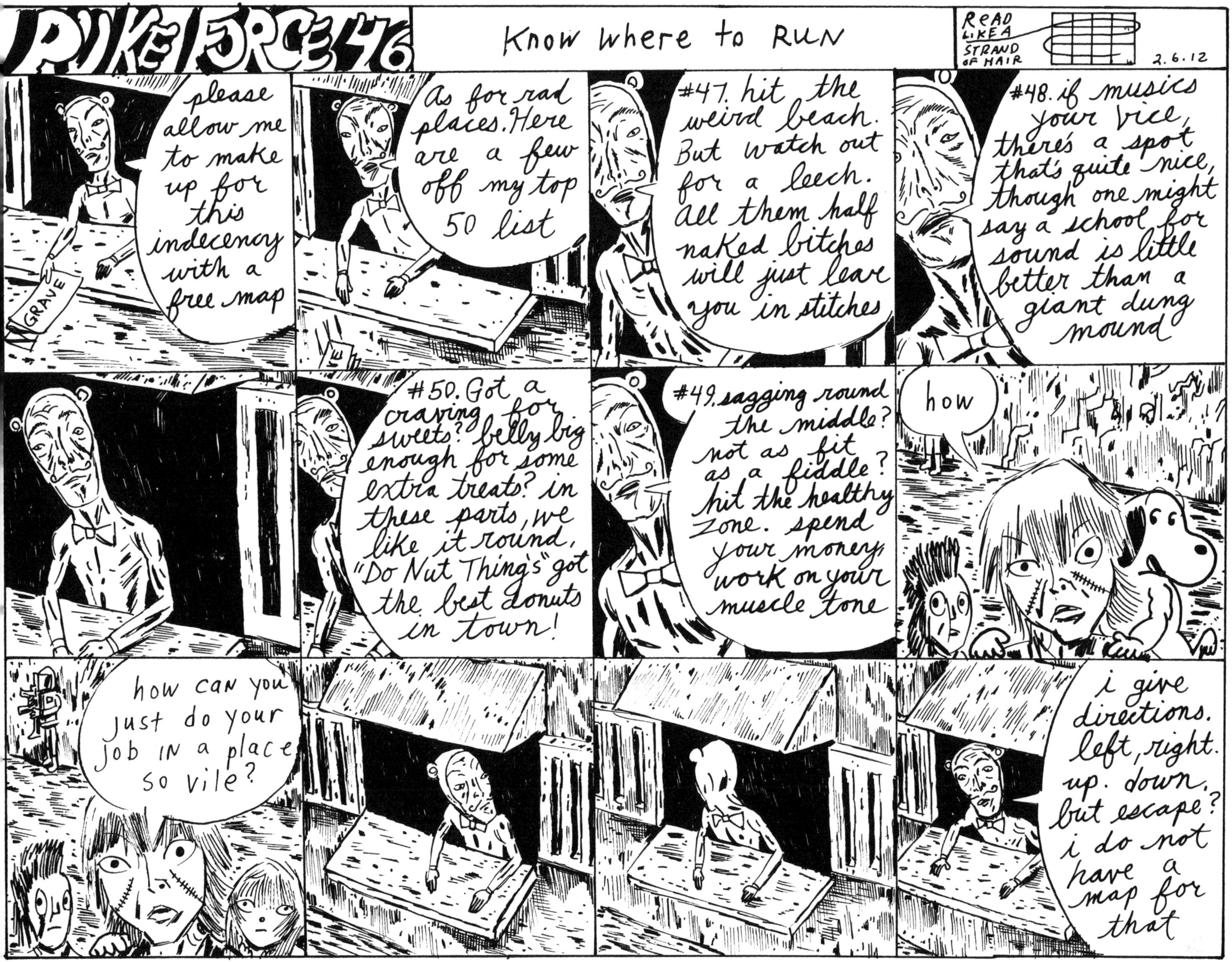
PIKE FORCE 46
Know where to RUN
READ LIKE A STRAND OF HAIR
2.6.12
please allow me to make up for this indecency with a free map
GRAVE
As for rad places. Here are a few off my top 50 list
#47. hit the weird beach. But watch out for a leech. All them half naked bitches will just leave you in stitches
#48. if musics your vice, there's a spot that's quite nice, though one might say a school for sound is little better than a giant dung mound
how
#49. sagging round the middle? not as fit as a fiddle? hit the healthy zone. spend your money work on your muscle tone
#50. Got a craving for sweets? belly big enough for some extra treats? in these parts, we like it round. "Do Nut Thing's" got the best donuts in town!
how can you just do your job in a place so vile?
i give directions. left, right. up. down. but escape? i do not have a map for that

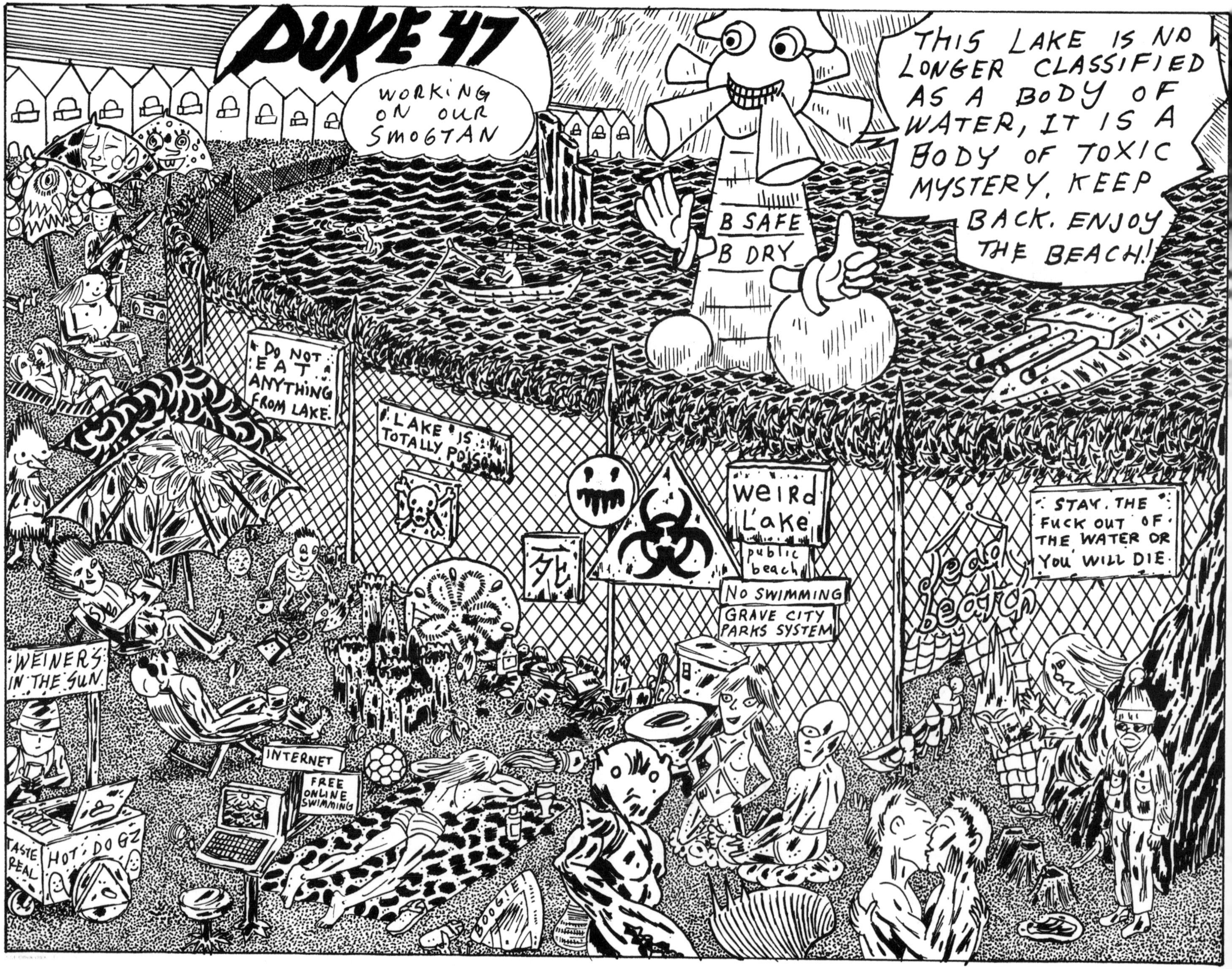
PUKE 47
WORKING ON OUR SMOGTAN
THIS LAKE IS NO LONGER CLASSIFIED AS A BODY OF WATER, IT IS A BODY OF TOXIC MYSTERY. KEEP BACK. ENJOY THE BEACH!
B SAFE
B DRY
DO NOT EAT ANYTHING FROM LAKE.
LAKE IS TOTALLY POISON
死
weird Lake
public beach
NO SWIMMING
GRAVE CITY PARKS SYSTEM
STAY THE FUCK OUT OF THE WATER OR YOU WILL DIE
dead beach
WEINERS IN THE SUN
INTERNET
FREE ONLINE SWIMMING
TASTE REAL
HOT DOGZ
BOOGIE

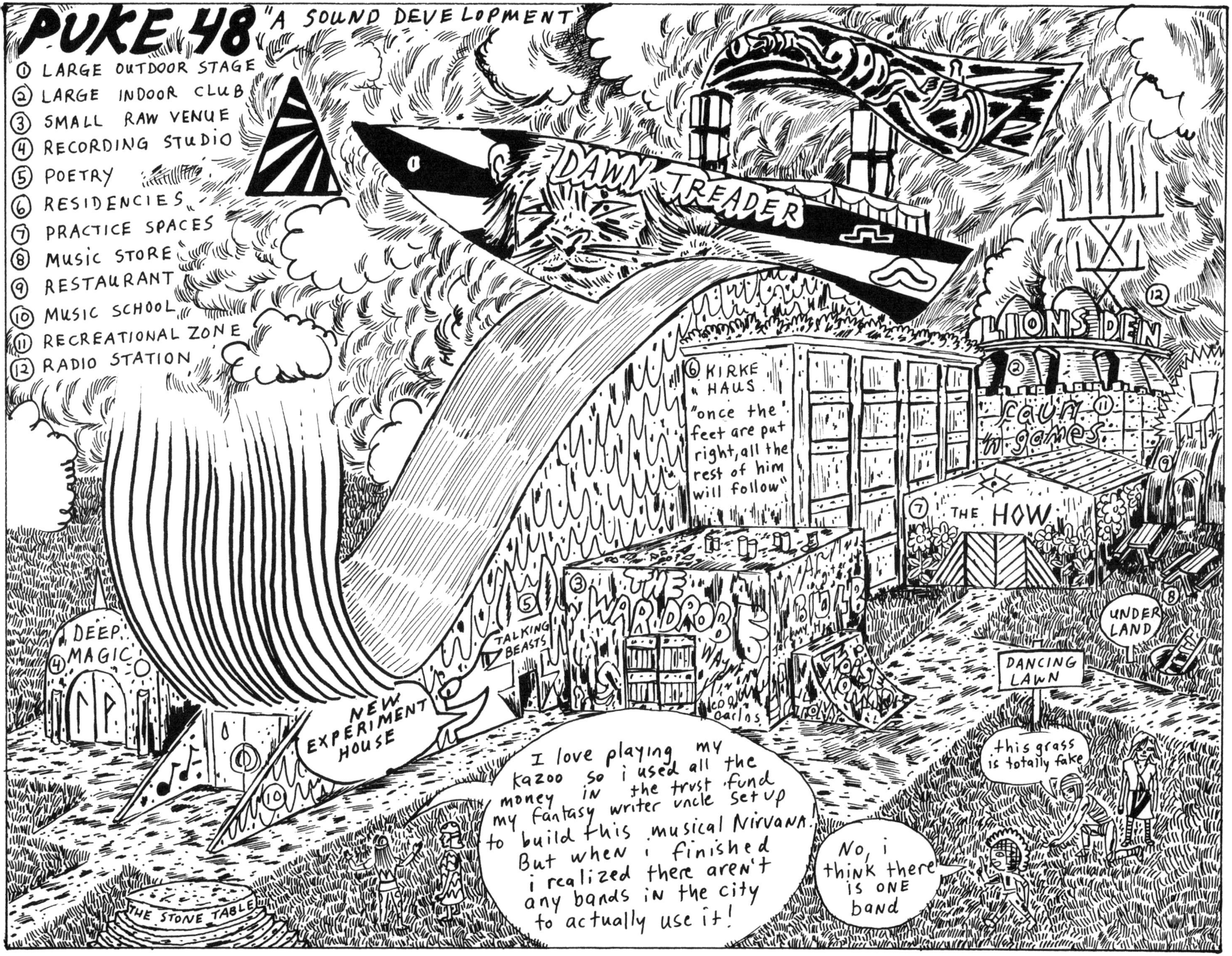

PUKE 48
"A SOUND DEVELOPMENT"
① LARGE OUTDOOR STAGE
② LARGE INDOOR CLUB
③ SMALL RAW VENUE
④ RECORDING STUDIO
⑤ POETRY
⑥ RESIDENCIES
⑦ PRACTICE SPACES
⑧ MUSIC STORE
⑨ RESTAURANT
⑩ MUSIC SCHOOL
⑪ RECREATIONAL ZONE
⑫ RADIO STATION
DAWN TREADER
LIONS DEN
⑥ KIRKE HAUS
"once the feet are put right, all the rest of him will follow"
faun games
⑦ THE HOW
③ THE WARDROBE
TALKING BEASTS
DEEP MAGIC
NEW EXPERIMENT HOUSE
UNDER LAND
DANCING LAWN
THE STONE TABLE
I love playing my kazoo so i used all the money in the trust fund my fantasy writer uncle set up to build this musical Nirvana. But when i finished i realized there aren't any bands in the city to actually use it!
No, i think there is ONE band
this grass is totally fake

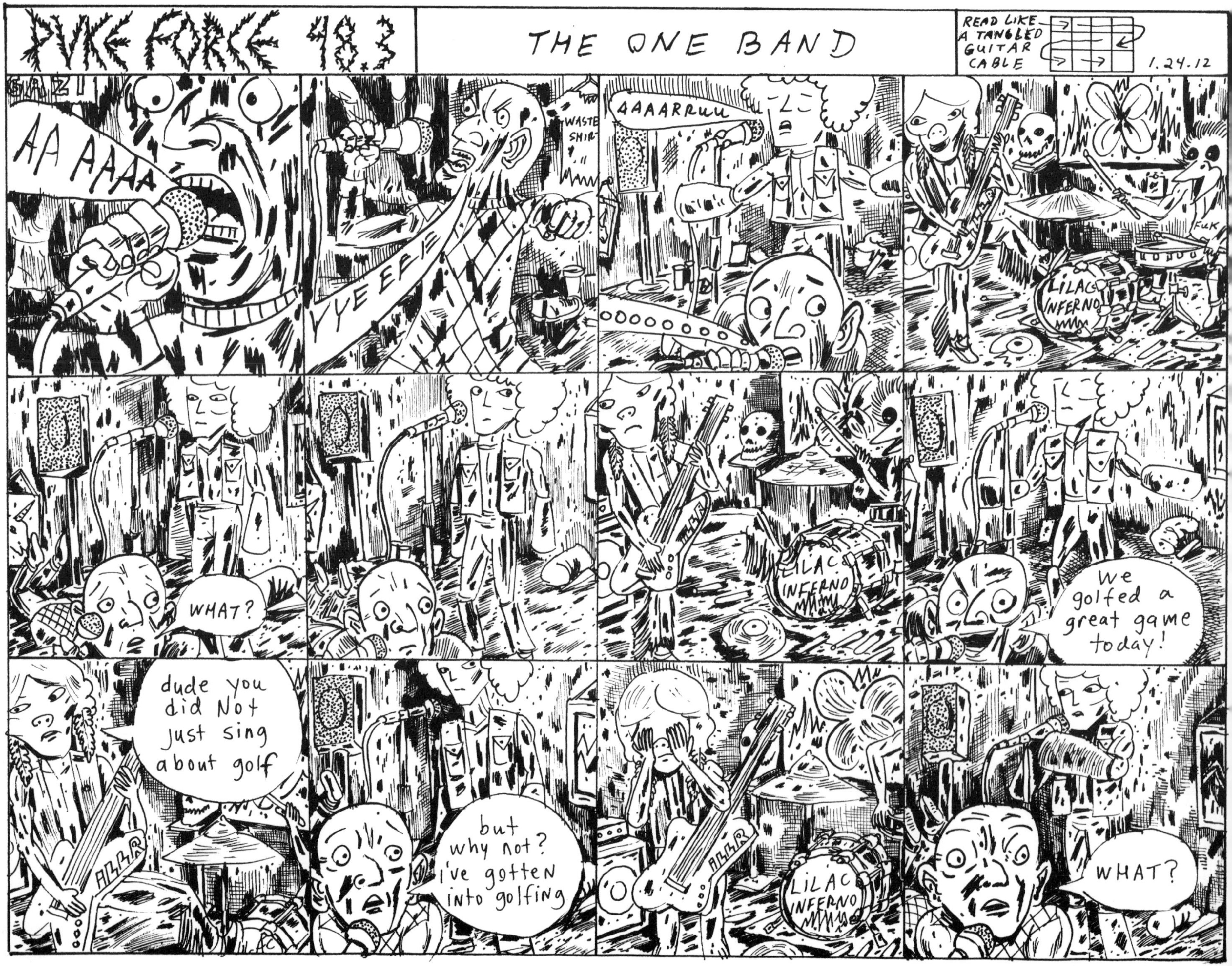
PUKE FORCE 48.3
THE ONE BAND
READ LIKE A TANGLED GUITAR CABLE
1.24.12
AA AAAA
YYEEEE
WASTE SHIR
AAAARRUU
OOOOOOOO
LILAC INFERNO
FUK
we golfed a great game today!
LILAC INFERNO
WHAT?
dude you did Not just sing about golf
but why not? I've gotten into golfing
LILAC INFERNO
WHAT?

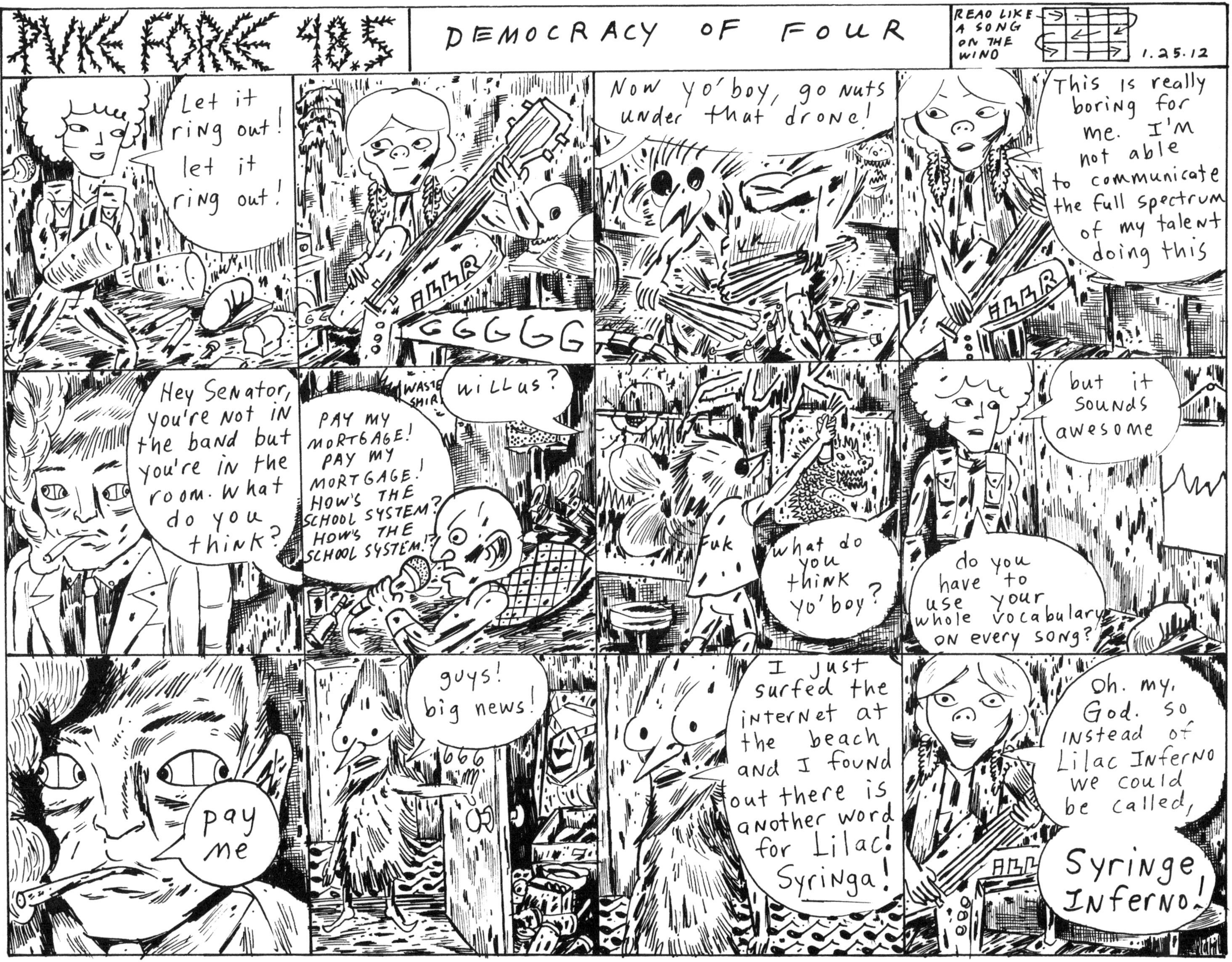
PVKE FORCE 18.5
DEMOCRACY OF FOUR
READ LIKE A SONG ON THE WIND
1.25.12
Let it ring out! let it ring out!
ABBR
GGGGG
Now yo' boy, go nuts under that drone!
This is really boring for me. I'm not able to communicate the full spectrum of my talent doing this
but it sounds awesome
do you have to use your whole vocabulary on every song?
Fuk
what do you think yo' boy?
WASTE SHIR
willus?
PAY MY MORTGAGE! PAY MY MORTGAGE! HOW'S THE SCHOOL SYSTEM? HOW'S THE SCHOOL SYSTEM!?
Hey Senator, you're not in the band but you're in the room. What do you think?
pay me
guys! big news!
666
I just surfed the internet at the beach and I found out there is another word for Lilac! Syringa!
Oh. my. God. so instead of Lilac Inferno we could be called,
Syringe Inferno!

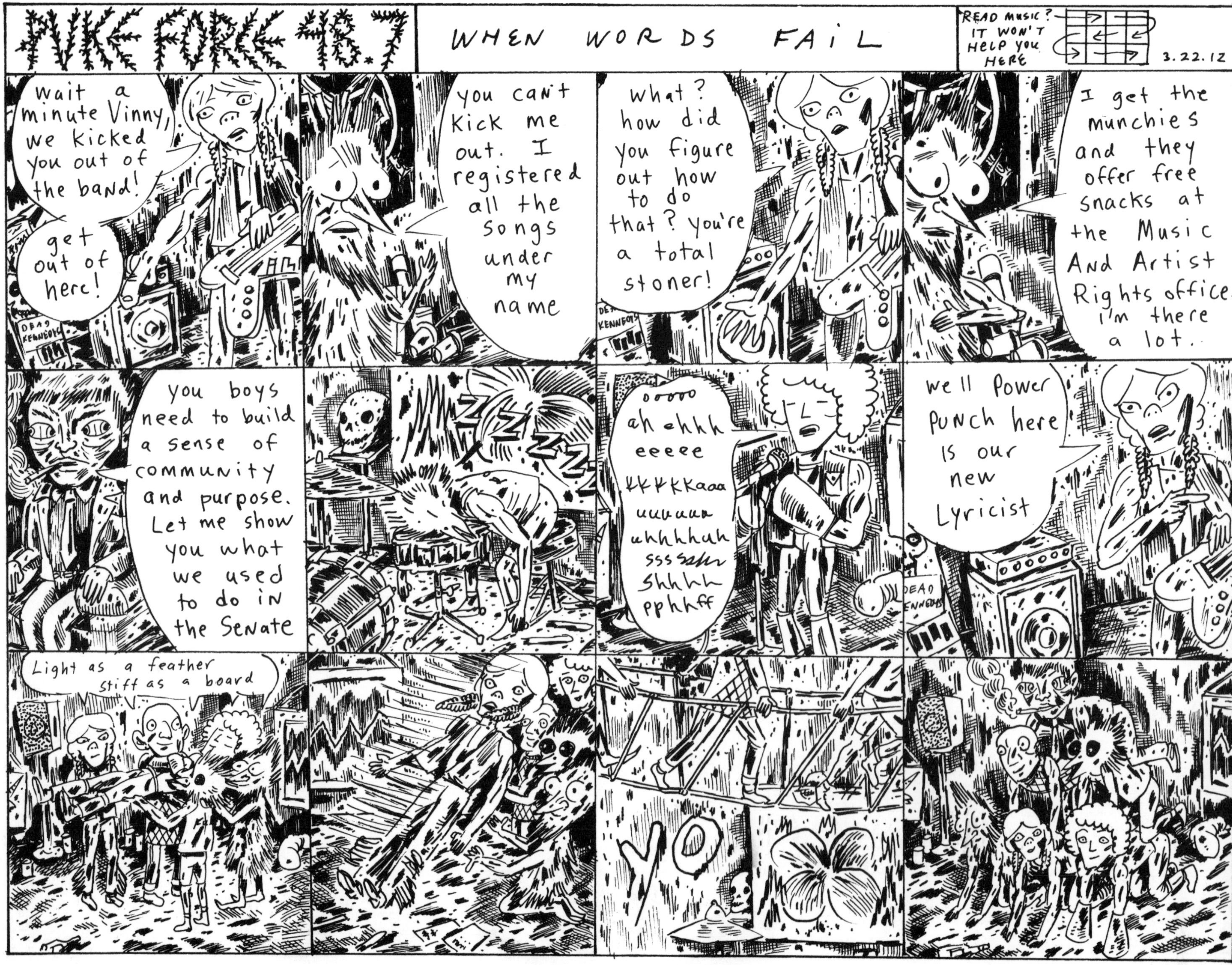
PYKE FORCE #18.7
WHEN WORDS FAIL
READ MUSIC? IT WON'T HELP YOU HERE
3.22.12
wait a minute Vinny, we kicked you out of the band!
get out of here!
you can't kick me out. I registered all the songs under my name
what? how did you figure out how to do that? you're a total stoner!
I get the munchies and they offer free snacks at the Music And Artist Rights office. I'm there a lot.
you boys need to build a sense of community and purpose. Let me show you what we used to do in the Senate
ZZZZ
ooooo ah ehhh eeeee KKKKKaaa uuuuuu uhhhhuh ssssshh Shhhh pphhff
well Power Punch here is our new Lyricist
Light as a feather stiff as a board
YO

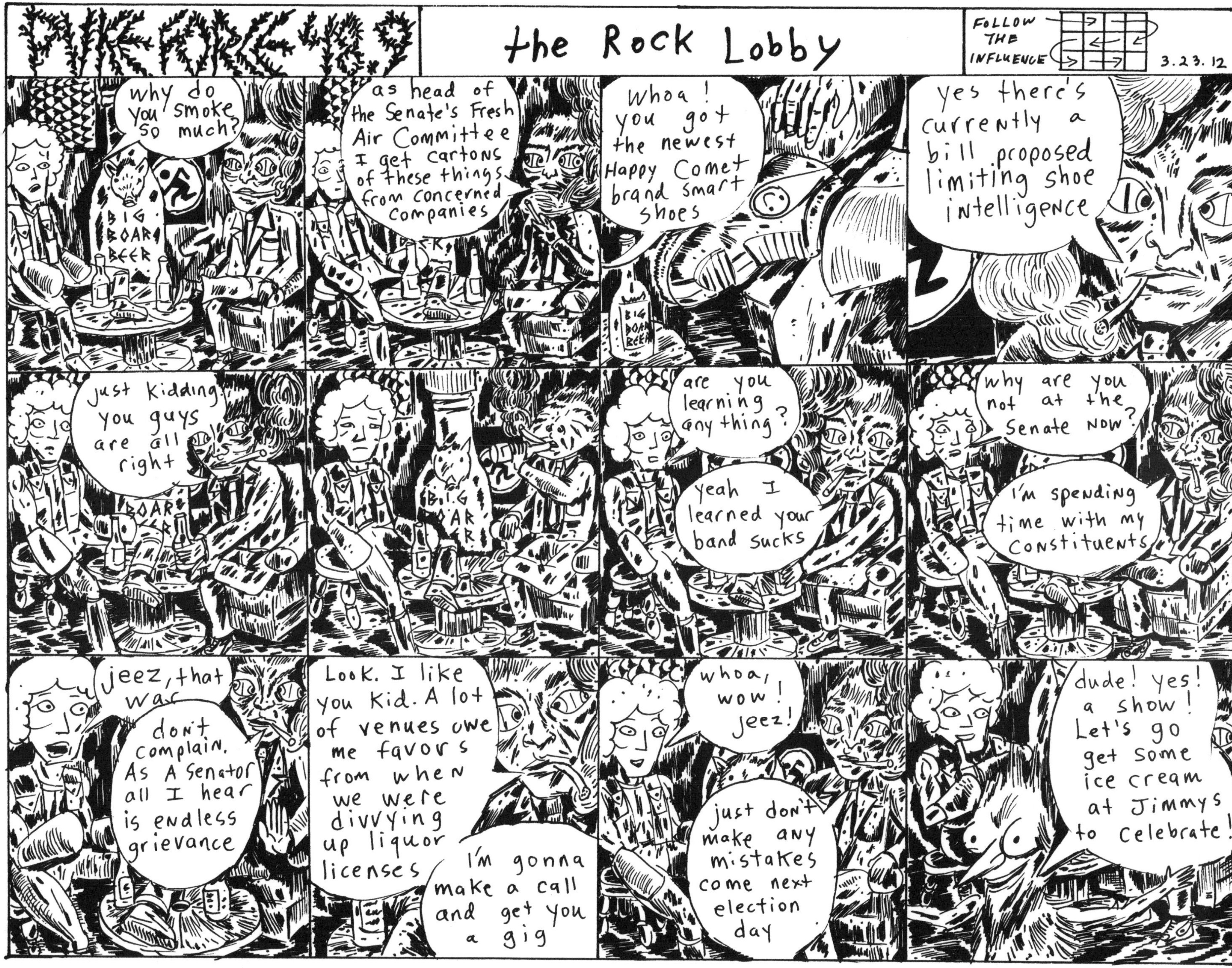

the Rock Lobby
FOLLOW THE INFLUENCE
3.23.12
why do you smoke so much?
BIG BOAR BEER
as head of the Senate's Fresh Air Committee I get cartons of these things from concerned companies
Whoa! you got the newest Happy Comet brand smart shoes
yes there's currently a bill proposed limiting shoe intelligence
just kidding. you guys are all right
are you learning any thing?
yeah I learned your band sucks
why are you not at the Senate now?
I'm spending time with my constituents
jeez, that war
don't complain. As A Senator all I hear is endless grievance
Look. I like you kid. A lot of venues owe me favors from when we were divvying up liquor licenses
I'm gonna make a call and get you a gig
whoa, wow! Jeez!
just don't make any mistakes come next election day
dude! yes! a show! Let's go get some ice cream at Jimmys to celebrate!

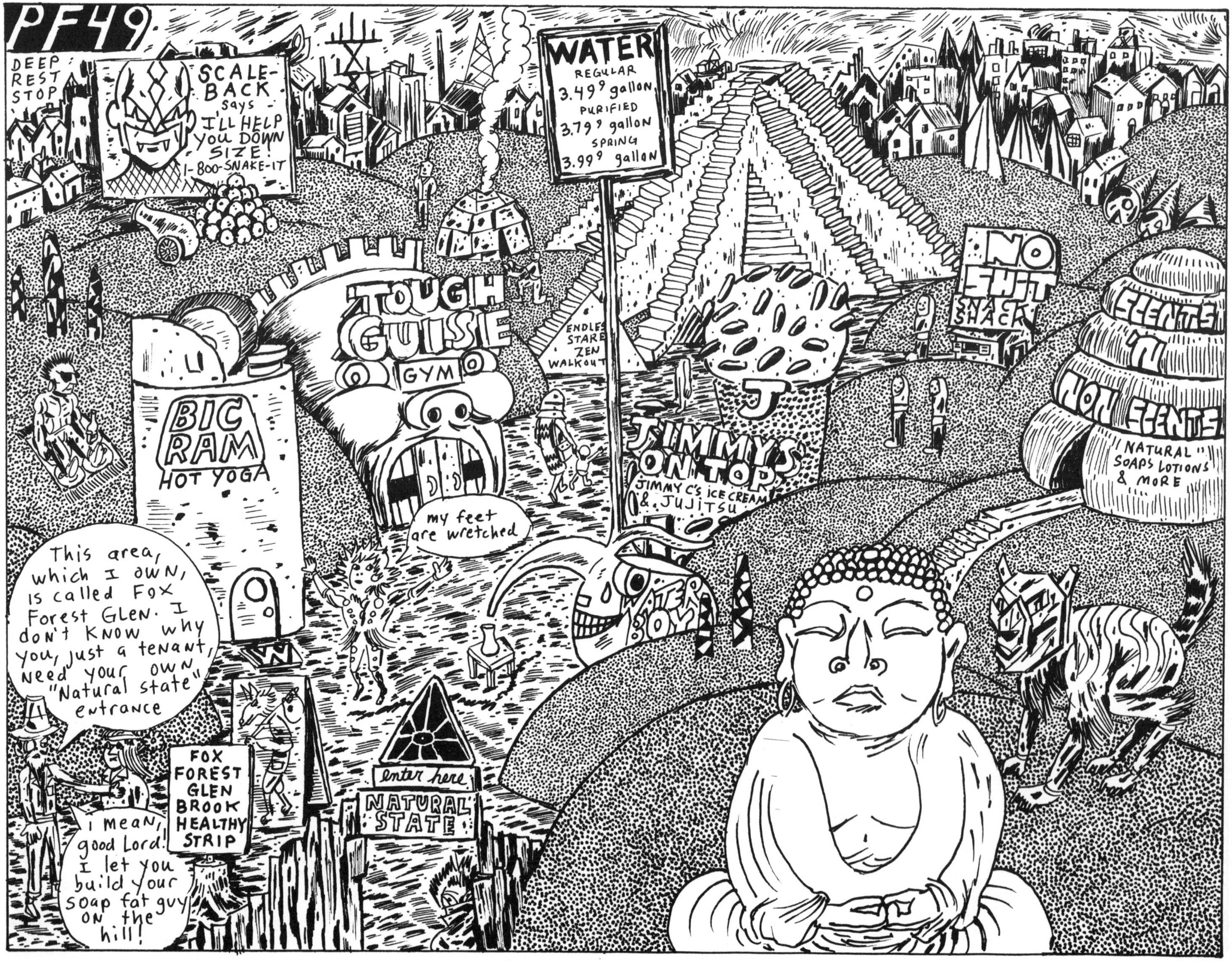
PF49
DEEP REST STOP
SCALE-BACK says I'LL HELP YOU DOWN SIZE 1-800-SNAKE-IT
WATER REGULAR 3.49⁹ gallon PURIFIED 3.79⁹ gallon SPRING 3.99⁹ gallon
NO SHIT SNACK SHACK
TOUGH GUISE GYM
ENDLESS STARE ZEN WALKOUT
CLEENTS 'N NON CLEENTS
NATURAL SOAPS LOTIONS & MORE
BIG RAM HOT YOGA
JIMMY'S ON TOP JIMMY C'S ICE CREAM & JUJITSU
my feet are wretched
WATER BOY
This area, which I OWN, is called Fox Forest Glen. I don't know you, just a tenant, need your own "Natural state" entrance
I mean, good Lord! I let you build your soap fat guy on the hill!
FOX FOREST GLEN BROOK HEALTHY STRIP
Enter here
NATURAL STATE

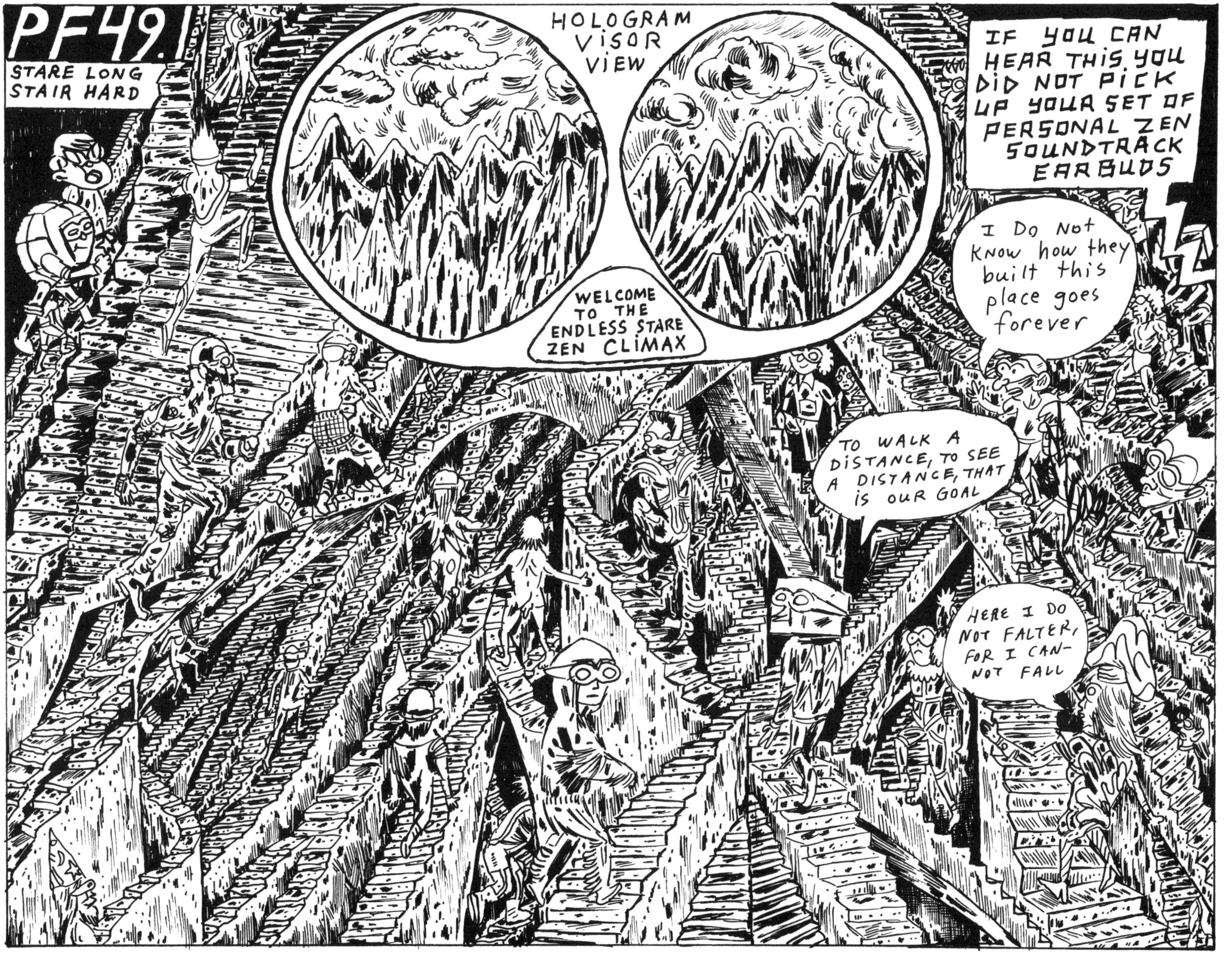
PF49.1
STARE LONG STAIR HARD
HOLOGRAM VISOR VIEW
WELCOME TO THE ENDLESS STARE ZEN CLIMAX
IF YOU CAN HEAR THIS YOU DID NOT PICK UP YOUR SET OF PERSONAL ZEN SOUNDTRACK EARBUDS
I Do Not Know how they built this place goes forever
TO WALK A DISTANCE, TO SEE A DISTANCE, THAT IS OUR GOAL
HERE I DO NOT FALTER, FOR I CAN-NOT FALL

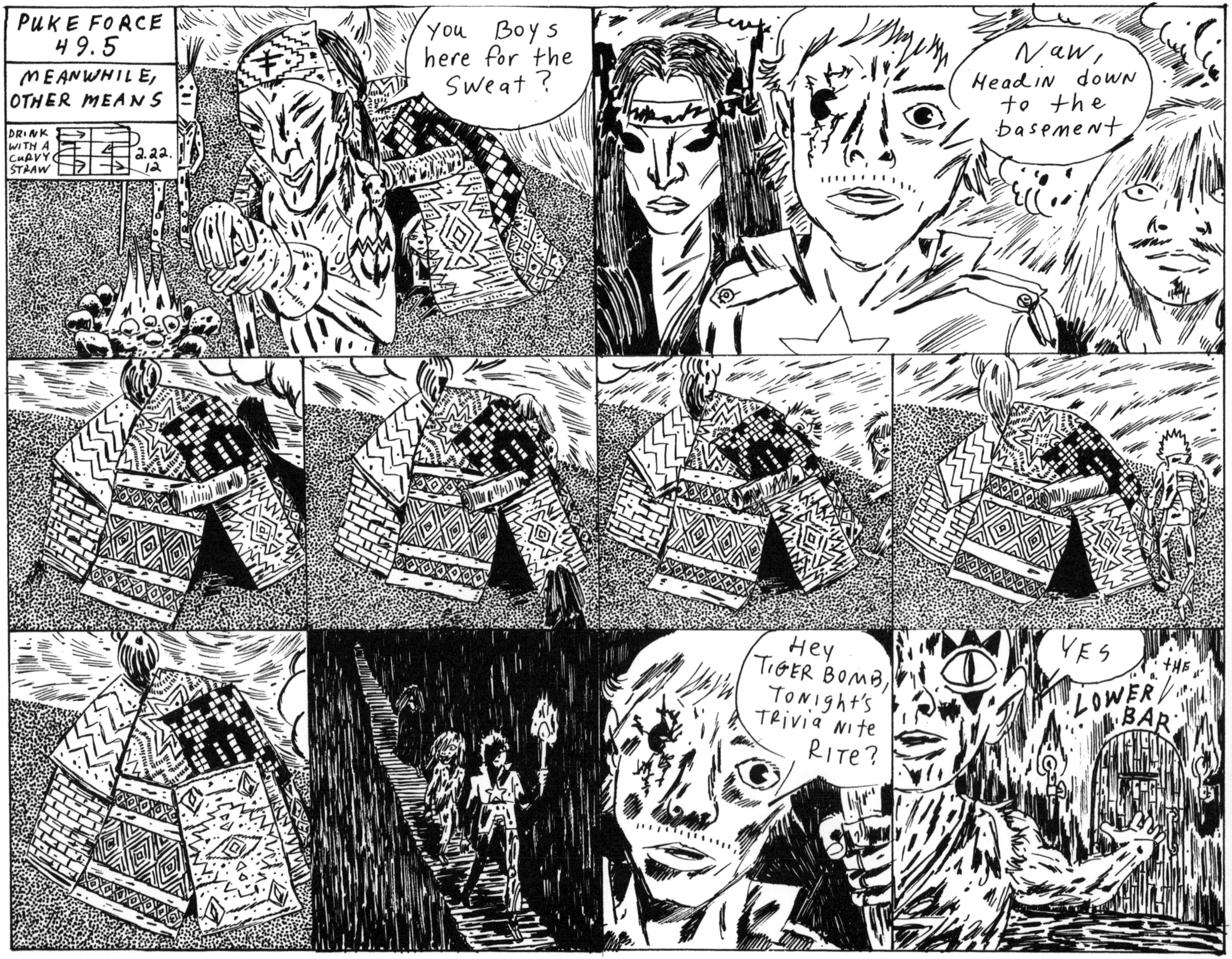
PUKE FORCE 49.5
MEANWHILE, OTHER MEANS
DRINK WITH A CURVY STRAW
2.22.12
You Boys here for the Sweat?
Naw, Headin down to the basement
Hey TIGER BOMB, Tonight's Trivia Nite Rite?
YES
THE LOWER BAR

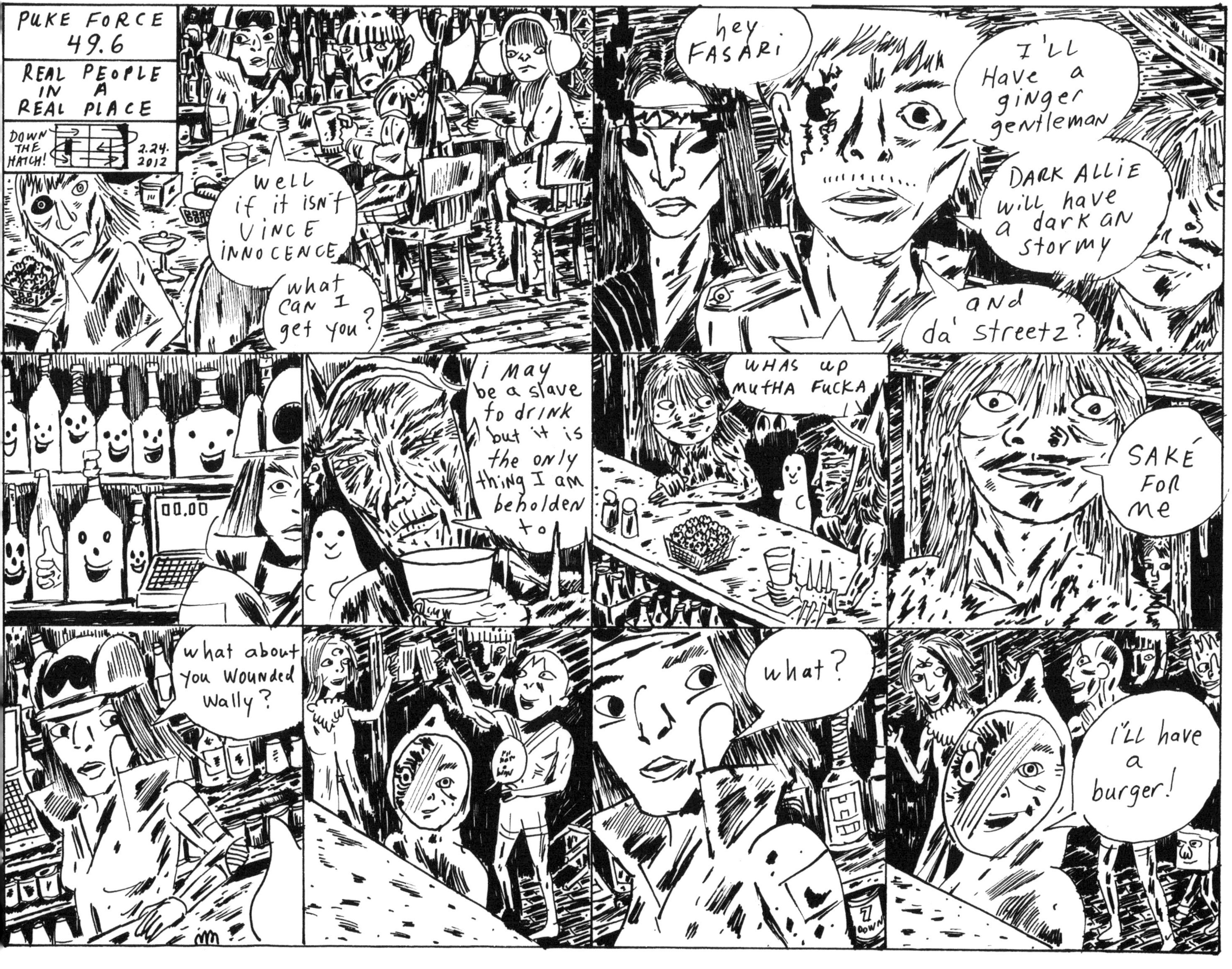
PUKE FORCE 49.6
REAL PEOPLE IN A REAL PLACE
DOWN THE HATCH!
2.24.2012
WELL if it isn't VINCE INNOCENCE
what CAN I get you?
hey FASARI
I'LL Have a ginger gentleman
DARK ALLIE will have a dark an stormy
and da' streetz?
00.00
i May be a slave to drink but it is the only thing I am beholden to
WHAS up MUTHA FUCKA
SAKÉ FOR me
what about you WOUNDED Wally?
what?
I'LL have a burger!

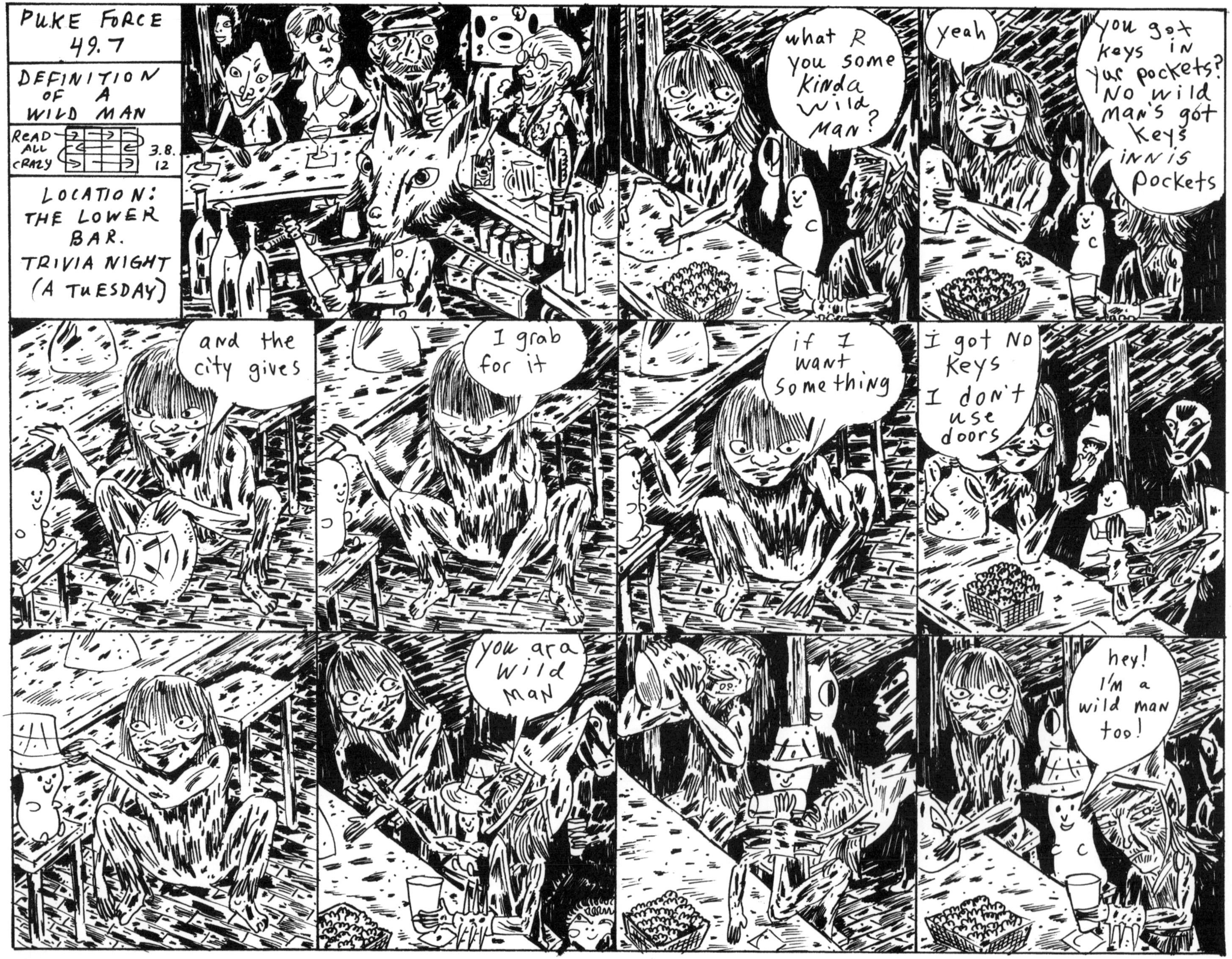
PUKE FORCE 49.7
DEFINITION OF A WILD MAN
READ ALL CRAZY
3.8.12
LOCATION: THE LOWER BAR. TRIVIA NIGHT (A TUESDAY)
what R you some Kinda wild man?
yeah
you got keys in yur pockets? No wild man's got keys innis pockets
and the city gives
I grab for it
if I want something
I got NO keys I don't use doors
you ara wild man
hey! I'M a wild man too!

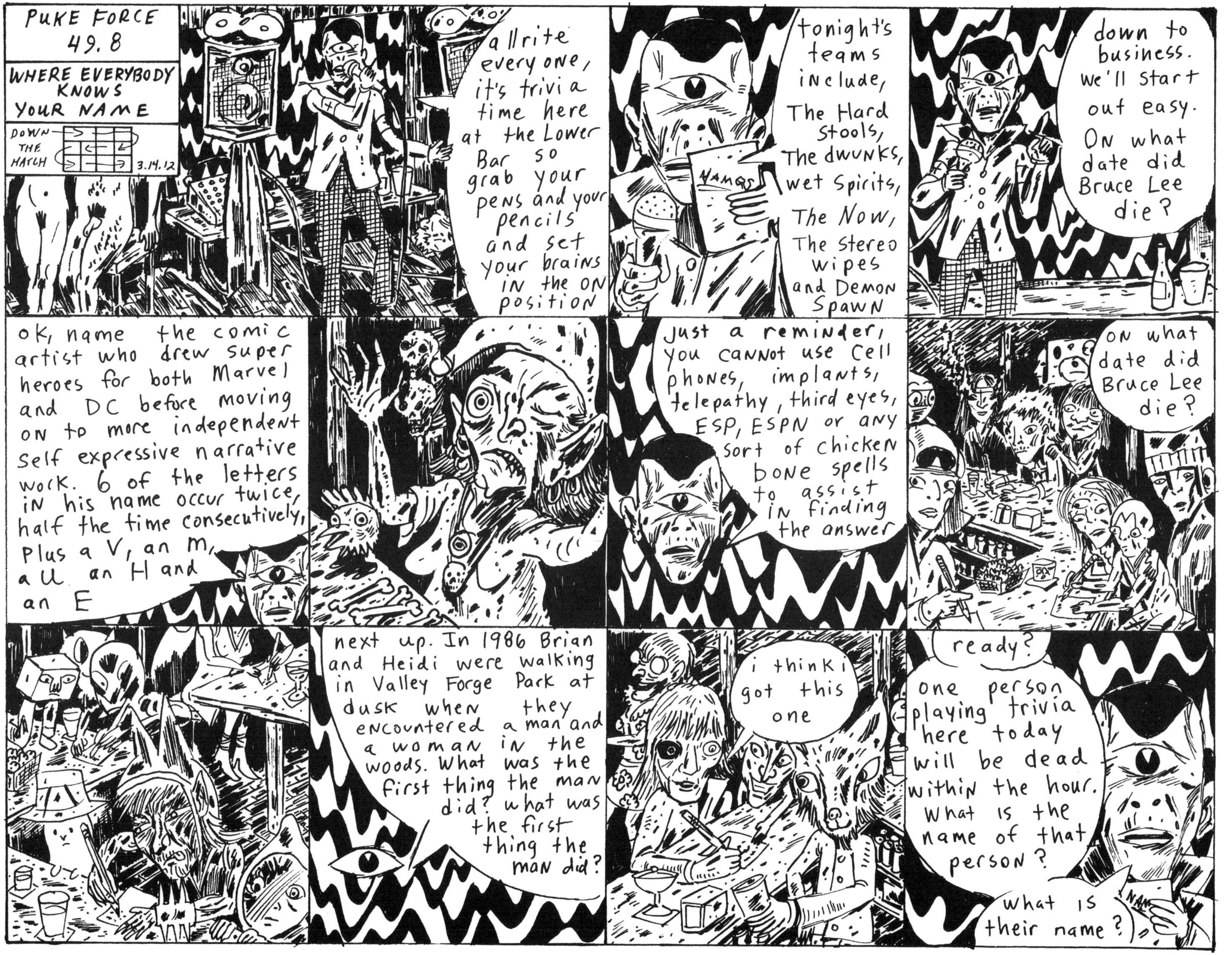

PUKE FORCE 49.8
WHERE EVERYBODY KNOWS YOUR NAME
DOWN THE HATCH
3.14.12
allrite everyone, it's trivia time here at the Lower Bar so grab your pens and your pencils and set your brains in the ON position
tonight's teams include, The Hard Stools, The dwunks, wet Spirits, The Now, The Stereo wipes and Demon Spawn
NAMES
down to business. we'll start out easy. On what date did Bruce Lee die?
ok, name the comic artist who drew super heroes for both Marvel and DC before moving on to more independent self expressive narrative work. 6 of the letters in his name occur twice, half the time consecutively, Plus a V, an M, a U, an H and an E
Just a reminder, you cannot use Cell phones, implants, telepathy, third eyes, ESP, ESPN or any sort of chicken bone spells to assist in finding the answer
On what date did Bruce Lee die?
next up. In 1986 Brian and Heidi were walking in Valley Forge Park at dusk when they encountered a man and a woman in the woods. What was the first thing the man did? what was the first thing the man did?
i think i got this one
ready?
one person playing trivia here today will be dead within the hour. What is the name of that person?
what is their name?

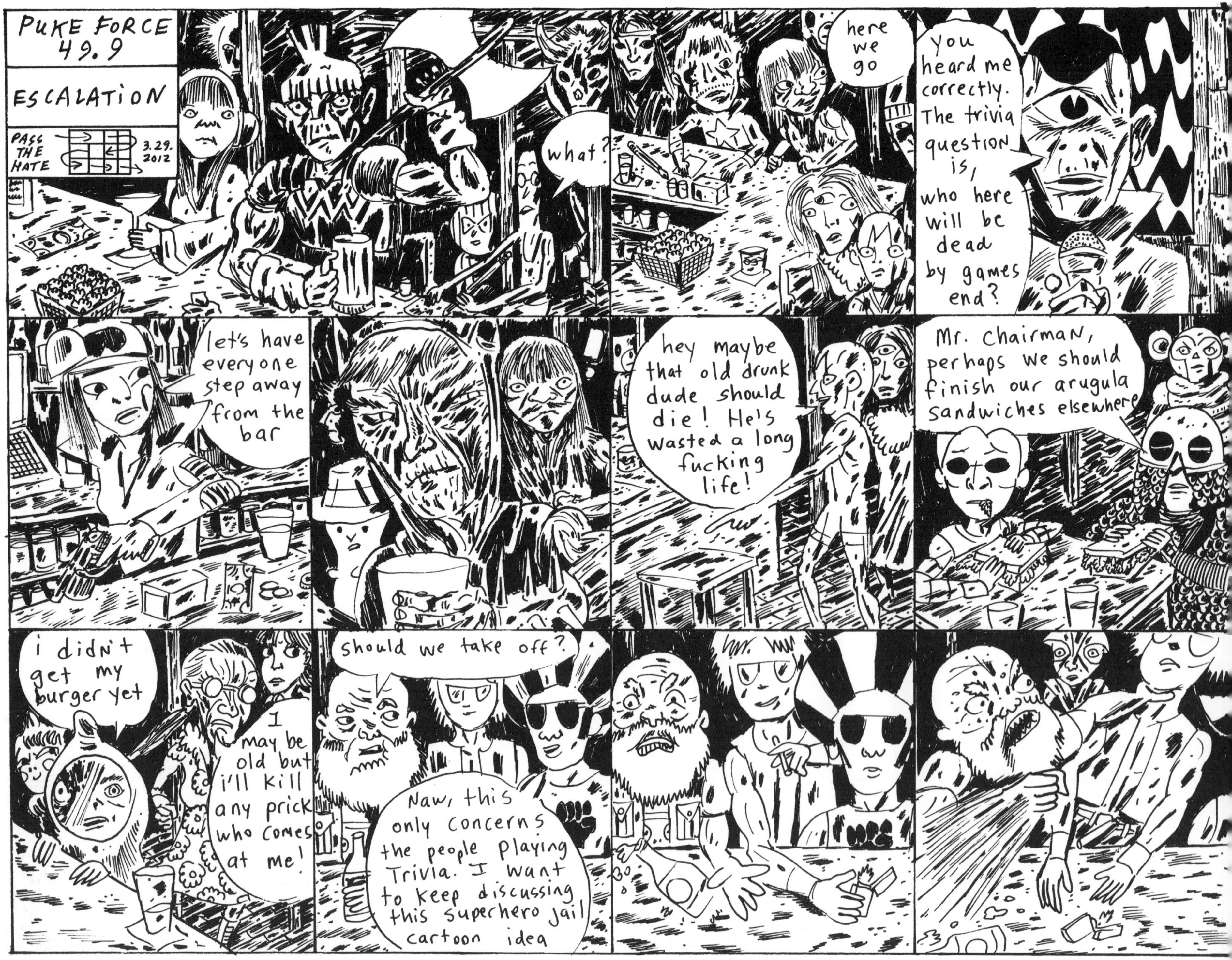
PUKE FORCE 49.9
ESCALATION
PASS THE HATE
3.29.2012
what?
here we go
you heard me correctly. The trivia question is, who here will be dead by games end?
let's have everyone step away from the bar
hey maybe that old drunk dude should die! He's wasted a long fucking life!
Mr. Chairman, perhaps we should finish our arugula sandwiches elsewhere
i didn't get my burger yet
I may be old but i'll kill any prick who comes at me!
should we take off?
Naw, this only concerns the people playing Trivia. I want to keep discussing this superhero jail cartoon idea

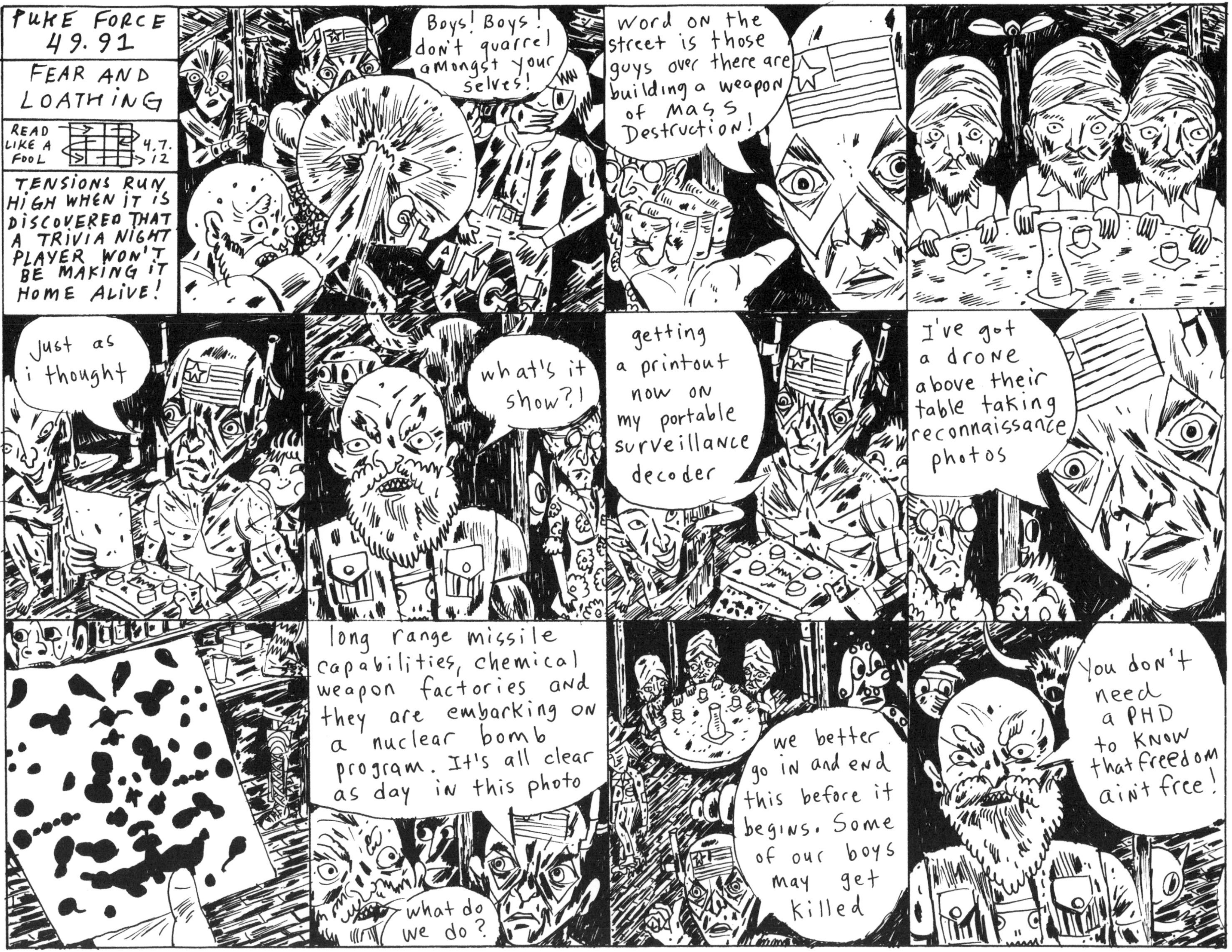
PUKE FORCE
49.91
FEAR AND LOATHING
READ LIKE A FOOL
4.7.12
TENSIONS RUN HIGH WHEN IT IS DISCOVERED THAT A TRIVIA NIGHT PLAYER WON'T BE MAKING IT HOME ALIVE!
Boys! Boys! don't quarrel amongst your selves!
Word on the street is those guys over there are building a weapon of Mass Destruction!
I've got a drone above their table taking reconnaissance photos
getting a printout now on my portable surveillance decoder
what's it show?!
Just as i thought
long range missile capabilities, chemical weapon factories and they are embarking on a nuclear bomb program. It's all clear as day in this photo
what do we do?
we better go in and end this before it begins. Some of our boys may get killed
You don't need a PHD to know that freedom ain't free!

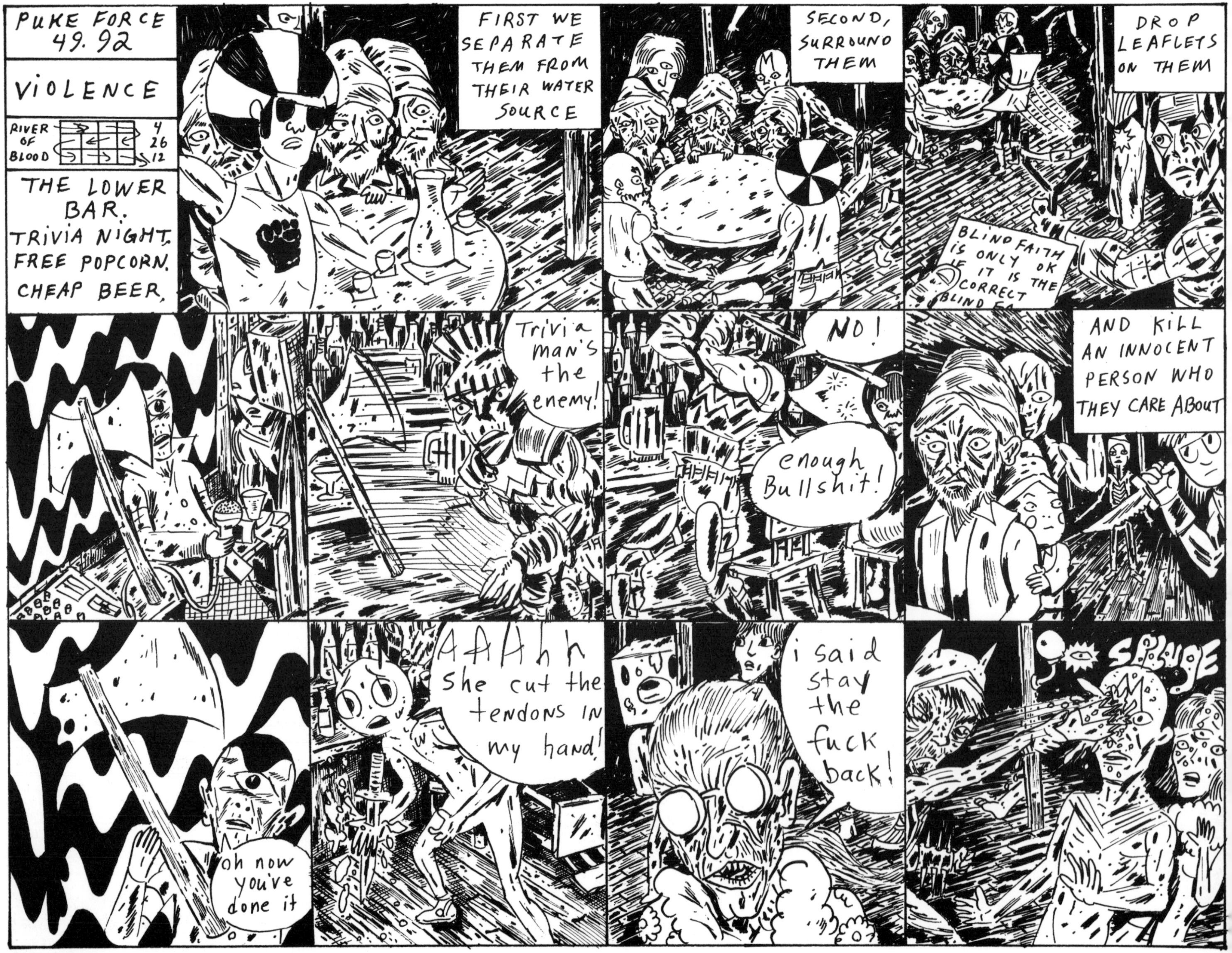
PUKE FORCE
49.92
VIOLENCE
RIVER OF BLOOD
4
26
12
THE LOWER BAR. TRIVIA NIGHT. FREE POPCORN. CHEAP BEER.
FIRST WE SEPARATE THEM FROM THEIR WATER SOURCE
SECOND, SURROUND THEM
DROP LEAFLETS ON THEM
BLIND FAITH IS ONLY OK IF IT IS THE CORRECT BLIND FA
Trivia man's the enemy!
NO!
enough Bullshit!
AND KILL AN INNOCENT PERSON WHO THEY CARE ABOUT
oh now you've done it
AAAhh She cut the tendons in my hand!
i said stay the fuck back!
SPLUGE

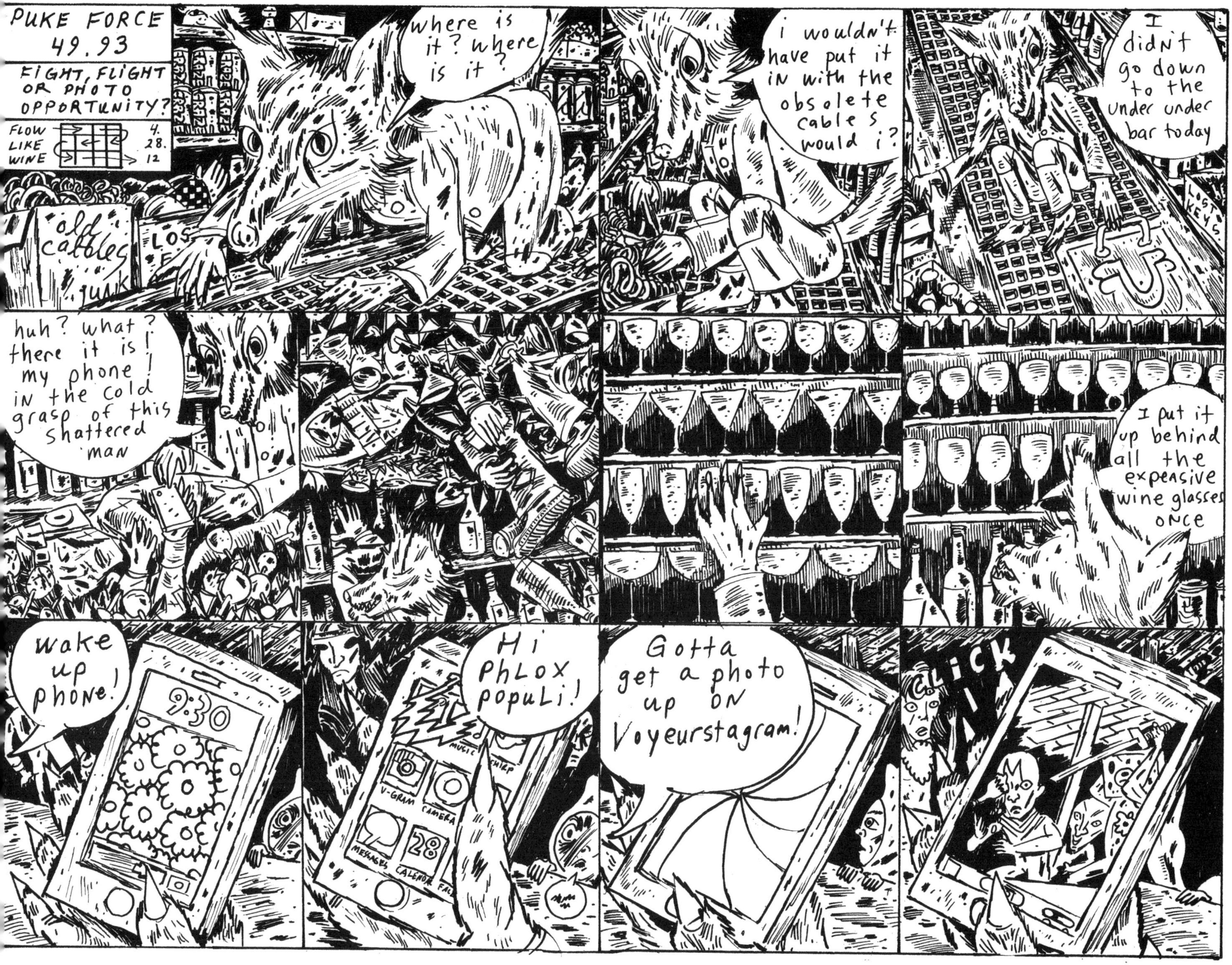

PUKE FORCE 49.93
FIGHT, FLIGHT OR PHOTO OPPORTUNITY?
FLOW LIKE WINE
4. 28. 12
where is it? where is it?
old cables
junk
i wouldn't have put it in with the obsolete cables would i?
I didn't go down to the under under bar today
LOST KEYS
huh? what? there it is! my phone! in the cold grasp of this shattered man
I put it up behind all the expensive wine glasses once
wake up phone!
9:30
Hi Phlox populi!
MUSIC
CHIRP
V-GRAM
CAMERA
MESSAGES
28
CALENDAR
Gotta get a photo up on Voyeurstagram!
CLICK

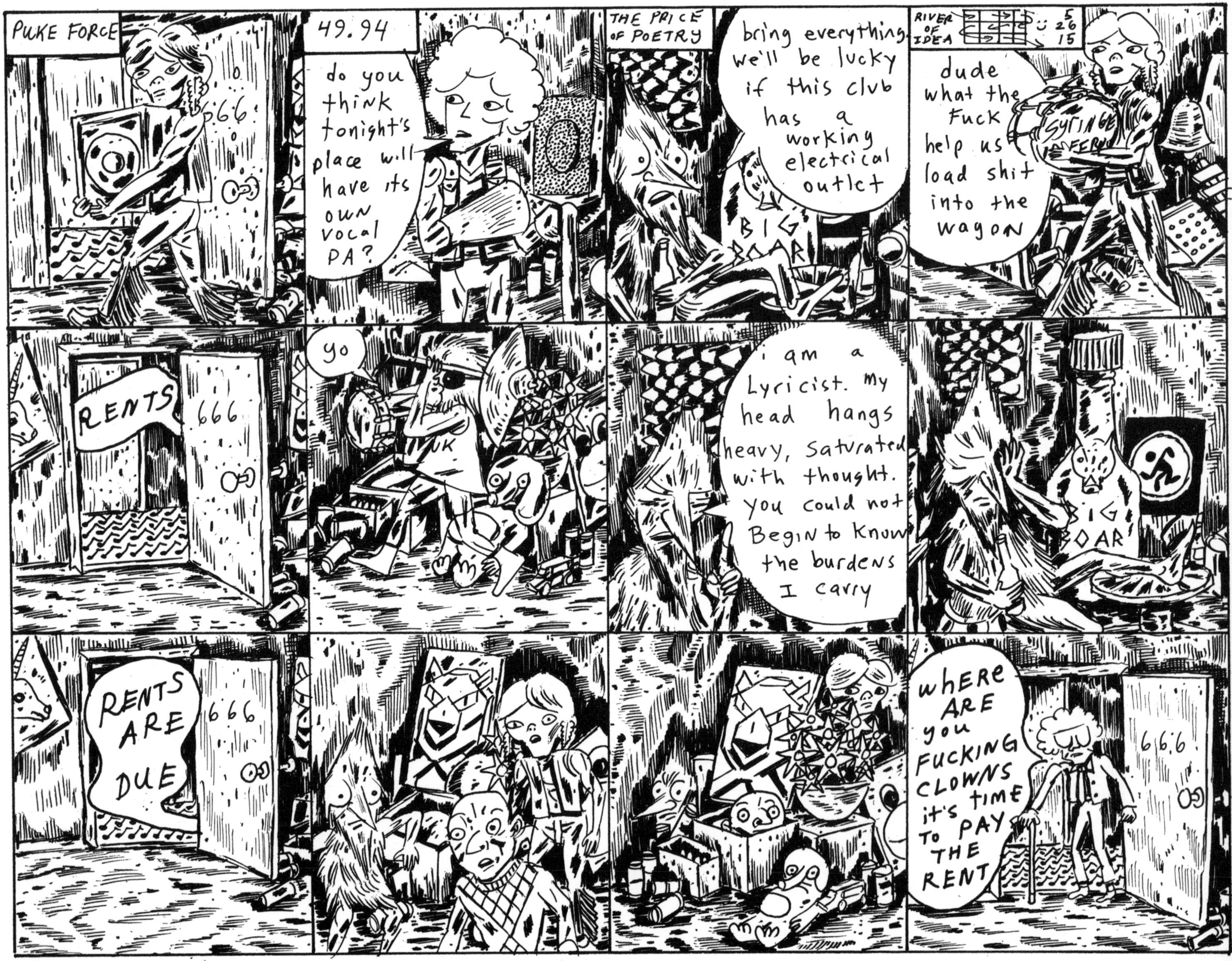
PUKE FORCE
666
49.94
do you think tonight's place will have its own vocal PA?
THE PRICE OF POETRY
bring everything. we'll be lucky if this club has a working electrical outlet
BIG BOAR
RIVER OF IDEA
5 26 15
dude what the Fuck help us load shit into the wagon
RENTS
666
yo
i am a Lyricist. My head hangs heavy, saturated with thought. you could not Begin to know the burdens I carry
BIG BOAR
RENTS ARE DUE
666
WHERE ARE you FUCKING CLOWNS it's time to PAY THE RENT
666

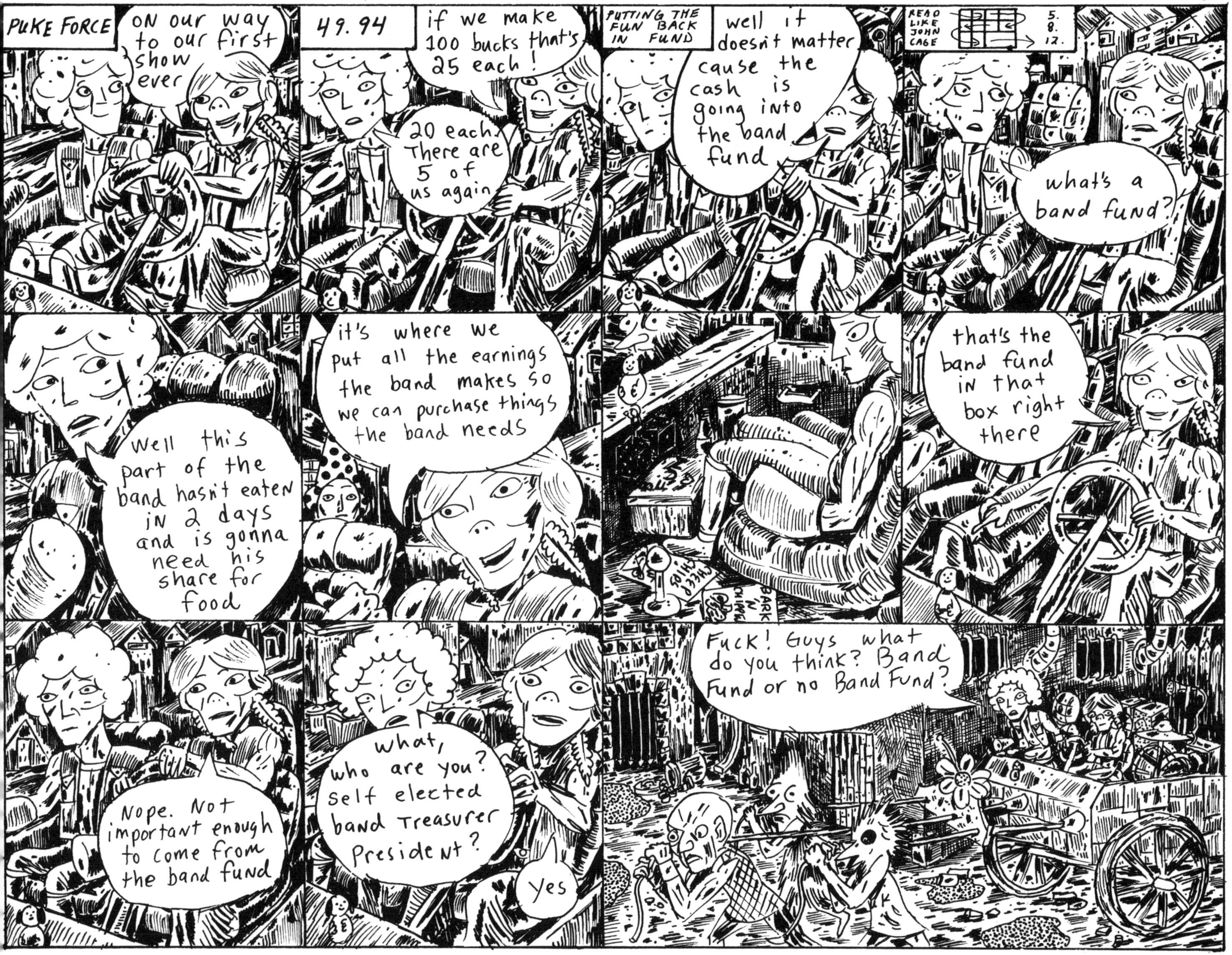
PUKE FORCE
ON our way to our first show ever
49.94
if we make 100 bucks that's 25 each!
20 each. There are 5 of us again
PUTTING THE FUN BACK IN FUND
well it doesn't matter cause the cash is going into the band fund
READ LIKE JOHN CAGE
5.
8.
12.
what's a band fund?
Well this part of the band hasn't eaten in 2 days and is gonna need his share for food
it's where we put all the earnings the band makes so we can purchase things the band needs
that's the band fund in that box right there
Nope. Not important enough to come from the band fund
what, who are you? self elected band Treasurer President?
yes
Fuck! Guys what do you think? Band Fund or no Band Fund?

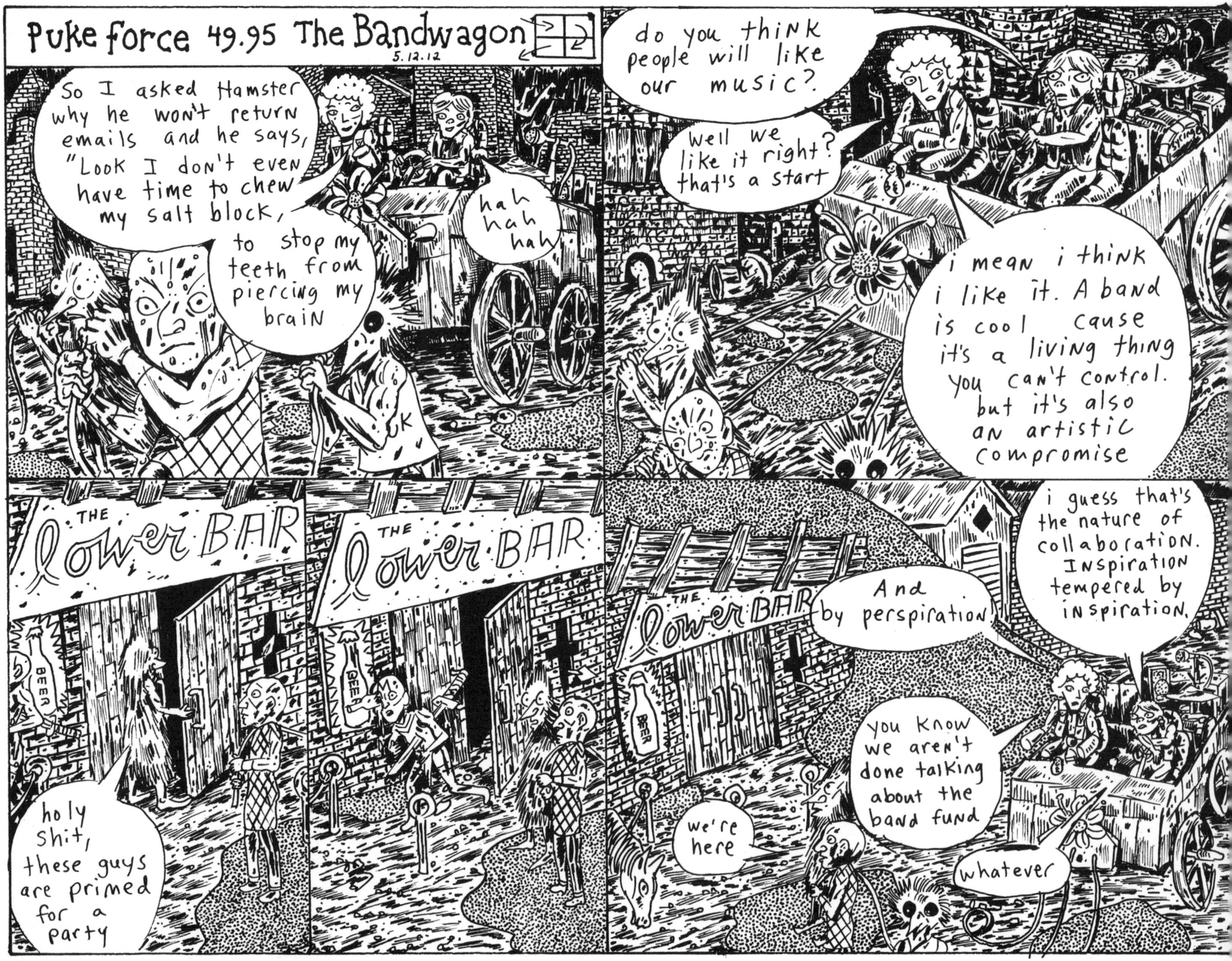
Puke force 49.95 The Bandwagon
5.12.12
So I asked Hamster why he won't return emails and he says, "Look I don't even have time to chew my salt block,
to stop my teeth from piercing my brain
hah hah hah
do you think people will like our music?
well we like it right? that's a start
i mean i think i like it. A band is cool cause it's a living thing you can't control. but it's also an artistic compromise
THE lower BAR
BEER
holy shit, these guys are primed for a party
THE lower BAR
BEER
THE lower BAR
BEER
i guess that's the nature of collaboration. Inspiration tempered by inspiration.
And by perspiration
you know we aren't done talking about the band fund
we're here
whatever

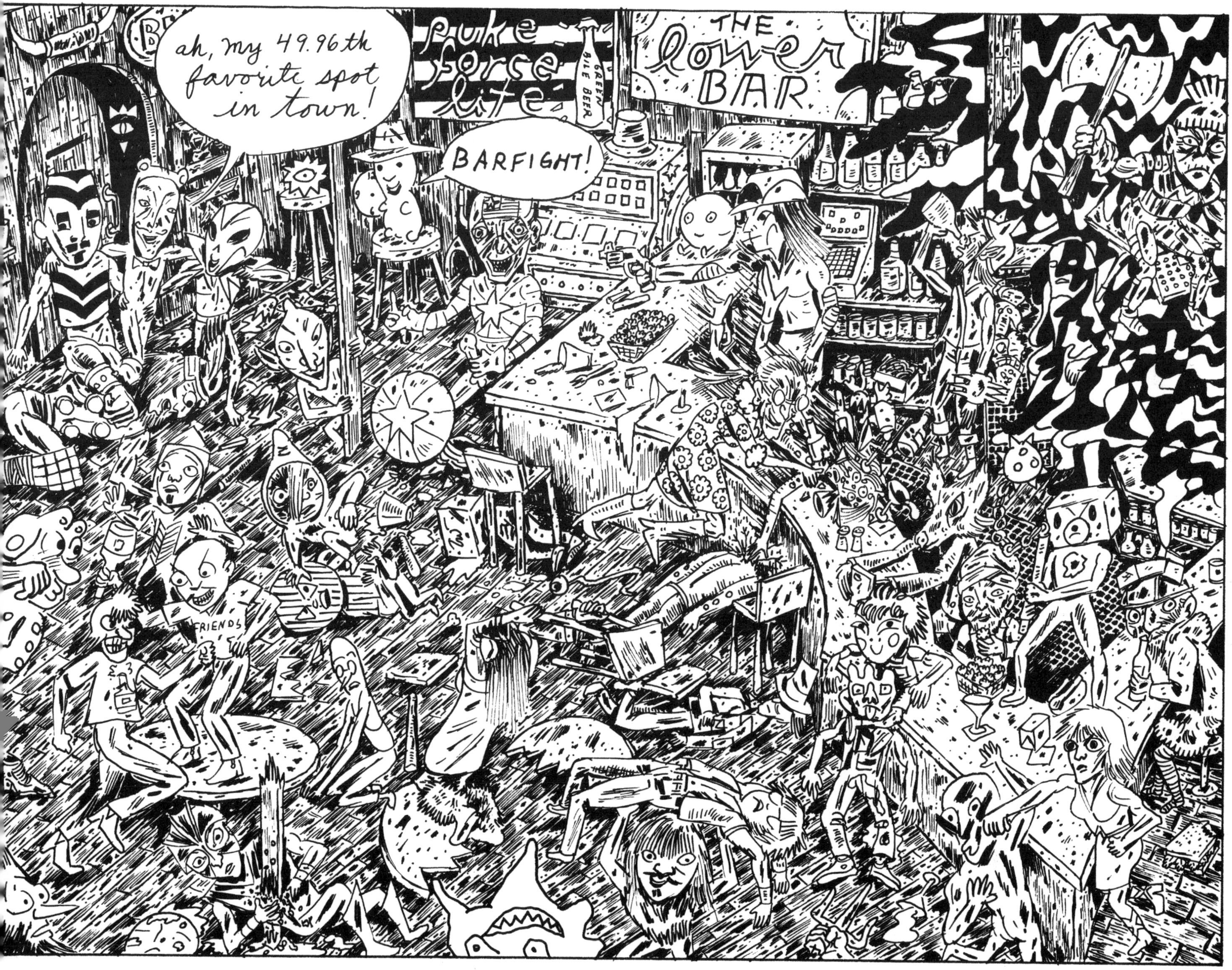
ah, my 49.96th favorite spot in town!
BARFIGHT!
puke force lite
GREEN BILE BEER
THE lower BAR
FRIENDS

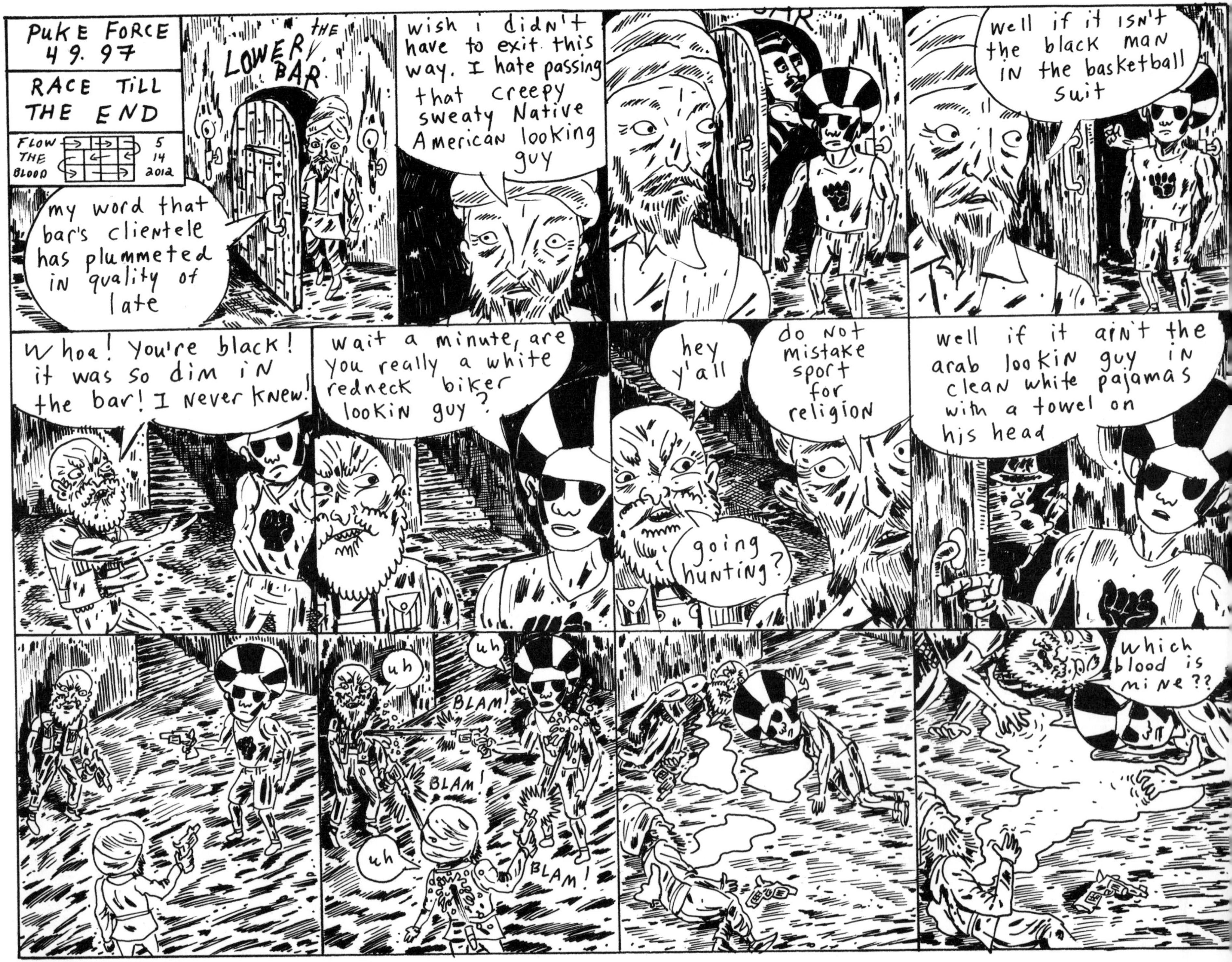
PUKE FORCE 49.97
RACE TILL THE END
FLOW THE BLOOD
5 14 2012
THE LOWER BAR
my word that bar's clientele has plummeted in quality of late
wish i didn't have to exit this way. I hate passing that creepy sweaty Native American looking guy
well if it isn't the black man in the basketball suit
Whoa! You're black! it was so dim in the bar! I never knew!
wait a minute, are you really a white redneck biker lookin guy?
hey y'all
do not mistake sport for religion
going hunting?
well if it ain't the arab lookin guy in clean white pajamas with a towel on his head
uh
uh
BLAM!
BLAM!
uh
BLAM!
which blood is mine??

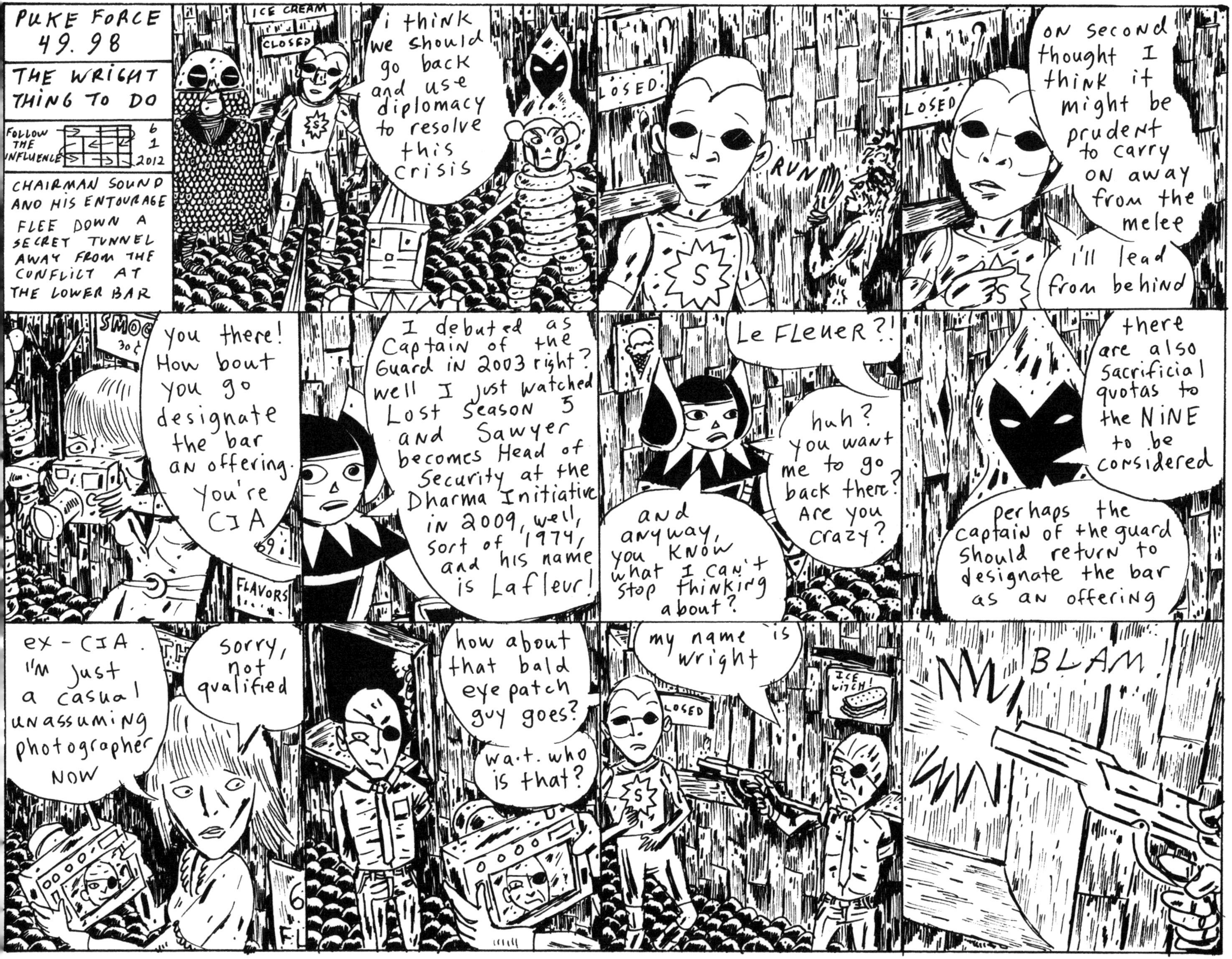

PUKE FORCE 49.98
THE WRIGHT THING TO DO
FOLLOW THE INFLUENCE 6 1 2012
CHAIRMAN SOUND AND HIS ENTOURAGE FLEE DOWN A SECRET TUNNEL AWAY FROM THE CONFLICT AT THE LOWER BAR
ICE CREAM
CLOSED
i think we should go back and use diplomacy to resolve this crisis
LOSED.
RUN
LOSED
on second thought I think it might be prudent to carry on away from the melee
I'll lead from behind
SMOO
30¢
you there! How bout you go designate the bar an offering. You're CIA
FLAVORS
I debuted as Captain of the Guard in 2003 right? well I just watched Lost Season 5 and Sawyer becomes Head of Security at the Dharma Initiative in 2009, well, sort of 1974, and his name is Lafleur!
Le FLEUER?!
huh? you want me to go back there? Are you crazy?
and anyway, you know what I can't stop thinking about?
there are also sacrificial quotas to the NINE to be considered
perhaps the captain of the guard should return to designate the bar as an offering
ex-CIA. I'm just a casual unassuming photographer now
sorry, not qualified
how about that bald eye patch guy goes?
wait. who is that?
my name is wright
LOSED
ICE WITCH!
BLAM!

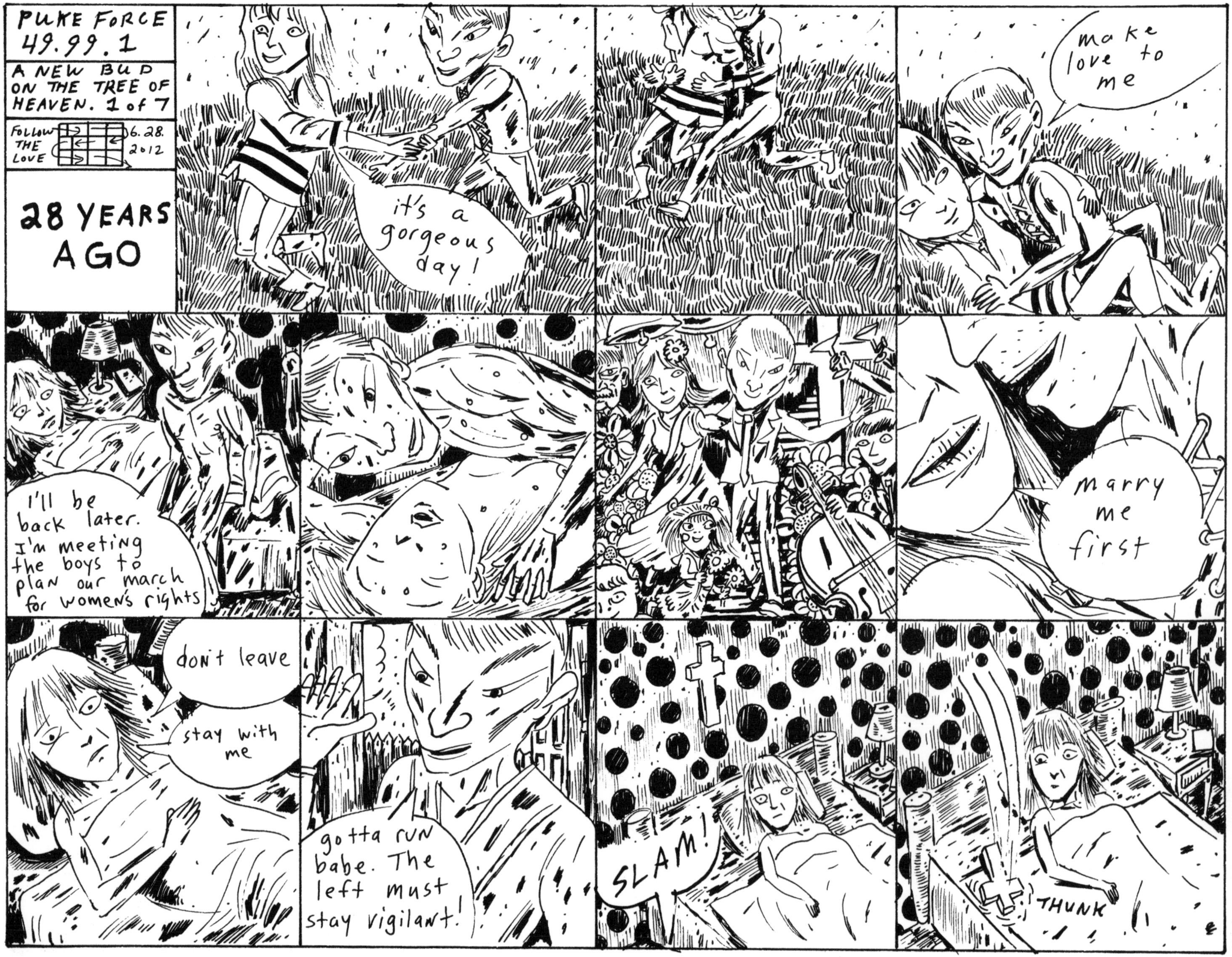
PUKE FORCE 49.99.1
A NEW BUD ON THE TREE OF HEAVEN. 1 of 7
FOLLOW THE LOVE
6.28.2012
28 YEARS AGO
it's a gorgeous day!
make love to me
I'll be back later. I'm meeting the boys to plan our march for women's rights
marry me first
don't leave
stay with me
gotta run babe. The left must stay vigilant!
SLAM!
THUNK

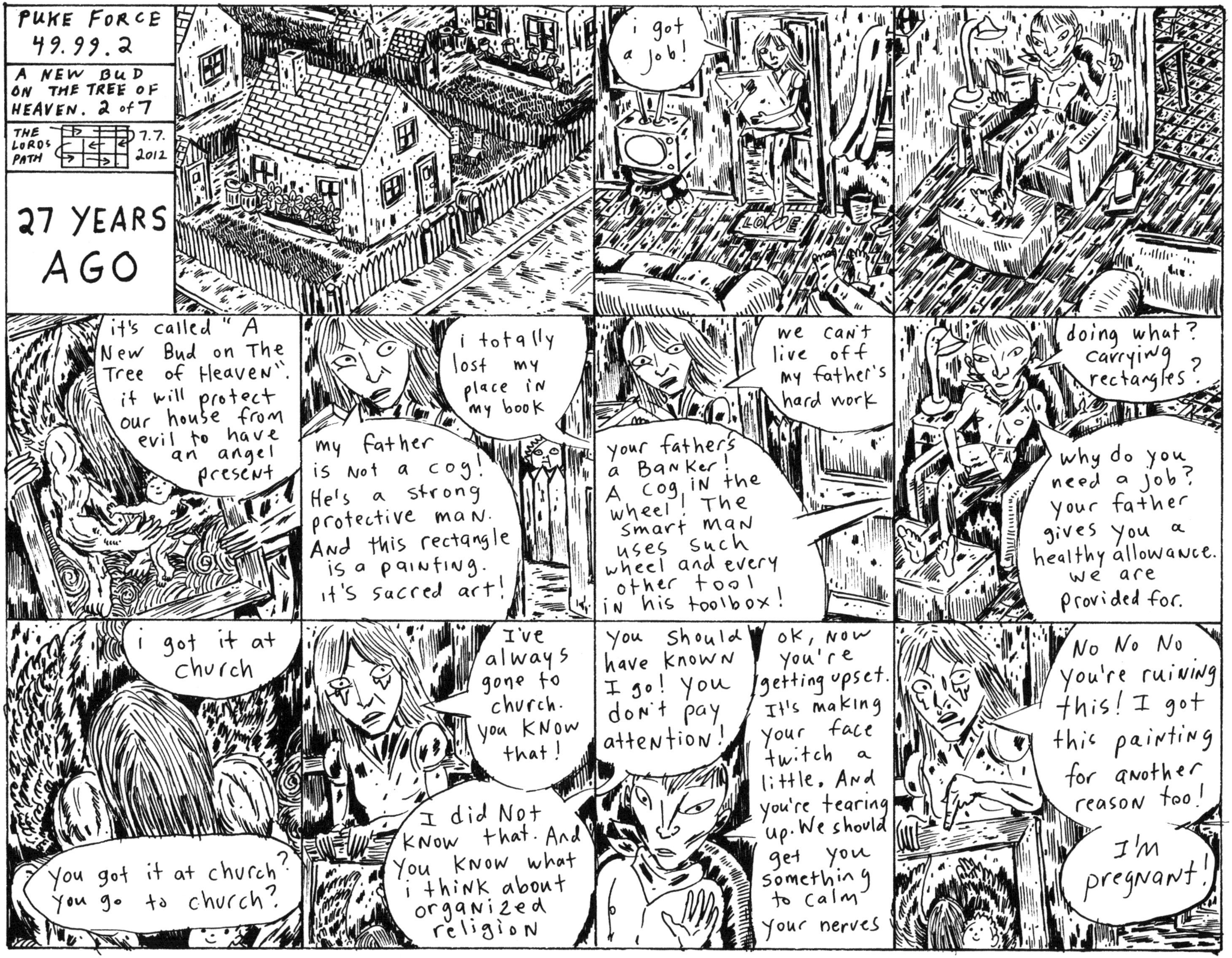

PUKE FORCE 49.99.2
A NEW BUD ON THE TREE OF HEAVEN. 2 of 7
THE LORDS PATH
7.7. 2012
27 YEARS AGO
i got a job!
it's called "A New Bud on The Tree of Heaven". it will protect our house from evil to have an angel present
i totally lost my place in my book
my father is not a cog! He's a strong protective man. And this rectangle is a painting. it's sacred art!
we can't live off my father's hard work
your father's a Banker! A cog in the wheel! The smart man uses such wheel and every other tool in his toolbox!
doing what? carrying rectangles?
why do you need a job? your father gives you a healthy allowance. we are provided for.
i got it at church
you got it at church? you go to church?
I've always gone to church. you KNOW that!
I did Not KNOW that. And You KNOW what i think about organized religion
You Should have KNOWN I go! you don't pay attention!
ok, now you're getting upset. It's making your face twitch a little. And you're tearing up. We should get you something to calm your nerves
No No No you're ruining this! I got this painting for another reason too!
I'M pregnant!

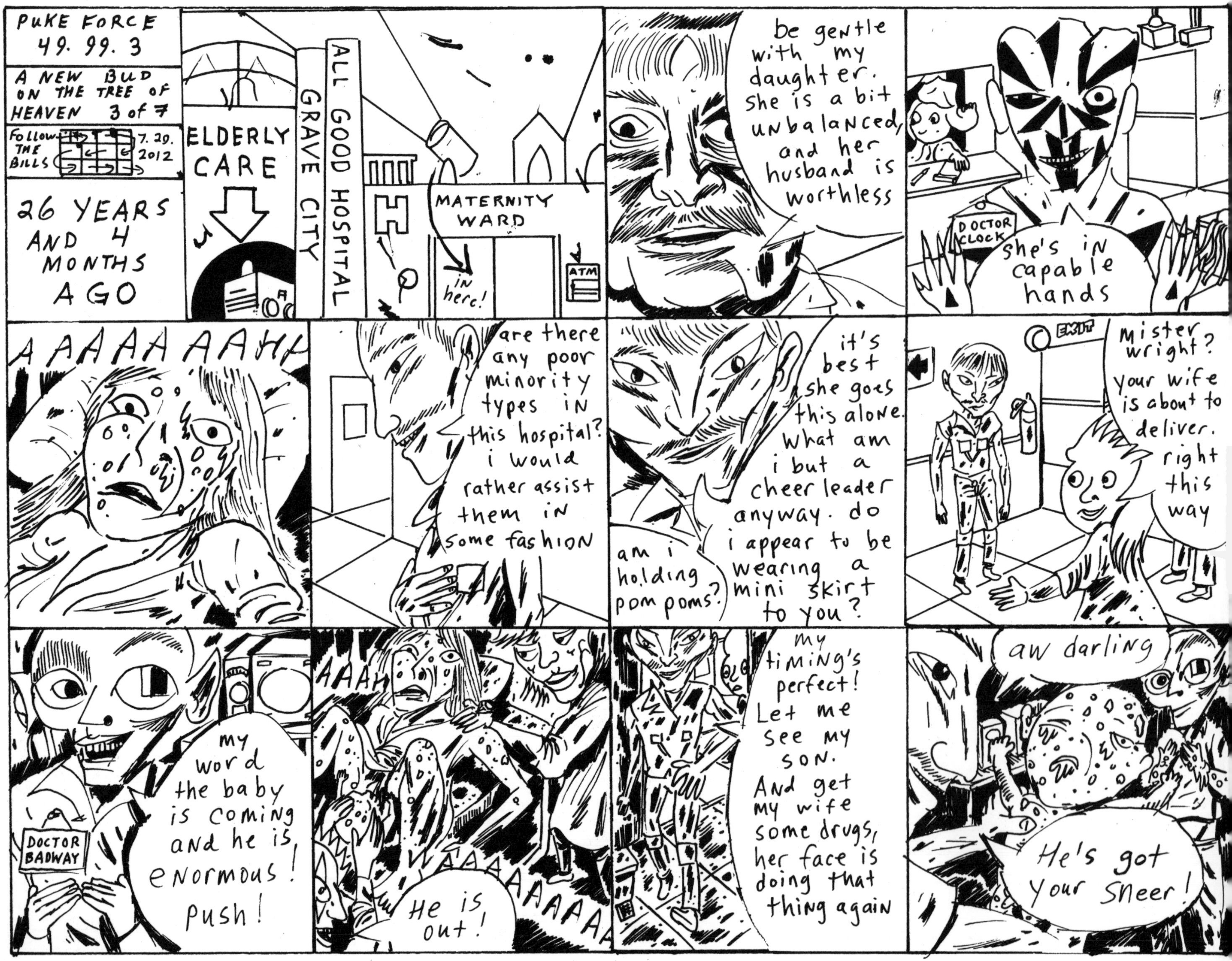
PUKE FORCE 49. 99. 3
A NEW BUD ON THE TREE OF HEAVEN 3 of 7
FOLLOW THE BILLS
7. 20. 2012
26 YEARS AND 4 MONTHS AGO
ELDERLY CARE
ALL GOOD HOSPITAL
GRAVE CITY
H
MATERNITY WARD
in here!
ATM
be gentle with my daughter. she is a bit unbalanced, and her husband is worthless
DOCTOR CLOCK
she's in capable hands
AAAAAAAHH
are there any poor minority types in this hospital? i would rather assist them in some fashion
it's best she goes this alone. what am i but a cheerleader anyway. do i appear to be wearing a mini skirt to you?
am i holding pom poms?
EXIT
mister wright? your wife is about to deliver. right this way
DOCTOR BADWAY
my word the baby is coming and he is enormous! push!
AAAH
WAAAAAAAAAA
He is out!
my timing's perfect! Let me see my son. And get my wife some drugs, her face is doing that thing again
aw darling
He's got your sneer!

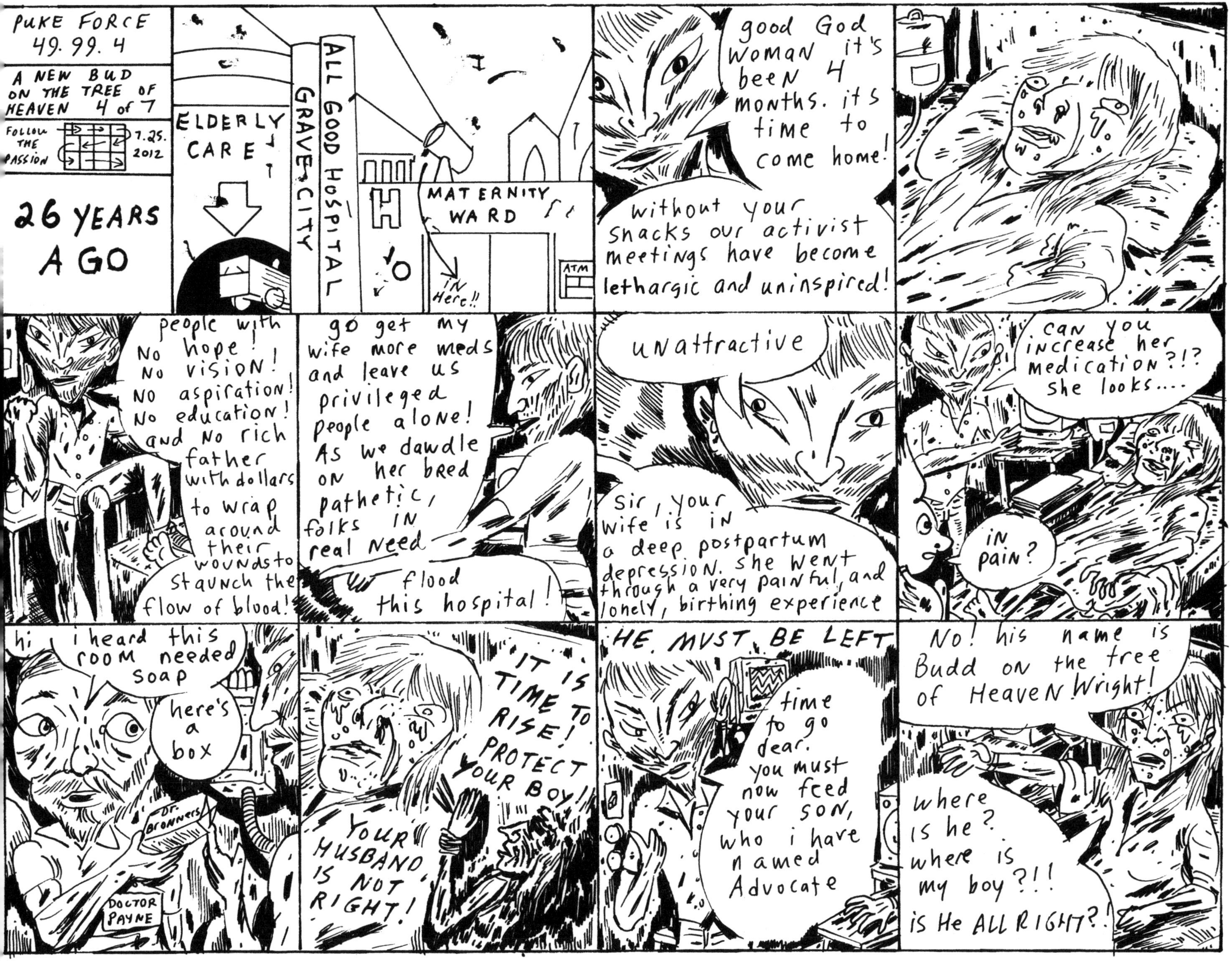
PUKE FORCE 49.99.4
A NEW BUD ON THE TREE OF HEAVEN 4 of 7
FOLLOW THE PASSION
7.25.2012
26 YEARS AGO
ELDERLY CARE
GRAVE CITY
ALL GOOD HOSPITAL
H
MATERNITY WARD
IN Here!!
ATM
good God woman it's been 4 months. it's time to come home!
without your snacks our activist meetings have become lethargic and uninspired!
people with No hope! No vision! No aspiration! No education! and No rich father with dollars to wrap around their wounds to staunch the flow of blood!
go get my wife more meds and leave us privileged people alone! As we dawdle on her bred pathetic, folks in real Need flood this hospital!
unattractive
Sir, your wife is in a deep postpartum depression. she went through a very painful, and lonely, birthing experience
can you increase her medication?!? she looks....
in pain?
hi
i heard this room needed soap
here's a box
DR. BRONNERS
DOCTOR PAYNE
IT IS TIME TO RISE! PROTECT YOUR BOY
YOUR HUSBAND IS NOT RIGHT!
HE MUST BE LEFT
time to go dear. you must now feed your son, who i have named Advocate
No! his name is Budd on the tree of Heaven Wright!
where is he? where is my boy?!! is He ALL RIGHT?!

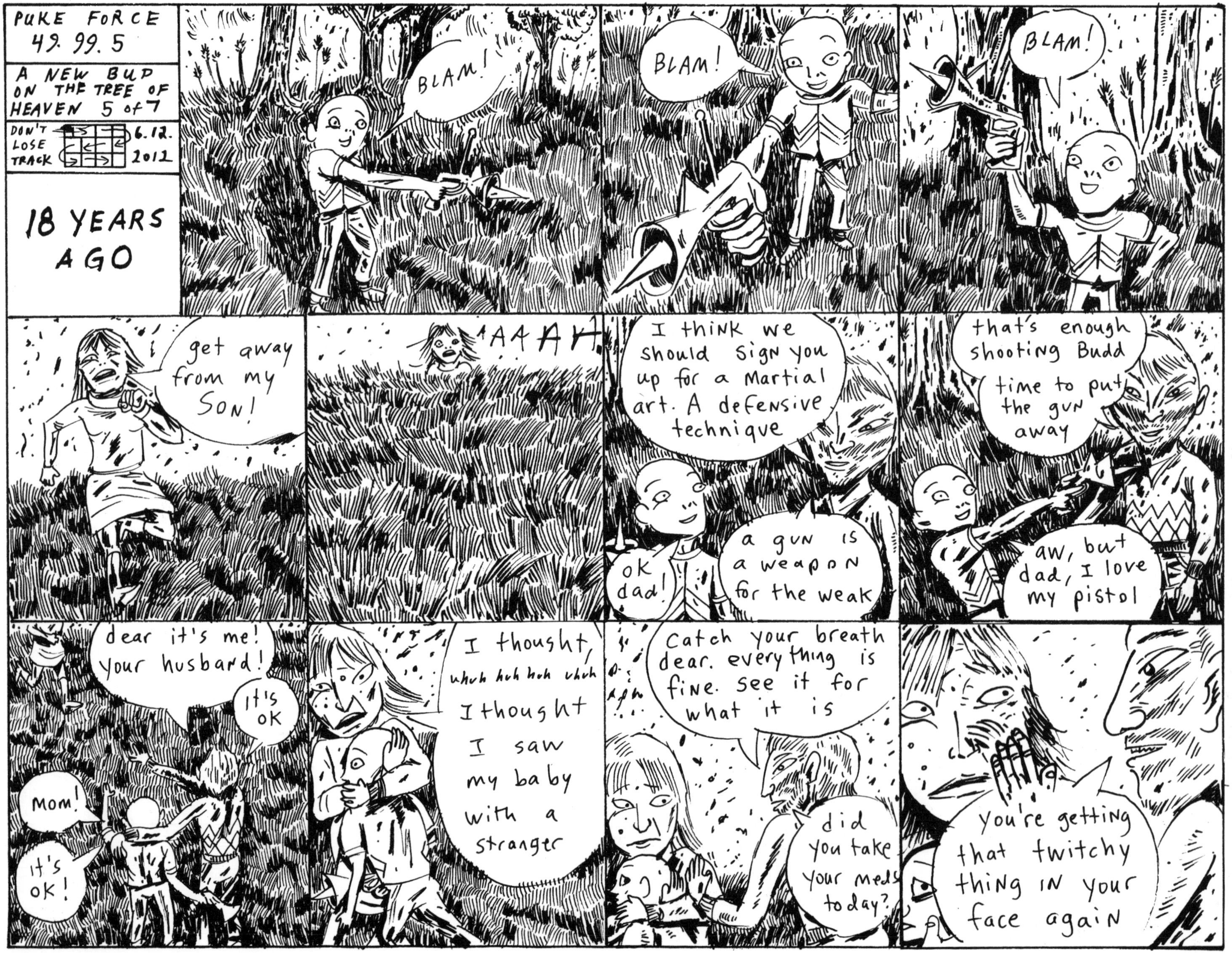
PUKE FORCE
49. 99. 5
A NEW BUD ON THE TREE OF HEAVEN 5 of 7
DON'T LOSE TRACK
6.12. 2012
18 YEARS AGO
BLAM!
BLAM!
BLAM!
get away from my son!
AAAAH
I think we should sign you up for a martial art. A defensive technique
ok dad!
a gun is a weapon for the weak
that's enough shooting Budd
time to put the gun away
aw, but dad, I love my pistol
dear it's me! your husband!
it's ok
Mom!
it's ok!
I thought, uhuh huh huh uhuh I thought I saw my baby with a stranger
Catch your breath dear. everything is fine. see it for what it is
did you take your meds today?
you're getting that twitchy thing in your face again

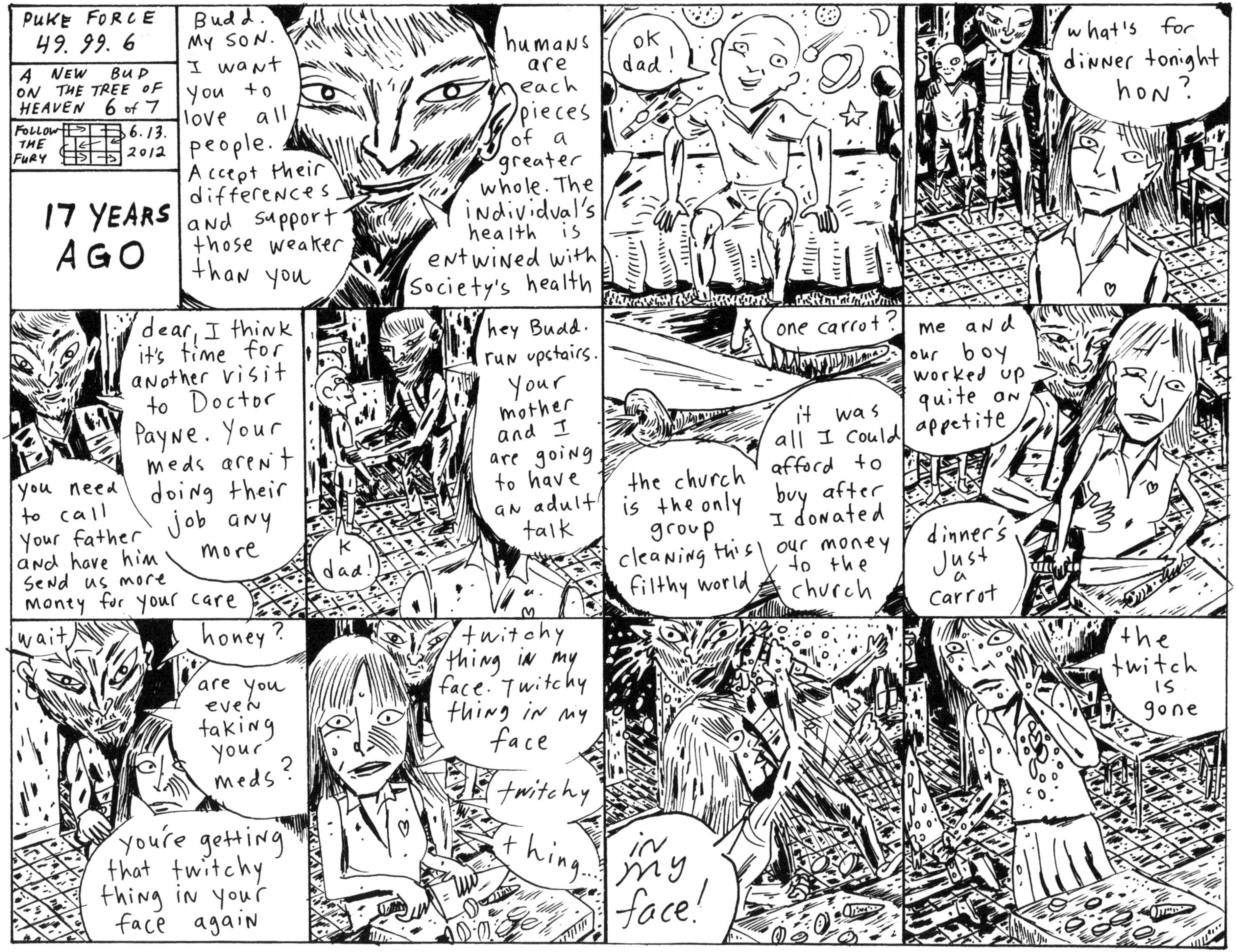
PUKE FORCE 49. 99. 6
A NEW BUD ON THE TREE OF HEAVEN 6 of 7
FOLLOW THE FURY
6. 13. 2012
17 YEARS AGO
Budd. My son. I want you to love all people. Accept their differences and support those weaker than you
humans are each pieces of a greater whole. The individual's health is entwined with society's health
ok dad!
what's for dinner tonight hon?
dear, I think it's time for another visit to Doctor Payne. Your meds aren't doing their job any more
you need to call your father and have him send us more money for your care
hey Budd. run upstairs. Your mother and I are going to have an adult talk
k dad!
one carrot?
the church is the only group cleaning this filthy world
it was all I could afford to buy after I donated our money to the church
me and our boy worked up quite an appetite
dinner's just a carrot
wait honey?
are you even taking your meds?
you're getting that twitchy thing in your face again
twitchy thing in my face. Twitchy thing in my face
twitchy
thing...
in my face!
the twitch is gone

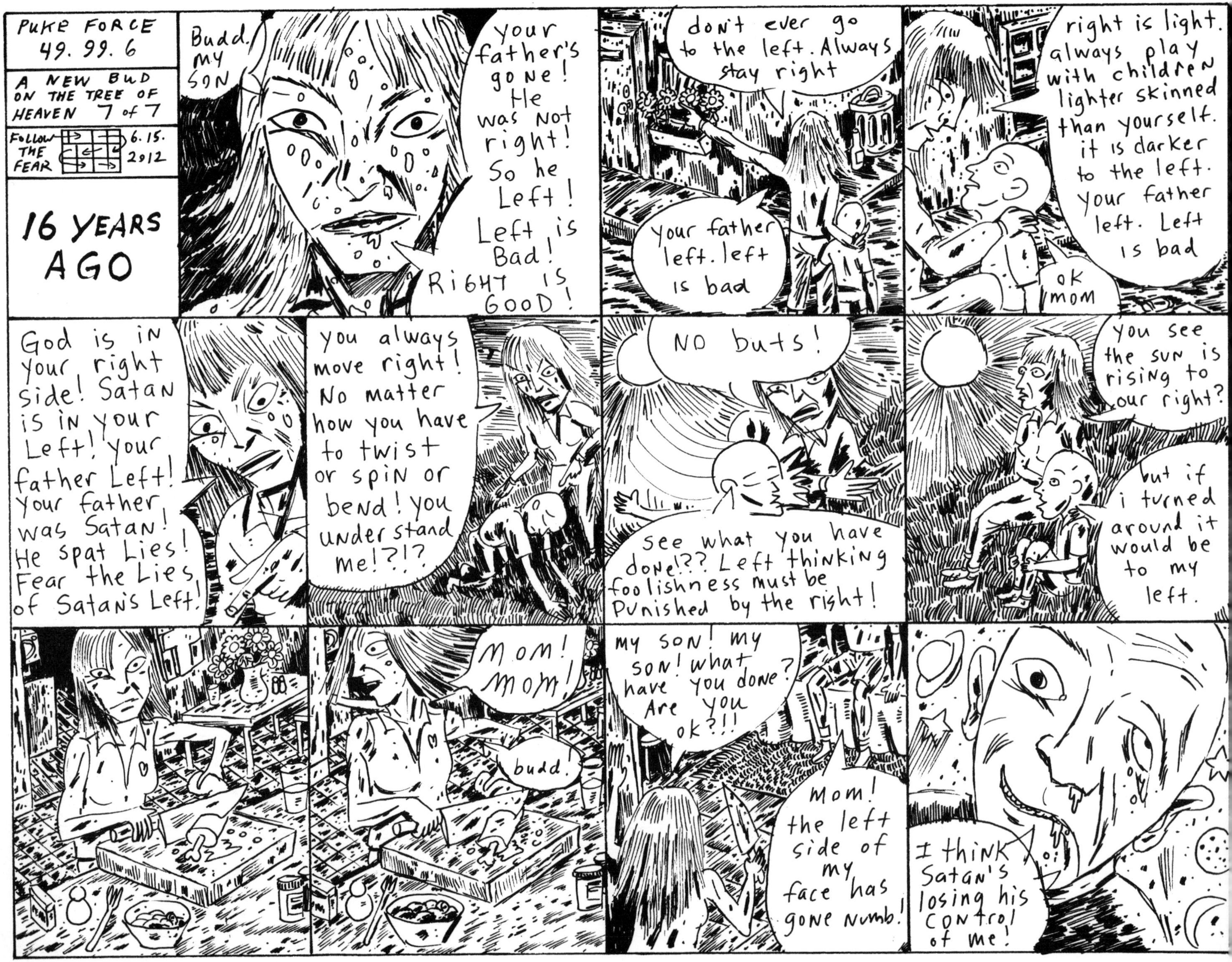

PUKE FORCE 49. 99. 6
A NEW BUD ON THE TREE OF HEAVEN 7 of 7
FOLLOW THE FEAR 6. 15. 2012
16 YEARS AGO
Budd. MY SON
your father's gone! He was not right! So he Left! Left is Bad! RIGHT IS GOOD!
don't ever go to the left. Always stay right
your father left. left is bad
right is light. always play with children lighter skinned than yourself. it is darker to the left. your father left. Left is bad
ok MOM
God is in your right side! Satan is in your Left! your father Left! your father was Satan! He spat Lies! Fear the Lies of Satan's Left!
you always move right! No matter how you have to twist or spin or bend! you understand me!?!?
NO buts!
see what you have done!?? Left thinking foolishness must be Punished by the right!
You see the sun is rising to our right?
but if i turned around it would be to my left.
MOM! MOM!
budd.
my son! my son! what have you done? Are you ok?!!
MOM! the left side of my face has gone numb!
I think Satan's losing his control of me!

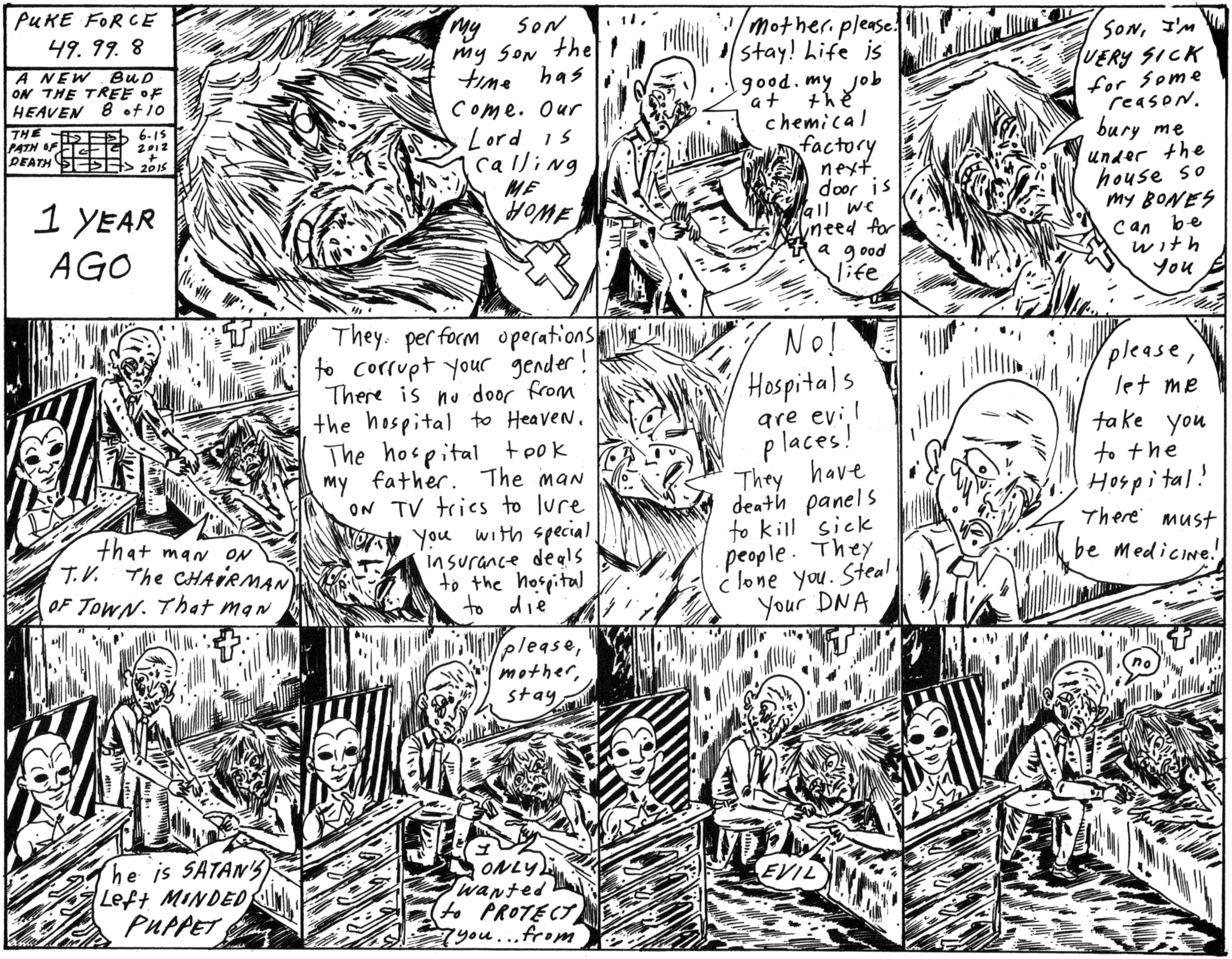
PUKE FORCE 49. 99. 8
A NEW BUD ON THE TREE OF HEAVEN 8 of 10
THE PATH OF DEATH 6-15 2012 + 2015
1 YEAR AGO
My son my son the time has come. Our Lord is calling ME HOME
Mother, please! stay! Life is good. my job at the chemical factory next door is all we need for a good life
Son, I'm VERY SICK for some reason. bury me under the house so my BONES can be with you
that man on T.V. The CHAIRMAN OF TOWN. That man
They perform operations to corrupt your gender! There is no door from the hospital to Heaven. The hospital took my father. The man on TV tries to lure you with special insurance deals to the hospital to die
No! Hospitals are evil places! They have death panels to kill sick people. They clone you. Steal your DNA
please, let me take you to the Hospital! There must be medicine!
he is SATAN'S Left MINDED PUPPET
please, mother, stay
I ONLY wanted to PROTECT you...from
EVIL
no

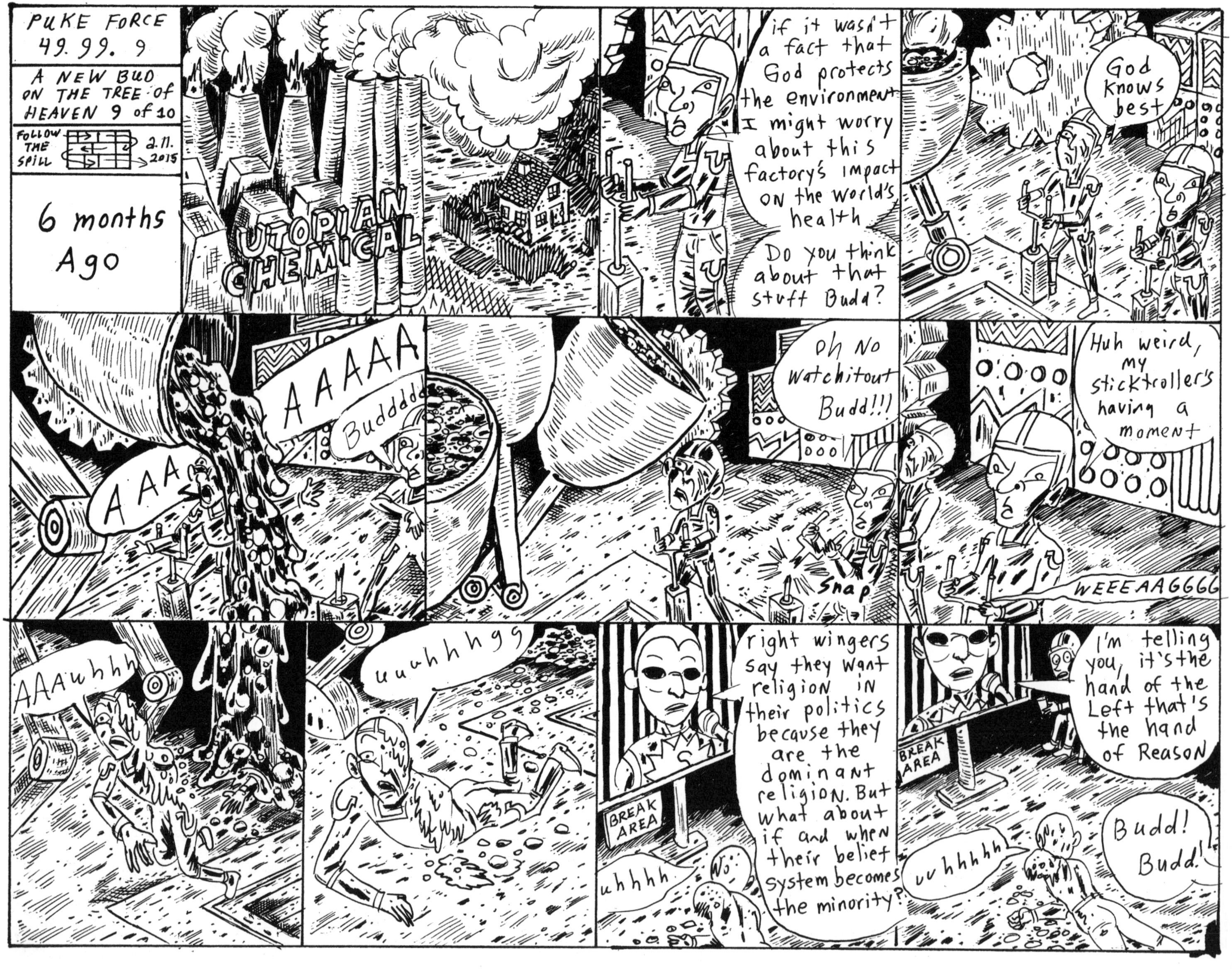
PUKE FORCE 49.99.9
A NEW BUD ON THE TREE OF HEAVEN 9 of 10
FOLLOW THE SPILL
2.11.2015
6 months Ago
UTOPIAN CHEMICAL
if it wasn't a fact that God protects the environment I might worry about this factory's impact on the world's health
Do you think about that stuff Budd?
God knows best
AAAAA
Buddddd
AAA
Oh No Watchitout Budd!!!
Snap
Huh weird, my sticktroller's having a moment
WEEEAAGGGG
AAAuhhh
uuuhhhgg
BREAK AREA
right wingers say they want religion in their politics because they are the dominant religion. But what about if and when their belief system becomes the minority?
uhhhh
BREAK AREA
I'm telling you, it's the hand of the Left that's the hand of Reason
uuhhhhh
Budd! Budd!

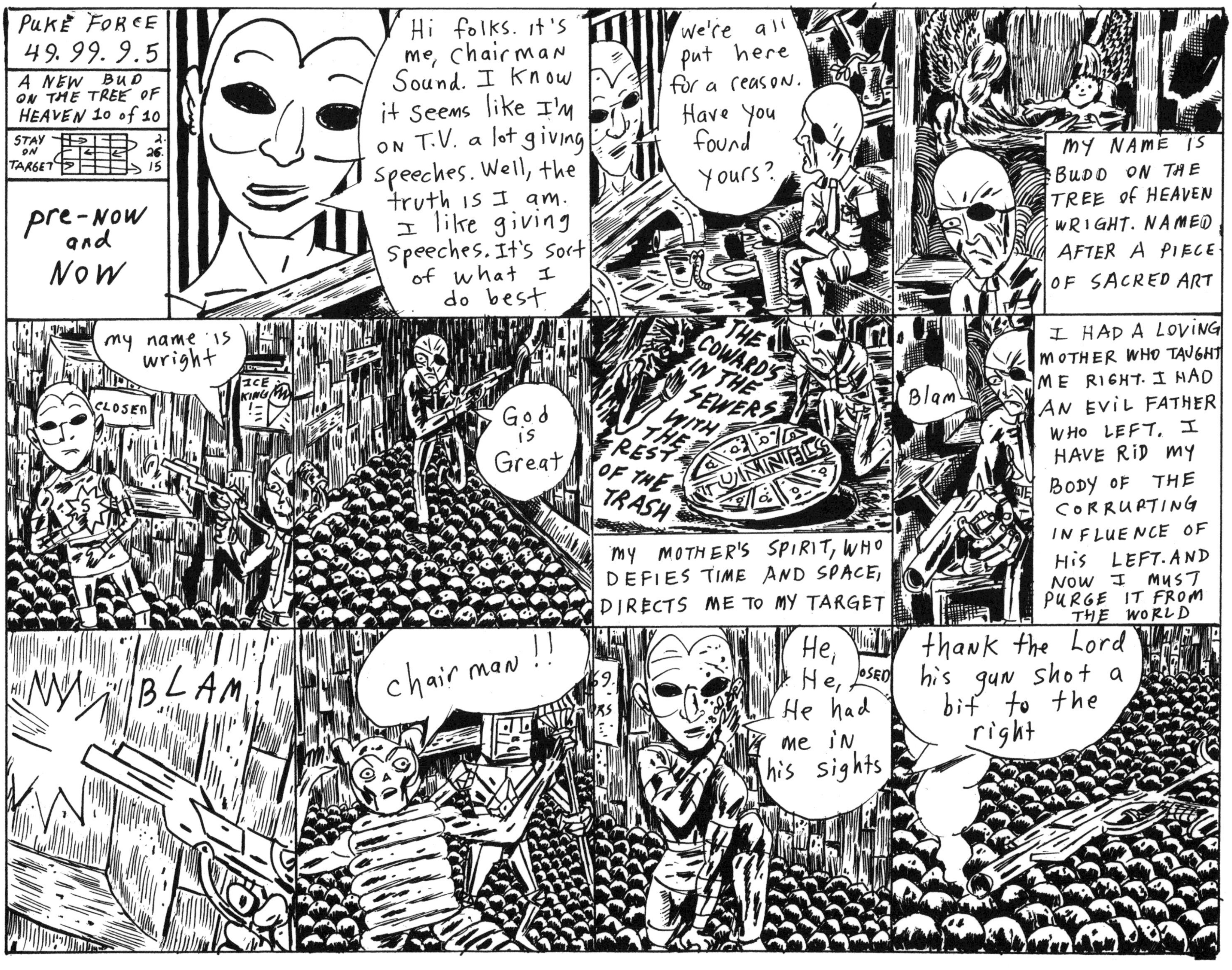
PUKE FORCE
49.99.9.5
A NEW BUD ON THE TREE OF HEAVEN 10 of 10
STAY ON TARGET
2.
26.
15
pre-NOW and NOW
Hi folks. it's me, Chairman Sound. I know it seems like I'm on T.V. a lot giving speeches. Well, the truth is I am. I like giving speeches. It's sort of what I do best
we're all put here for a reason. Have you found yours?
MY NAME IS BUDD ON THE TREE OF HEAVEN WRIGHT. NAMED AFTER A PIECE OF SACRED ART
my name is wright
CLOSED
ICE KING
God is Great
THE COWARDS IN THE SEWERS WITH THE REST OF THE TRASH
TUNNELS
MY MOTHER'S SPIRIT, WHO DEFIES TIME AND SPACE, DIRECTS ME TO MY TARGET
Blam
I HAD A LOVING MOTHER WHO TAUGHT ME RIGHT. I HAD AN EVIL FATHER WHO LEFT. I HAVE RID MY BODY OF THE CORRUPTING INFLUENCE OF HIS LEFT. AND NOW I MUST PURGE IT FROM THE WORLD
BLAM
chairman !!
He, He, He had me in his sights
thank the Lord his gun shot a bit to the right

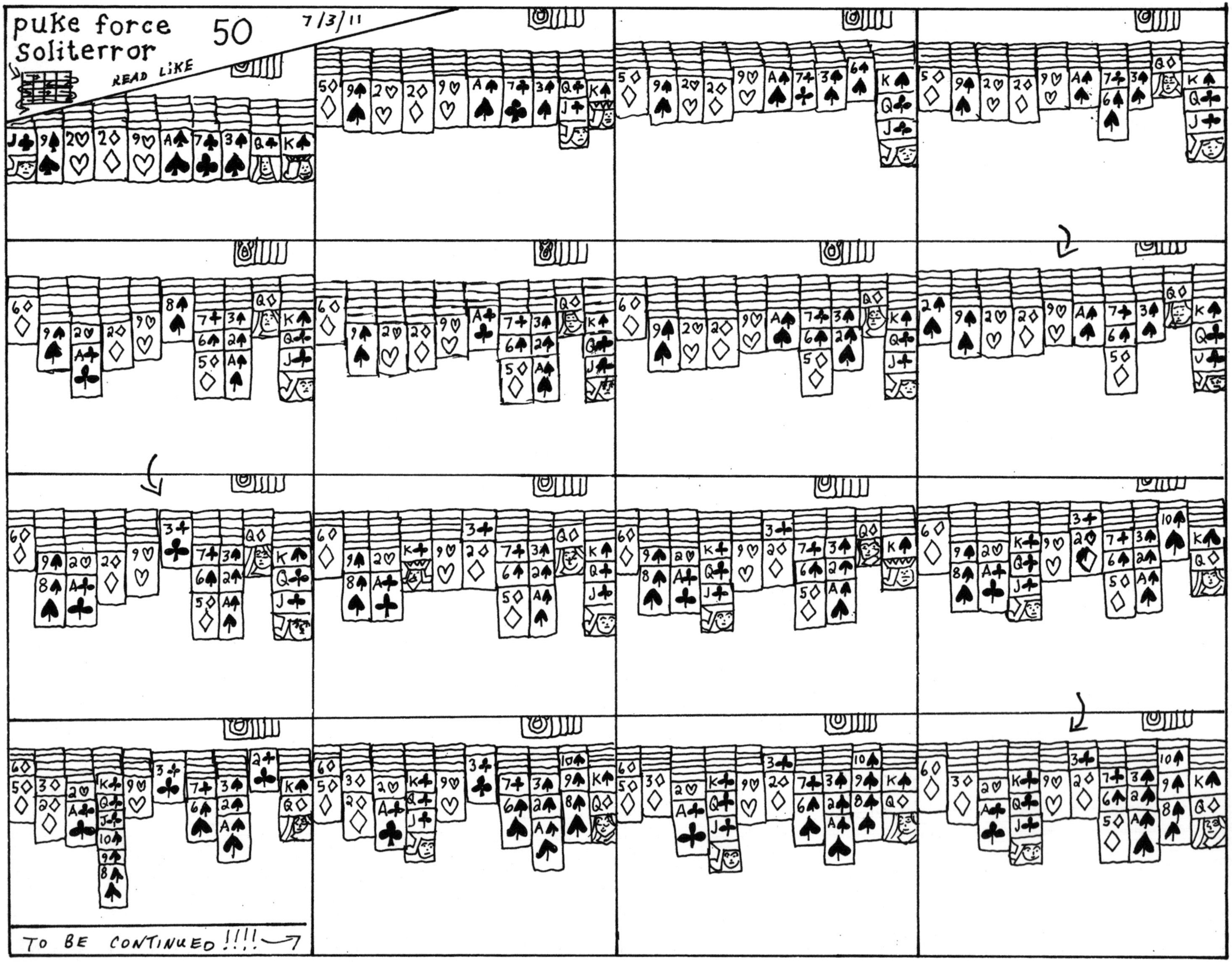
puke force
Soliterror
50
7/3/11
READ LIKE
TO BE CONTINUED!!!!

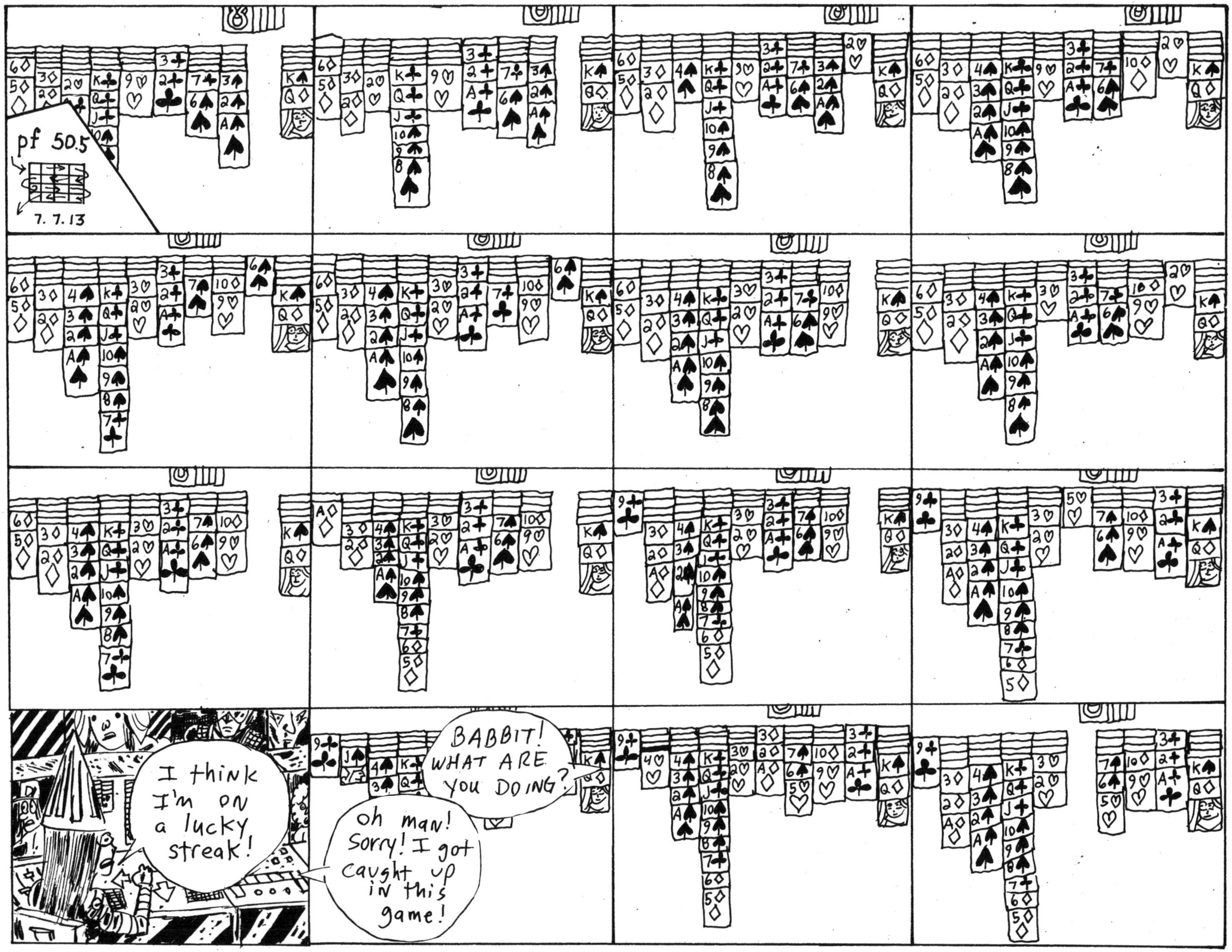
pf 50.5
7. 7. 13
I think I'm on a lucky streak!
BABBIT! WHAT ARE YOU DOING?
Oh man! Sorry! I got caught up in this game!

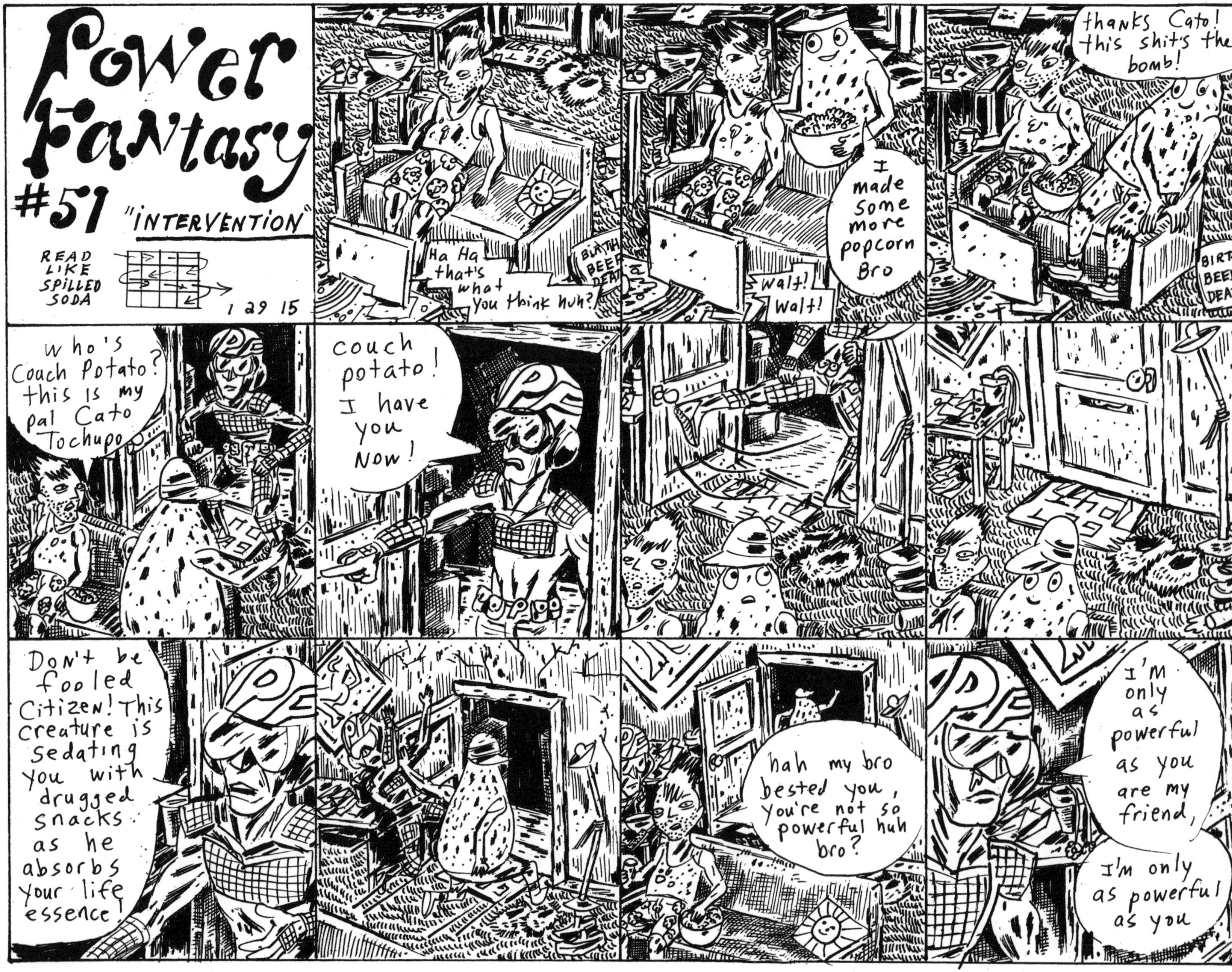
Power Fantasy
#51 "INTERVENTION"
READ LIKE SPILLED SODA
1 29 15
Ha Ha that's what you think huh?
Walt! Walt!
I made some more popcorn Bro
thanks Cato! this shit's the bomb!
Couch potato! I have you Now!
who's Couch Potato? this is my pal Cato Tochupo
Don't be fooled Citizen! This creature is sedating you with drugged snacks as he absorbs your life essence!
hah my bro bested you, you're not so powerful huh bro?
I'm only as powerful as you are my friend,
I'm only as powerful as you

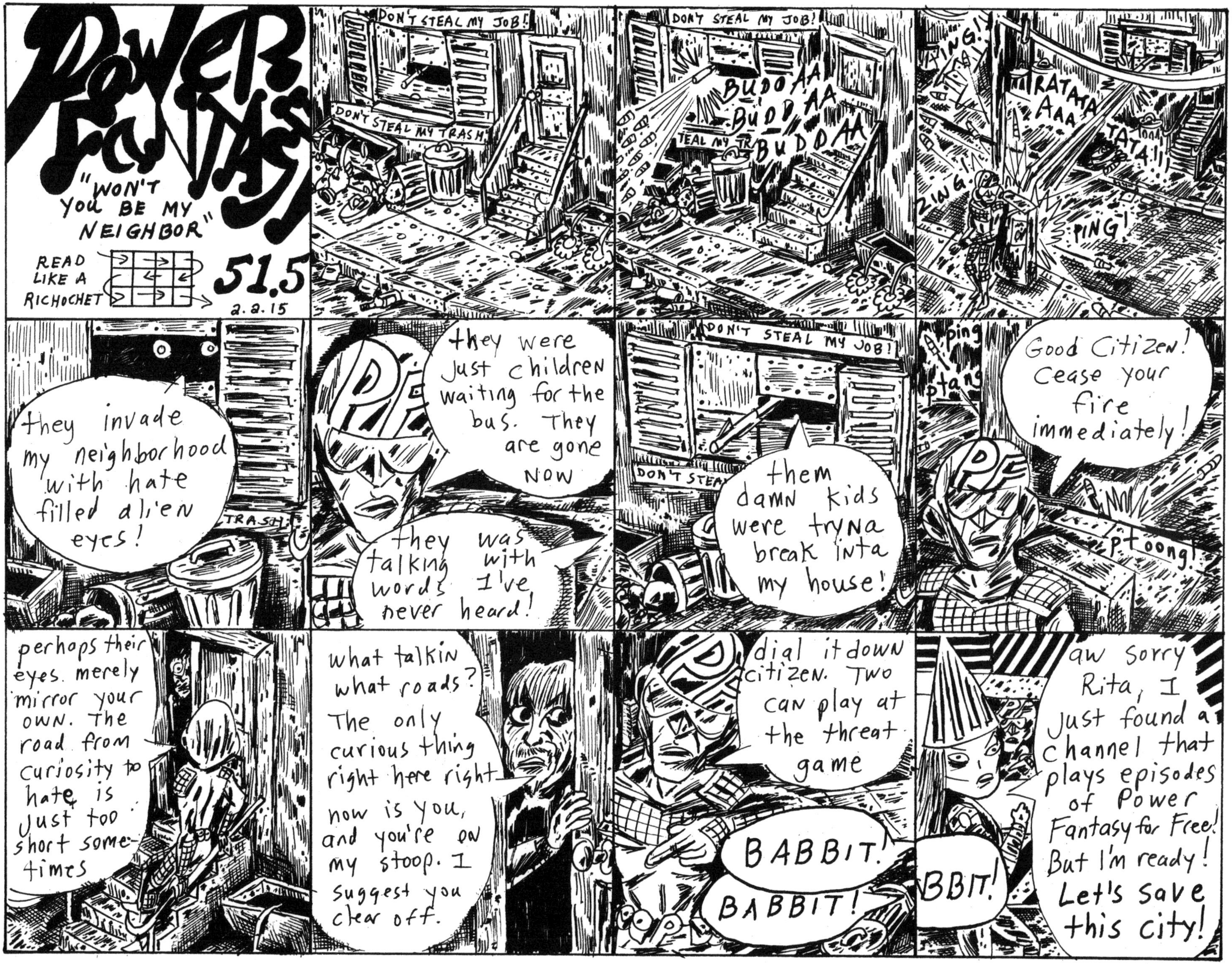
POWER FANTASY
"WON'T YOU BE MY NEIGHBOR"
READ LIKE A RICHOCHET
51.5
2.2.15
DON'T STEAL MY JOB!
DON'T STEAL MY TRASH
DON'T STEAL MY JOB!
TEAL MY TR
BUDDAA BUDDAA BUDDAA
PING!
RATATA AAA TATA!
ZING
PING!
ping
ptang
Good Citizen! Cease your fire immediately!
ptoong!
DON'T STEAL MY JOB!
DON'T STEA
them damn kids were tryna break inta my house!
they were just children waiting for the bus. They are gone now
they was talking with words I've never heard!
they invade my neighborhood with hate filled alien eyes!
TRASH
perhaps their eyes merely mirror your own. The road from curiosity to hate is just too short some-times
what talkin what roads? The only curious thing right here right now is you, and you're on my stoop. I suggest you clear off.
dial it down citizen. Two can play at the threat game
BABBIT!
BABBIT!
BBIT!
aw sorry Rita, I just found a channel that plays episodes of Power Fantasy for Free! But I'm ready! Let's save this city!

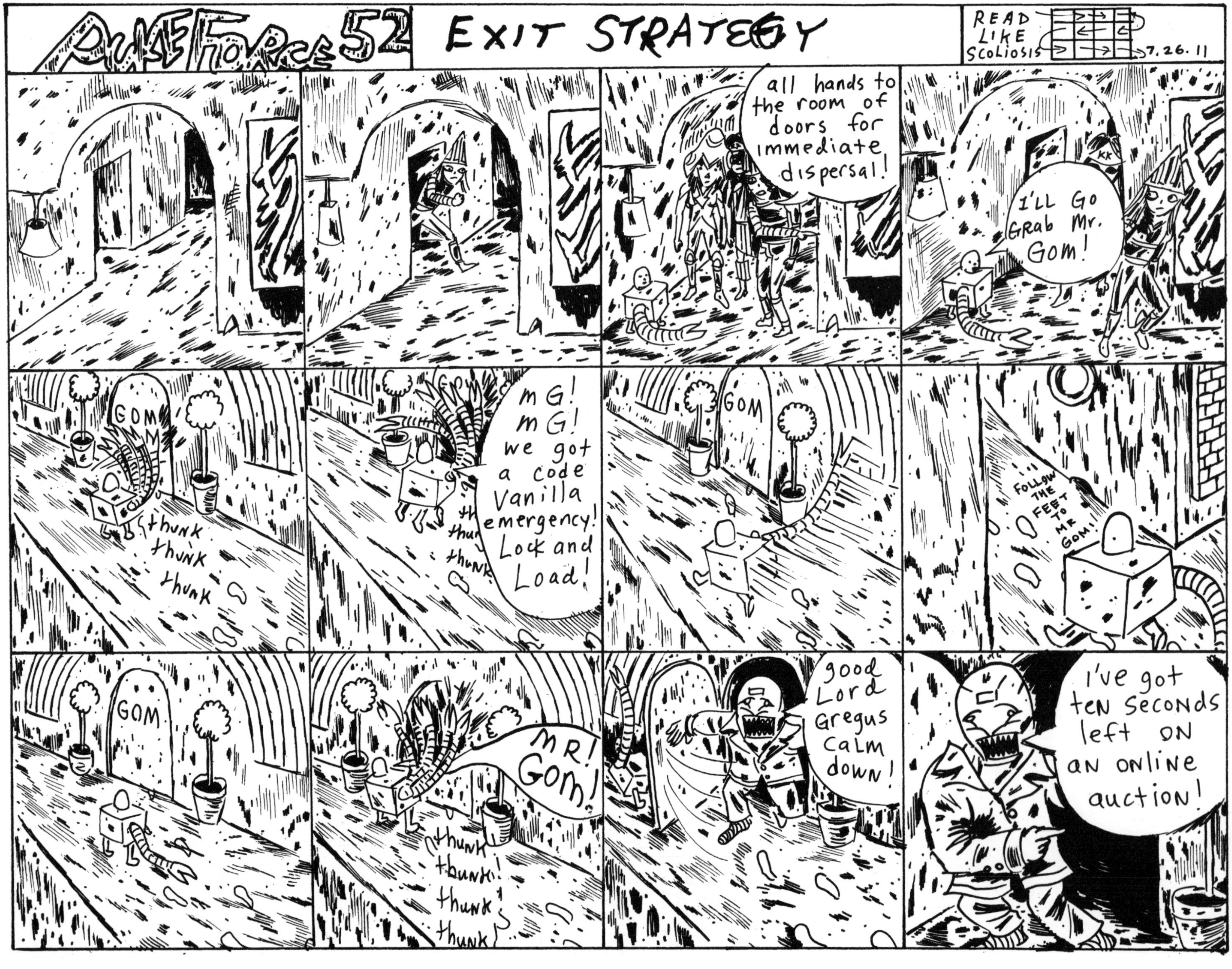
52
EXIT STRATEGY
READ LIKE SCOLIOSIS
7.26.11
all hands to the room of doors for immediate dispersal!
I'LL GO GRab Mr. GOM!
FOLLOW THE FEET TO MR GOM!
GOM
MG! MG! we got a code Vanilla emergency! Lock and Load!
GOM
thunk thunk thunk
GOM
MR! GOM!
thunk! thunk! thunk! thunk!
good Lord Gregus calm down!
I've got ten seconds left ON an ONLINE auction!

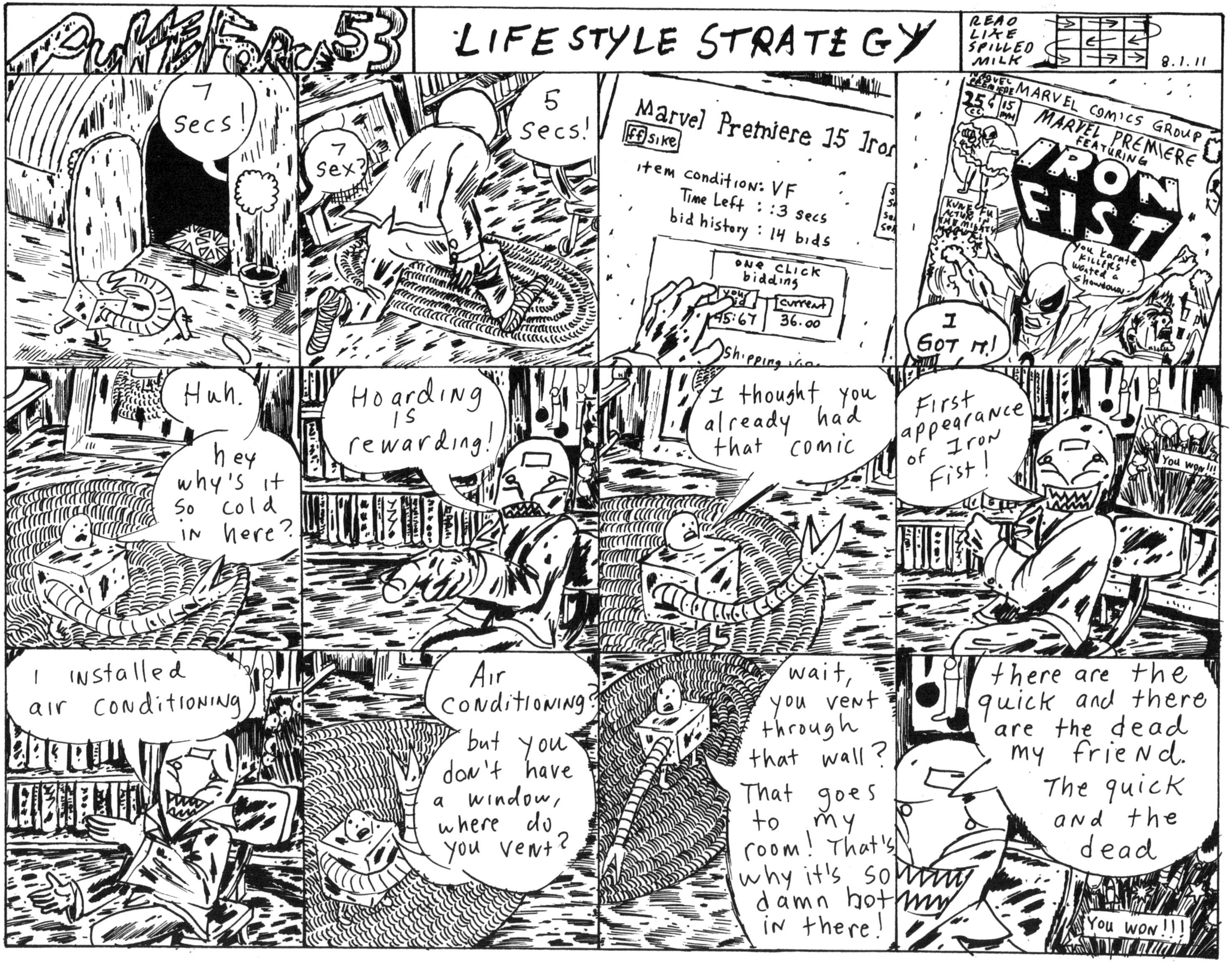

LIFESTYLE STRATEGY
READ LIKE SPILLED MILK
8.1.11
7 secs!
7 sex?
5 secs!
Marvel Premiere 15 Iron
item condition: VF
Time Left : :3 secs
bid history : 14 bids
one click bidding
current
36.00
MARVEL COMICS GROUP
MARVEL PREMIERE FEATURING
IRON FIST
I GOT IT!
First appearance of Iron Fist!
You won!!!
I thought you already had that comic
Hoarding is rewarding!
Huh.
hey why's it so cold in here?
I installed air conditioning
Air conditioning?
but you don't have a window, where do you vent?
wait, you vent through that wall? That goes to my room! That's why it's so damn hot in there!
there are the quick and there are the dead my friend. The quick and the dead
You won!!!

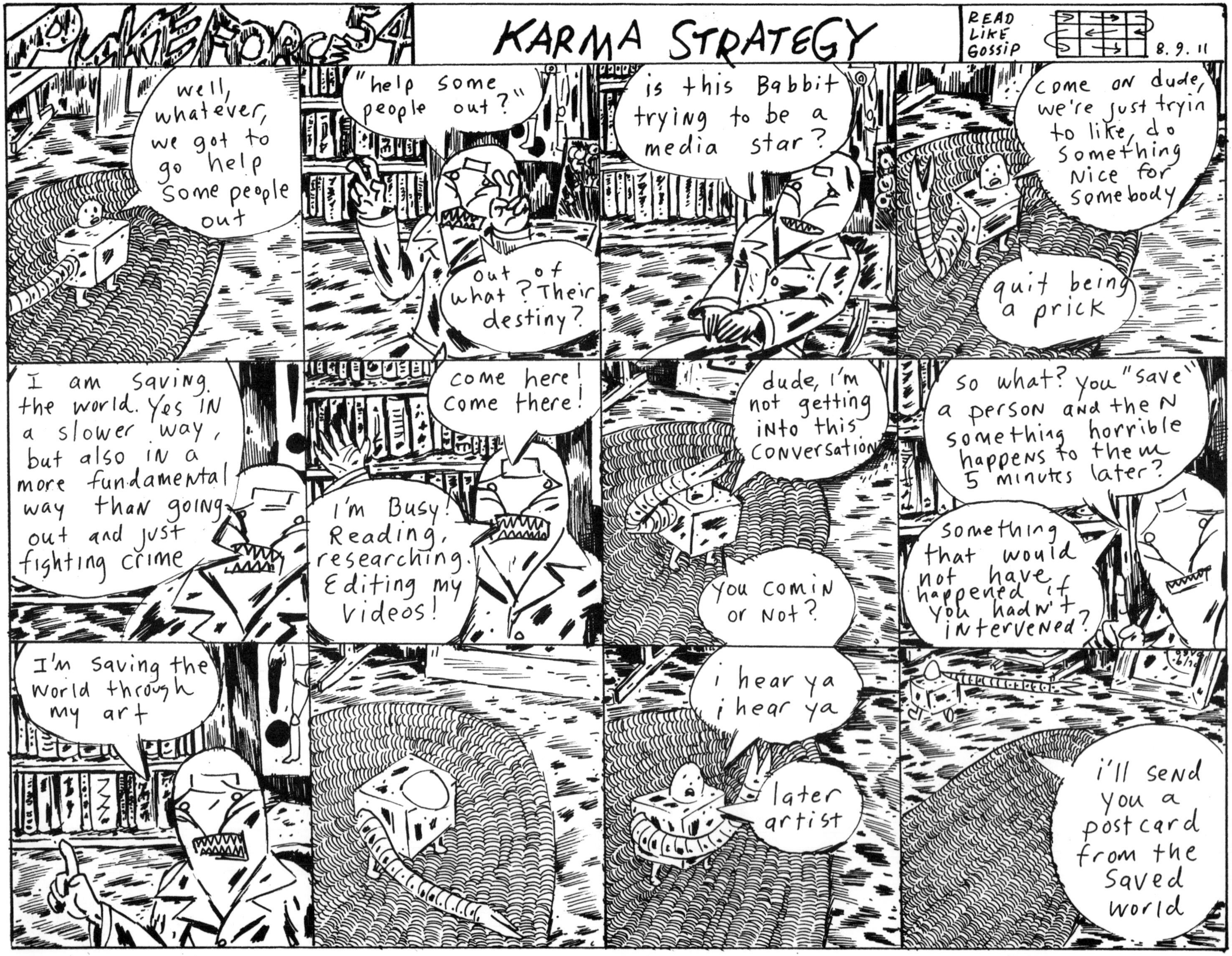
PUKE FORCE 54
KARMA STRATEGY
READ LIKE GOSSIP
8.9.11
well, whatever, we got to go help some people out
"help some people out?"
out of what? Their destiny?
is this Babbit trying to be a media star?
come on dude, we're just tryin to like, do something nice for somebody
quit being a prick
so what? you "save" a person and then something horrible happens to them 5 minutes later?
something that would not have happened if you hadn't intervened?
dude, I'm not getting into this conversation
you comin or not?
come here! come there!
I'm Busy! Reading, researching. Editing my videos!
I am saving the world. Yes in a slower way, but also in a more fundamental way than going out and just fighting crime
I'm saving the world through my art
i hear ya i hear ya
later artist
i'll send you a postcard from the saved world

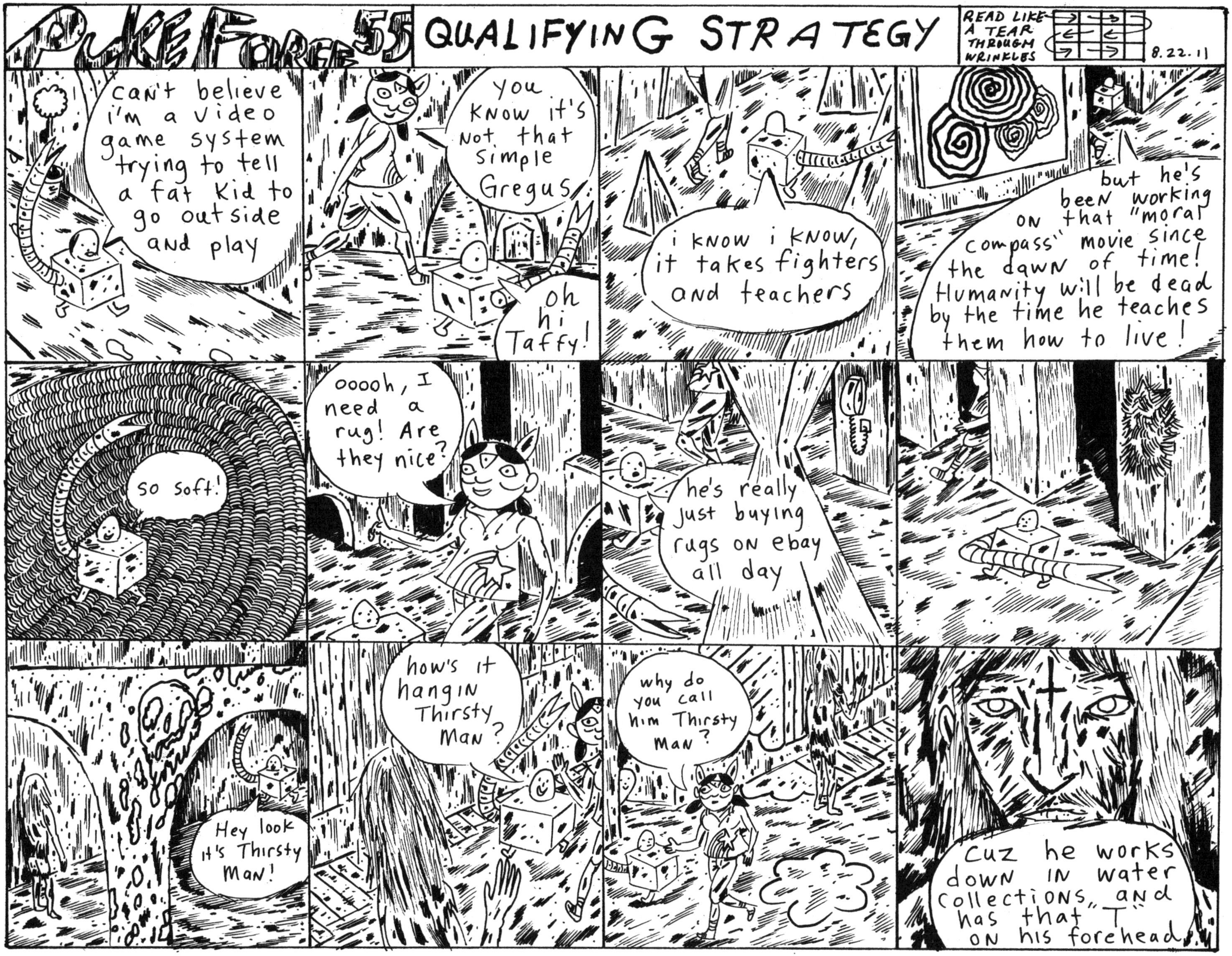
Puke Force 55
QUALIFYING STRATEGY
READ LIKE A TEAR THROUGH WRINKLES
8.22.11
can't believe i'm a video game system trying to tell a fat kid to go outside and play
you know it's not that simple Gregus
oh hi Taffy!
i know i know, it takes fighters and teachers
but he's been working on that "moral compass" movie since the dawn of time! Humanity will be dead by the time he teaches them how to live!
he's really just buying rugs on ebay all day
ooooh, I need a rug! Are they nice?
so soft!
Hey look it's Thirsty Man!
how's it hangin Thirsty Man?
why do you call him Thirsty Man?
Cuz he works down in water collections, and has that "T" on his forehead

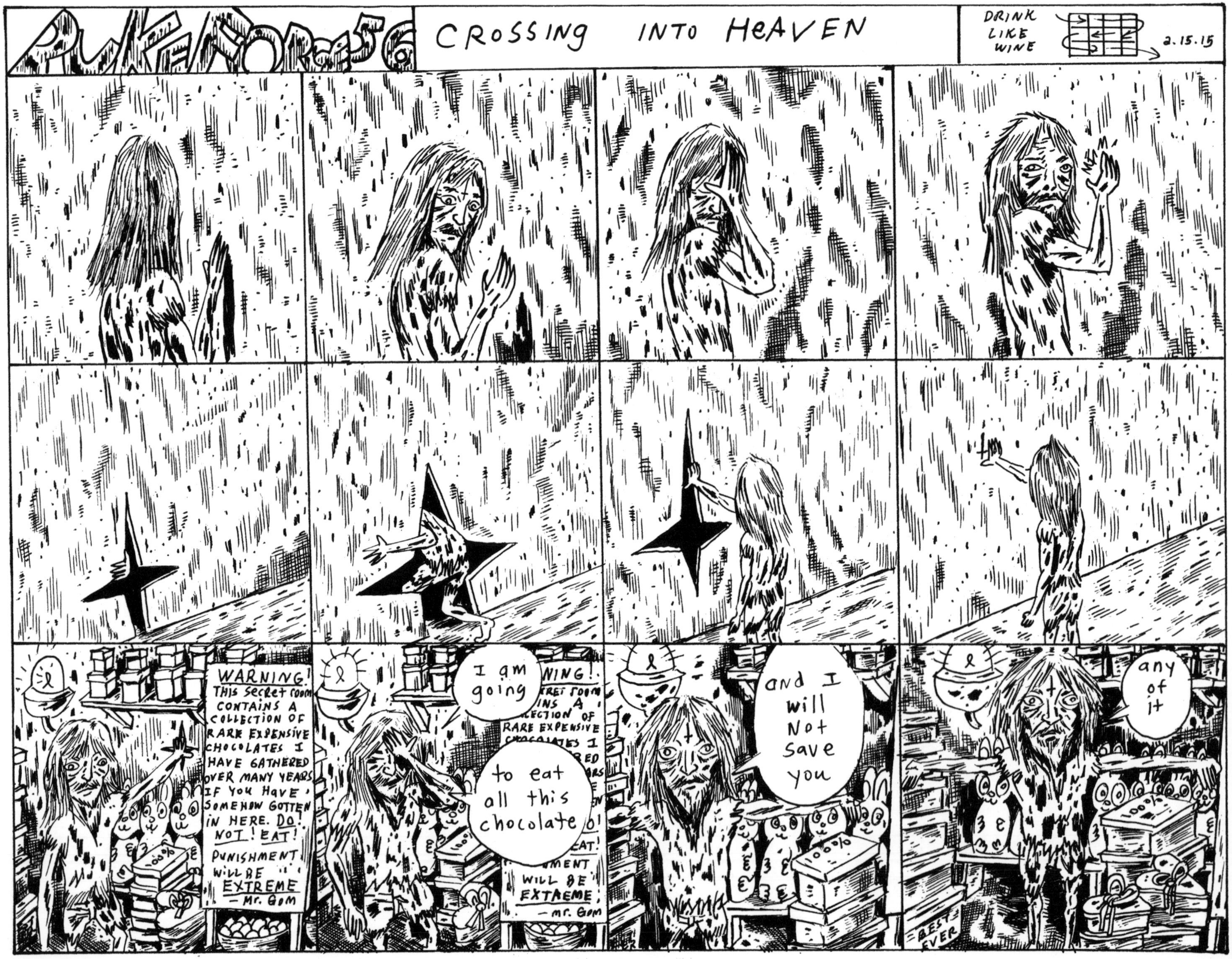
PUKEFORCE 56
CROSSING INTO HEAVEN
DRINK LIKE WINE
2.15.15
WARNING! THIS SECRET ROOM CONTAINS A COLLECTION OF RARE EXPENSIVE CHOCOLATES I HAVE GATHERED OVER MANY YEARS IF YOU HAVE SOMEHOW GOTTEN IN HERE. DO! NOT! EAT! PUNISHMENT WILL BE EXTREME — MR. GOM
I am going
to eat all this chocolate
and I will Not save you
any of it
100%
BEST EVER

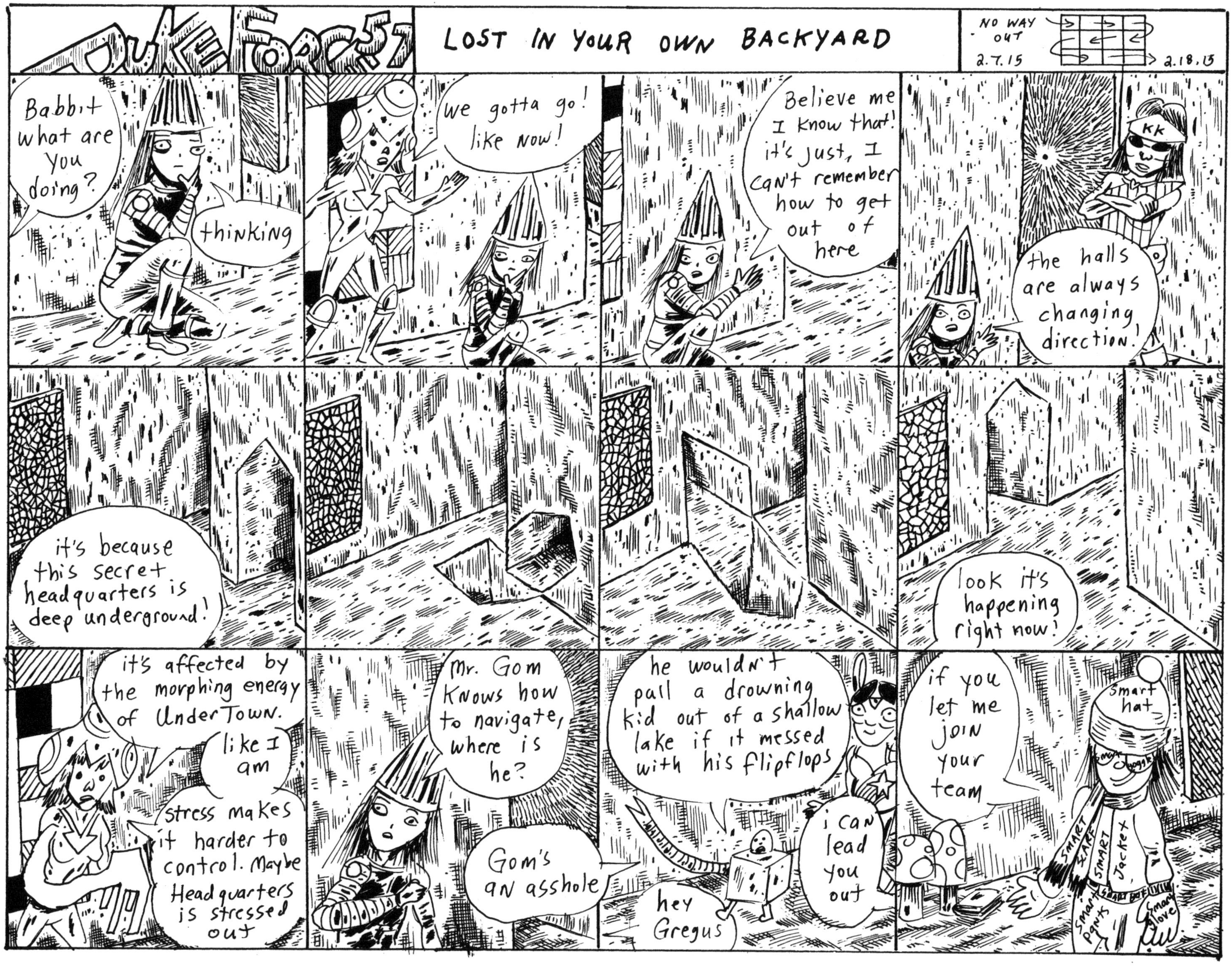

DukeForce 57
LOST IN YOUR OWN BACKYARD
NO WAY OUT
2.7.15
2.18.15
Babbit what are you doing?
thinking
we gotta go! like now!
Believe me I know that! it's just, I can't remember how to get out of here
KK
the halls are always changing direction!
it's because this secret headquarters is deep underground!
look it's happening right now!
it's affected by the morphing energy of UnderTown.
like I am
stress makes it harder to control. Maybe Headquarters is stressed out
Mr. Gom knows how to navigate, where is he?
Gom's an asshole
he wouldn't pull a drowning kid out of a shallow lake if it messed with his flipflops
hey Gregus
i can lead you out
if you let me join your team
smart hat
SMART SCARF
SMART Jacket
Smart pants
Smart glove

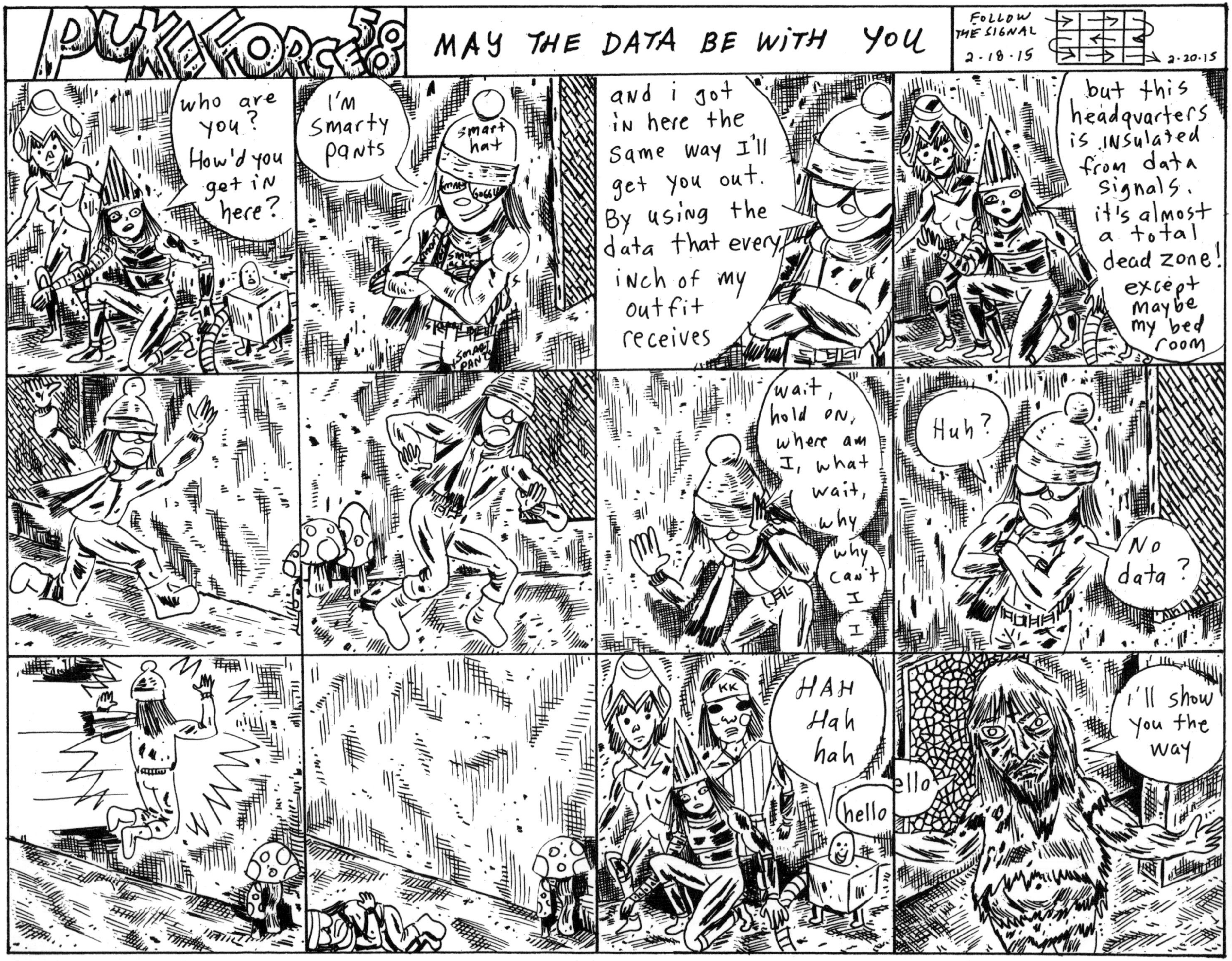
PUKE FORCE 58
MAY THE DATA BE WITH YOU
FOLLOW THE SIGNAL
2·18·15
2·20·15
who are you? How'd you get in here?
I'M Smarty pants
smart hat
and i got in here the same way I'll get you out. By using the data that every inch of my outfit receives
but this headquarters is insulated from data signals. it's almost a total dead zone! except maybe my bed room
Huh?
No data?
wait, hold on, where am I, what wait, why why can't I I
HAH Hah hah
KK
hello
ello
I'll show you the way

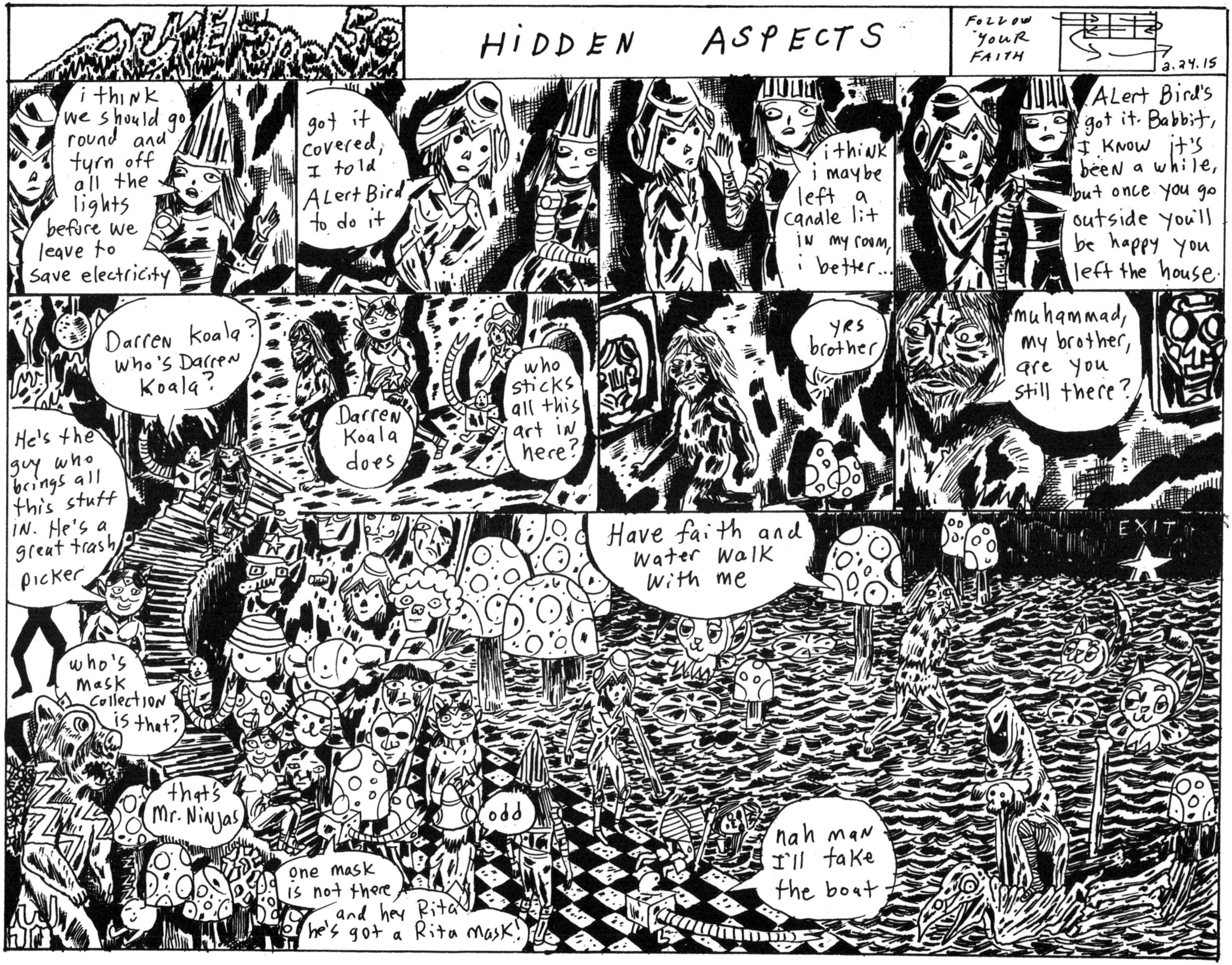
HIDDEN ASPECTS
FOLLOW YOUR FAITH
2.24.15
i think we should go round and turn off all the lights before we leave to save electricity
got it covered, I told Alert Bird to do it
i think i maybe left a candle lit in my room, i better...
Alert Bird's got it. Babbit, I know it's been a while, but once you go outside you'll be happy you left the house.
Darren koala? Who's Darren Koala?
He's the guy who brings all this stuff in. He's a great trash picker
Darren Koala does
who sticks all this art in here?
yes brother
muhammad, my brother, are you still there?
Have faith and water walk with me
EXIT
who's mask collection is that?
that's Mr. Ninjas
odd
one mask is not there
and hey Rita he's got a Rita mask!
nah man I'll take the boat

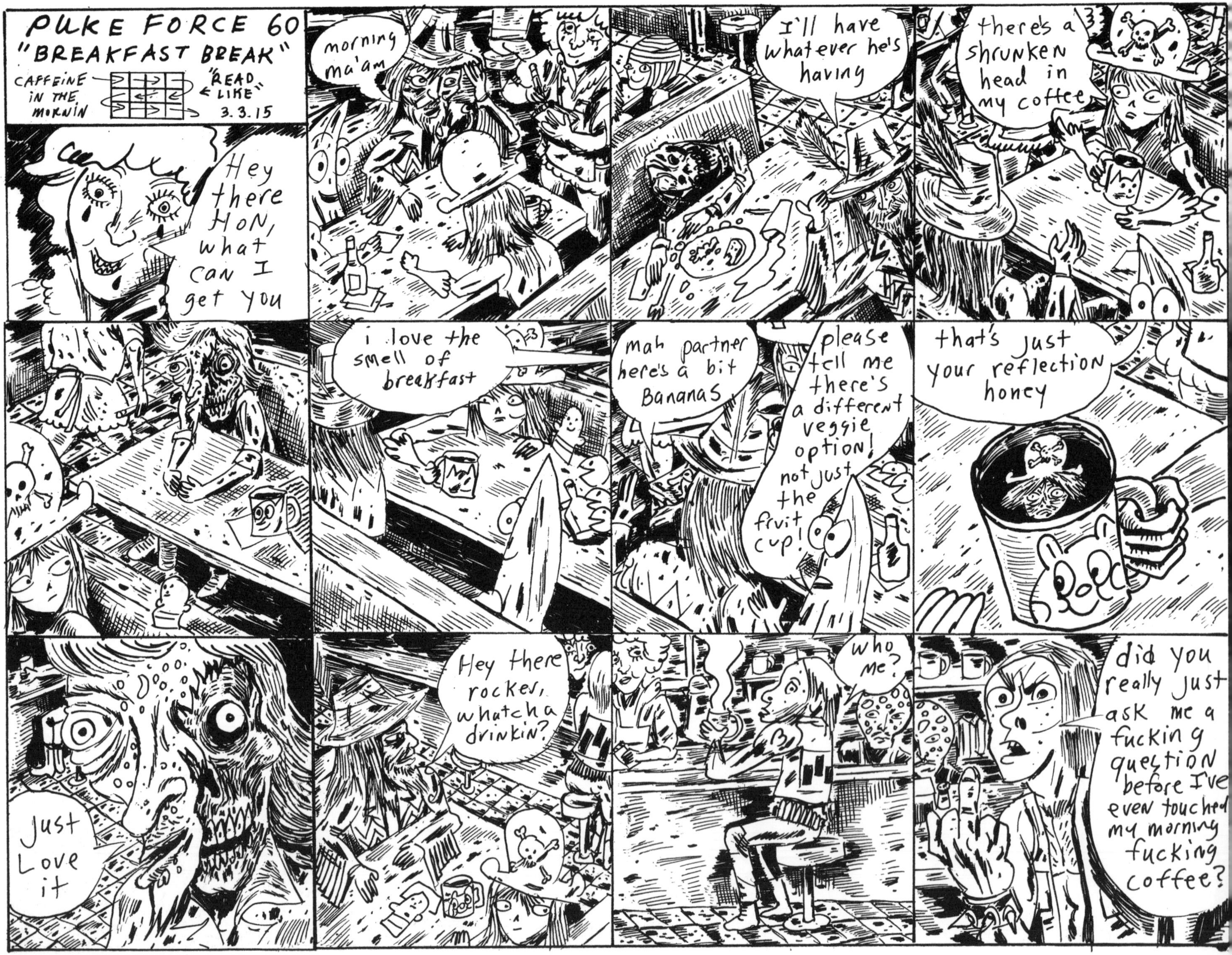
PUKE FORCE 60
"BREAKFAST BREAK"
CAFFEINE IN THE MORNIN
"READ LIKE"
3.3.15
Hey there HON, what can I get you
morning ma'am
I'll have whatever he's having
there's a shrunken head in my coffee
i love the smell of breakfast
mah partner here's a bit Bananas
please tell me there's a different veggie option! not just the fruit cup!
that's just your reflection honey
Just Love it
Hey there rockers, whatcha drinkin?
who me?
did you really just ask me a fucking question before I've even touched my morning fucking coffee?

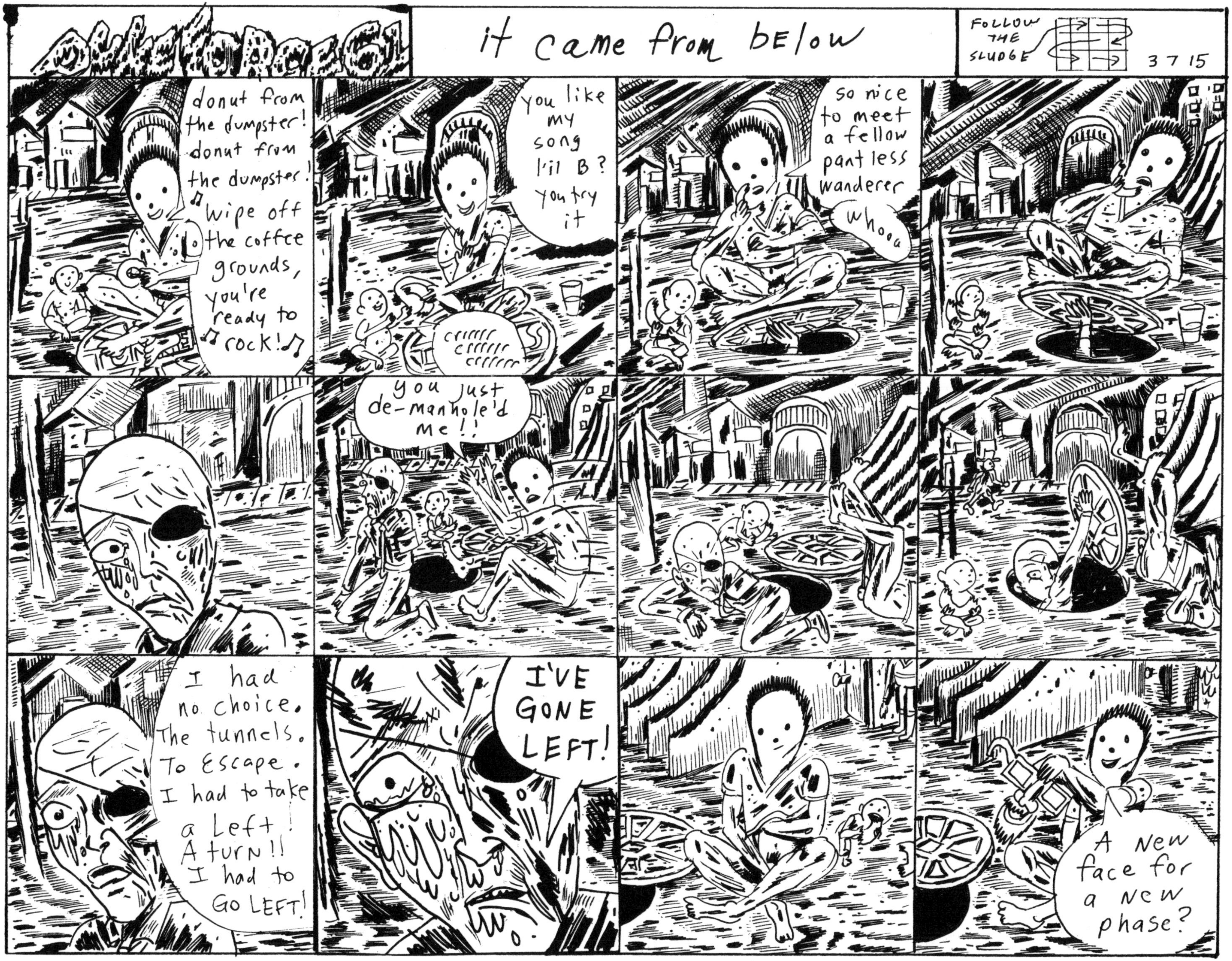
it came from below
FOLLOW THE SLUDGE
3 7 15
donut from the dumpster! donut from the dumpster! wipe off the coffee grounds, you're ready to rock!
you like my song lil B? you try it
crrrrrr crrrrrr crrrrrrr
so nice to meet a fellow pantless wanderer
whooa
you just de-manhole'd me!!
I had no choice. The tunnels. To Escape. I had to take a Left! A turn!! I had to GO LEFT!
I'VE GONE LEFT!
A New face for a New phase?

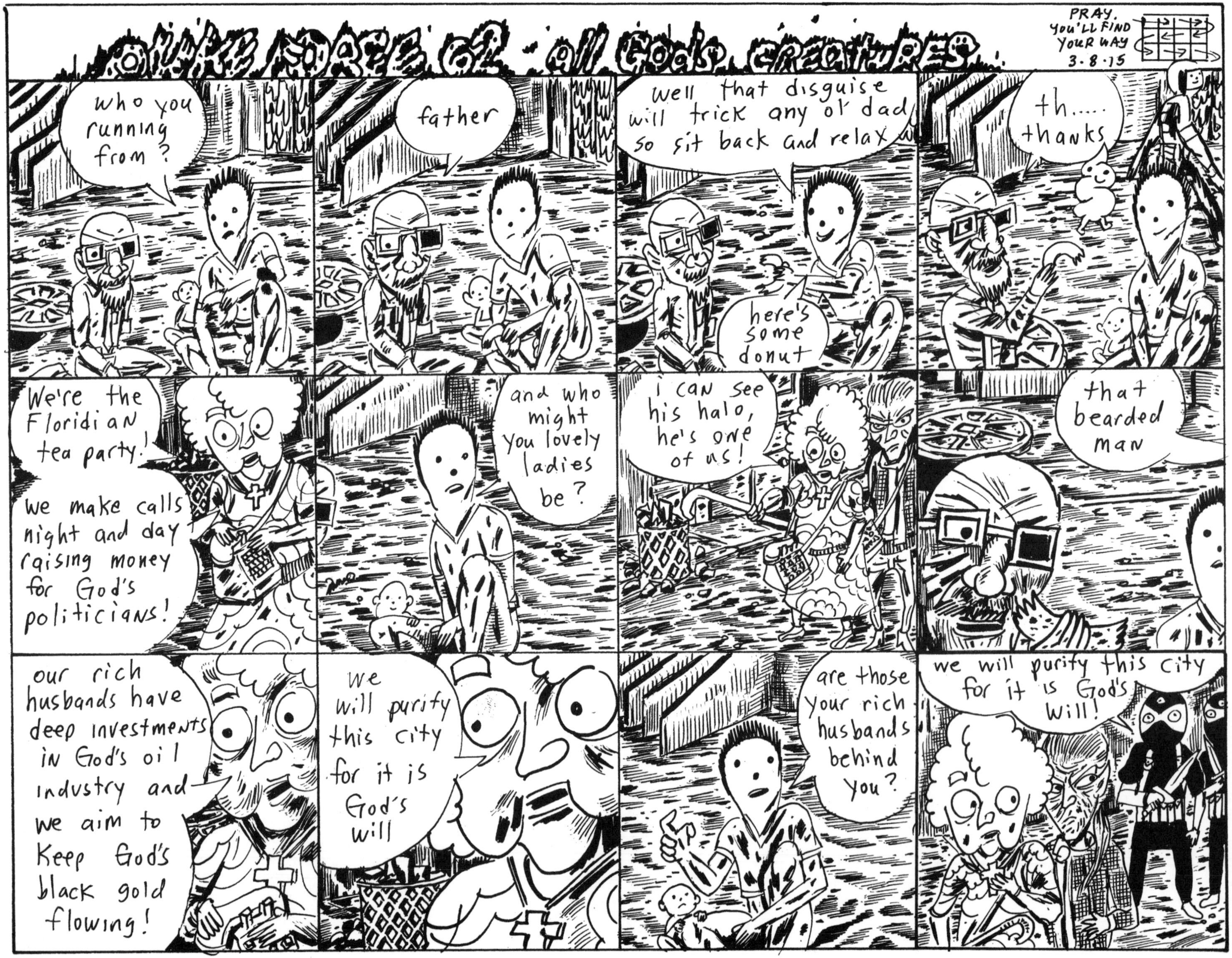
62 · all God's creatures
PRAY. YOU'LL FIND YOUR WAY
3·8·15
who you running from?
father
well that disguise will trick any ol' dad so sit back and relax
here's some donut
th..... thanks
We're the Floridian tea party!
we make calls night and day raising money for God's politicians!
and who might you lovely ladies be?
i can see his halo, he's one of us!
that bearded man
our rich husbands have deep investments in God's oil industry and we aim to keep God's black gold flowing!
we will purify this city for it is God's will
are those your rich husbands behind you?
we will purify this city for it is God's Will!

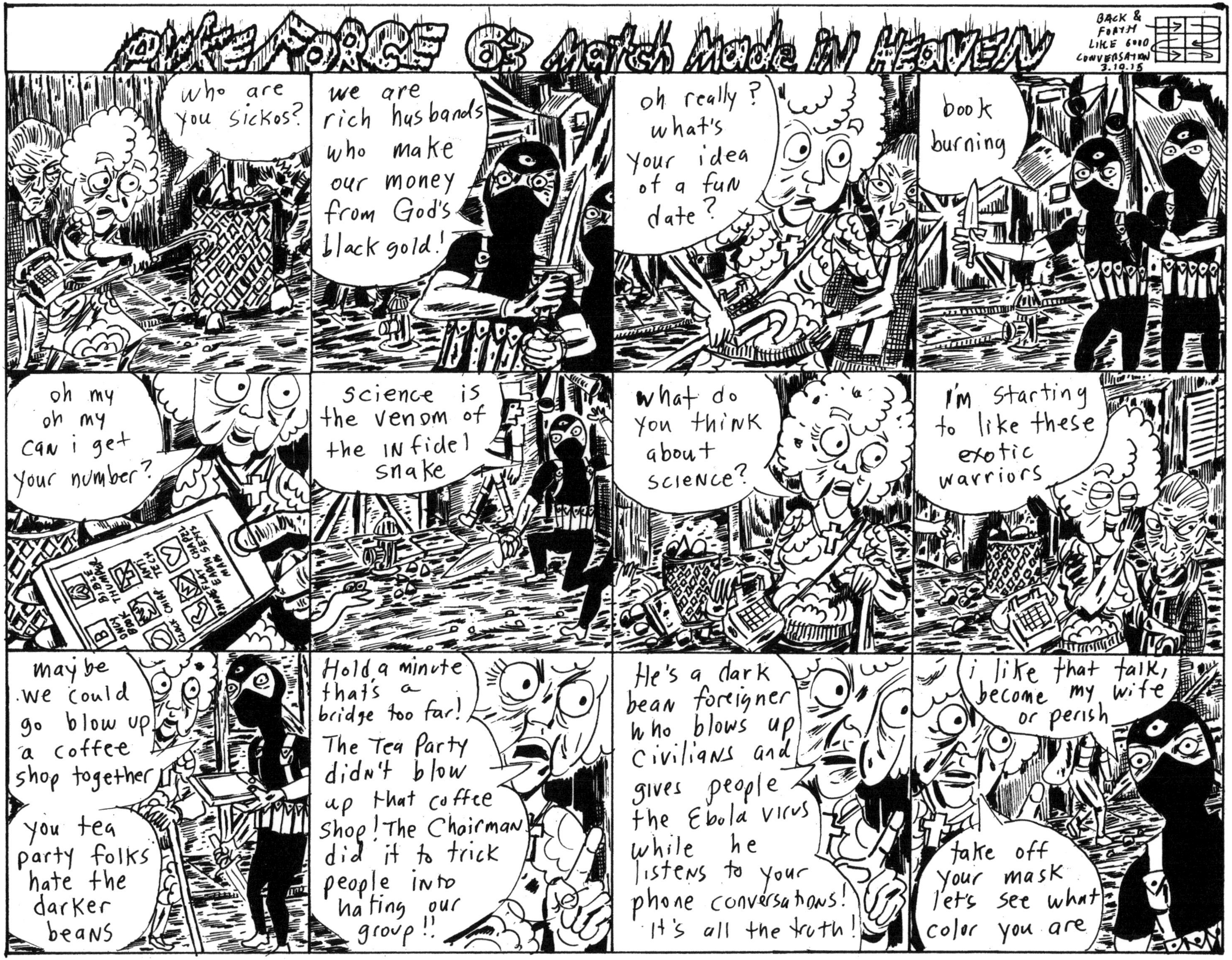
PUKE FORCE 63 MATCH MADE IN HEAVEN
BACK & FORTH LIKE GOOD CONVERSATION 3.19.15
who are you sickos?
we are rich husbands who make our money from God's black gold!
oh really? what's your idea of a fun date?
book burning
I'm starting to like these exotic warriors
what do you think about science?
science is the venom of the infidel snake
oh my oh my can i get your number?
maybe we could go blow up a coffee shop together
you tea party folks hate the darker beans
Hold a minute that's a bridge too far!
The Tea Party didn't blow up that coffee shop! The Chairman did it to trick people into hating our group!!
He's a dark bean foreigner who blows up civilians and gives people the Ebola virus while he listens to your phone conversations! It's all the truth!
i like that talk, become my wife or perish
take off your mask let's see what color you are

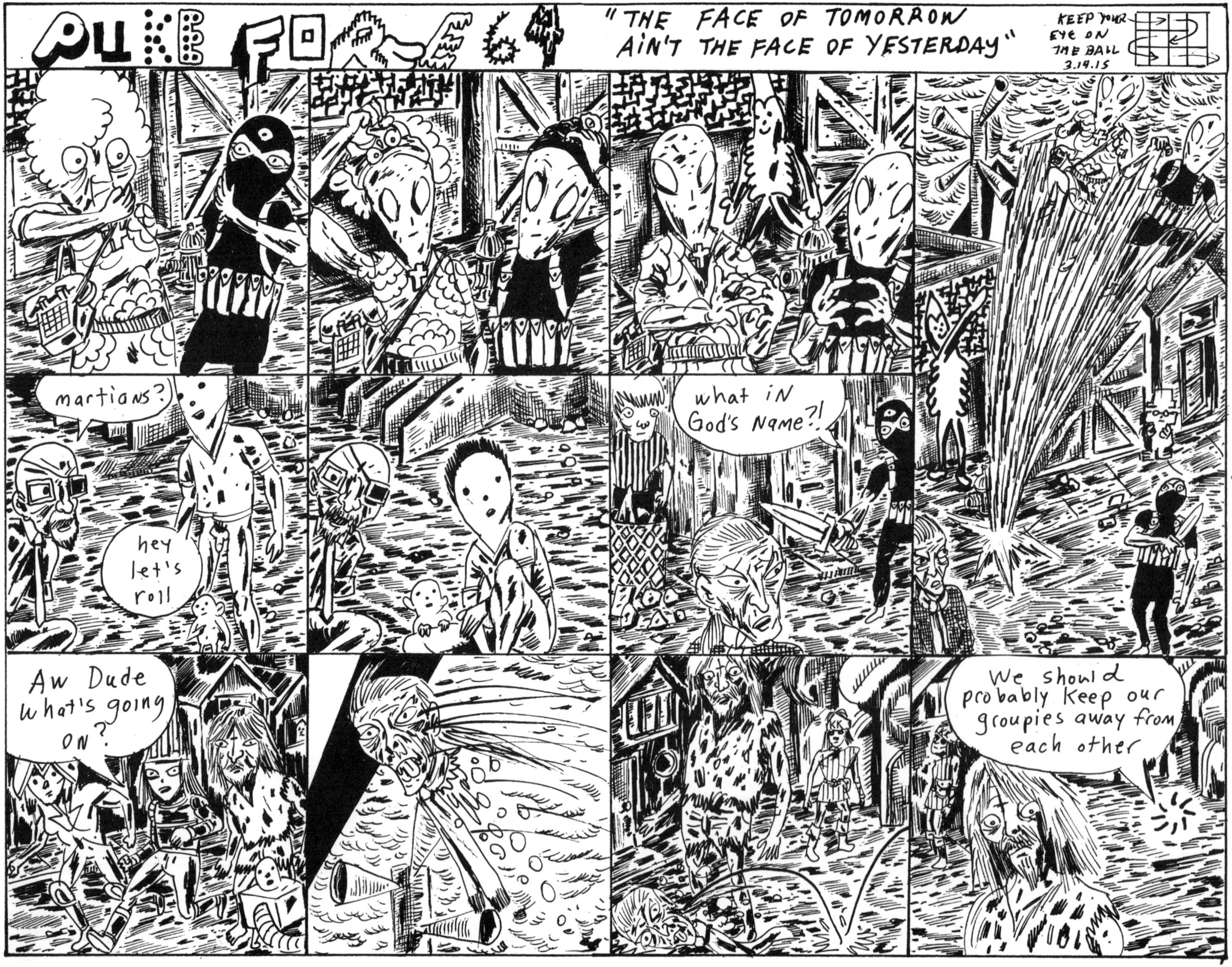
PUKE FORCE 64
"THE FACE OF TOMORROW AIN'T THE FACE OF YESTERDAY"
KEEP YOUR EYE ON THE BALL
3.14.15
martians?
hey let's roll
what IN God's Name?!
Aw Dude what's going on?
We should probably keep our groupies away from each other

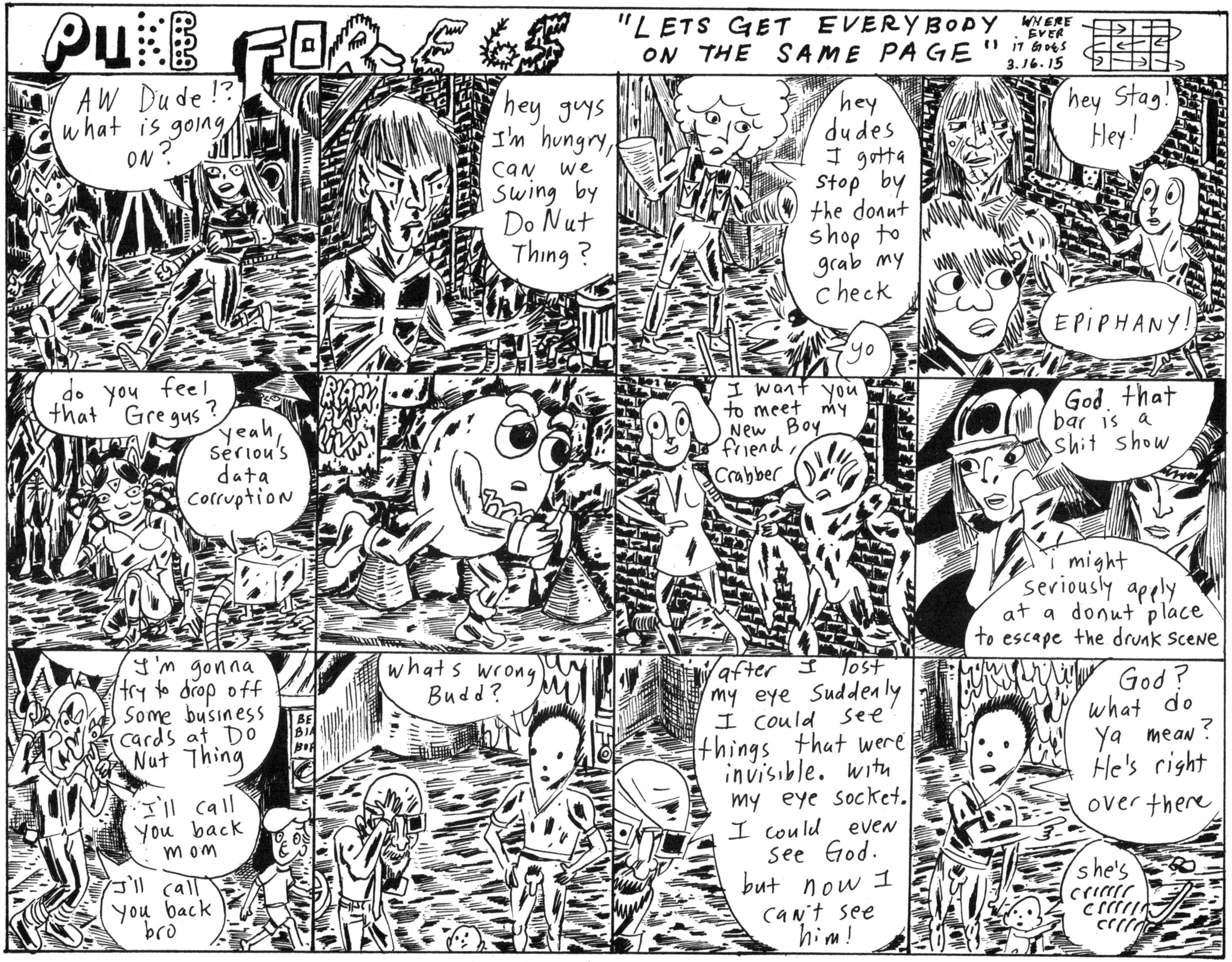
PUKE FORCES
"LETS GET EVERYBODY ON THE SAME PAGE"
WHERE EVER IT GOES 3.16.15
AW Dude!? what is going ON?
hey guys I'm hungry, can we swing by Do Nut Thing?
hey dudes I gotta stop by the donut shop to grab my check
yo
hey Stag! Hey!
EPIPHANY!
God that bar is a shit show
I might seriously apply at a donut place to escape the drunk scene
I want you to meet my New Boy friend, Crabber
do you feel that Gregus?
yeah, serious data corruption
I'm gonna try to drop off some business cards at Do Nut Thing
I'll call you back mom
I'll call you back bro
whats wrong Budd?
after I lost my eye Suddenly I could see things that were invisible. with my eye socket. I could even see God.
but now I can't see him!
God? what do ya mean? He's right over there
she's crrrrr crrrrr crrrr

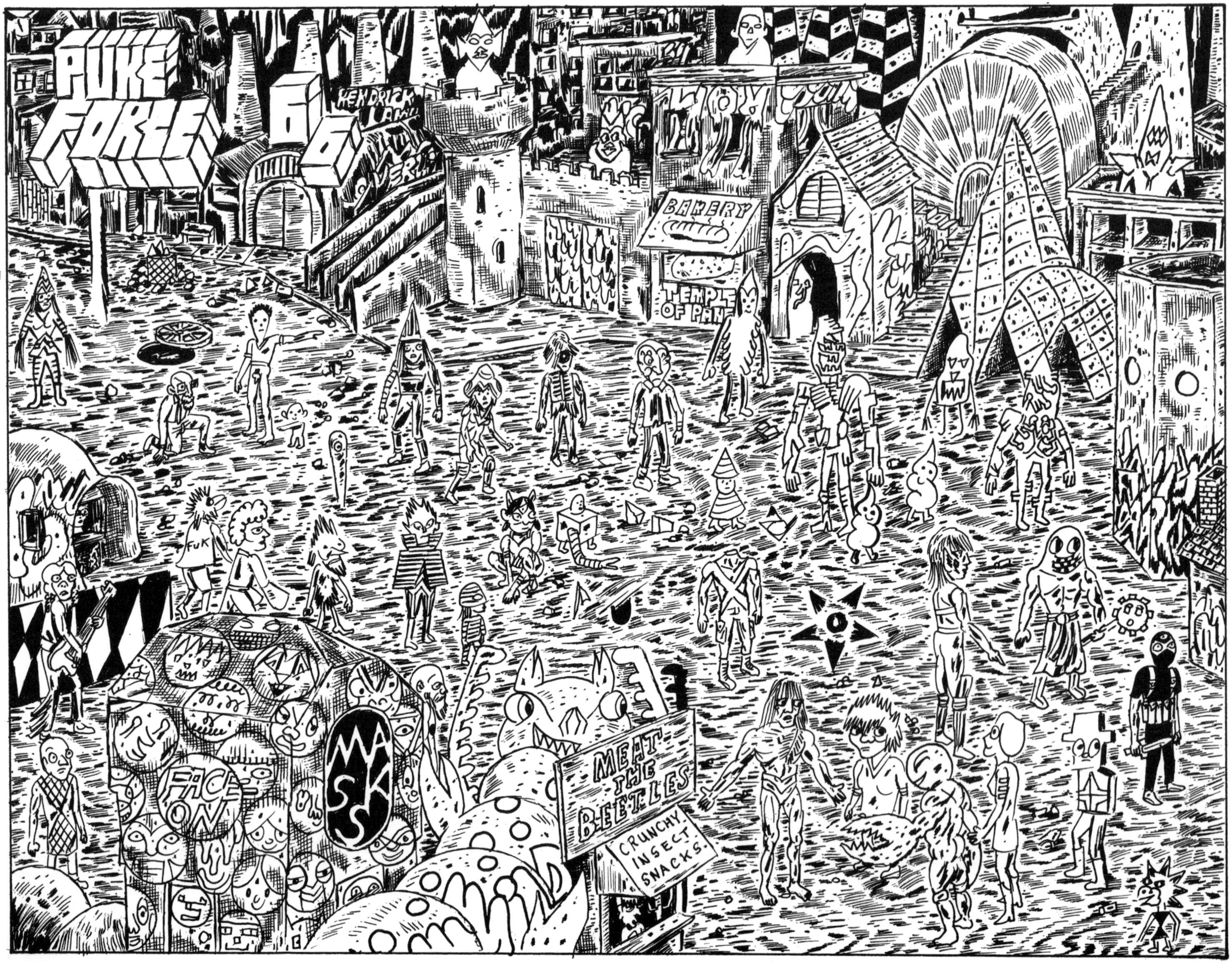
PUKE FORCE
BAKERY
TEMPLE OF PAN
FUK
FACE ON
MASKS
MEAT THE BEETLES
CRUNCHY INSECT SNACKS.

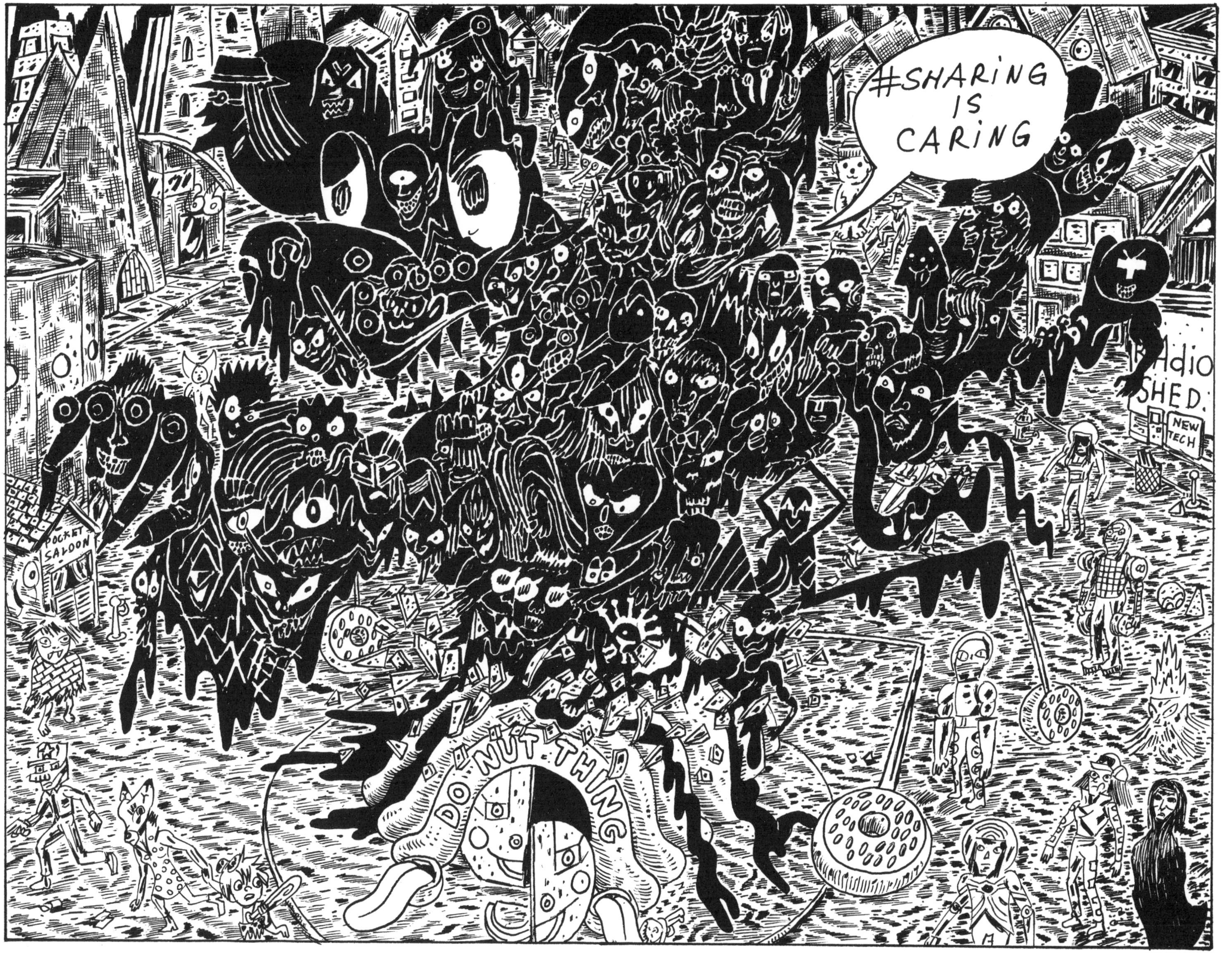
#SHARING IS CARING
POCKET SALOON
RAdio SHED.
NEW TECH
DO NUT THING

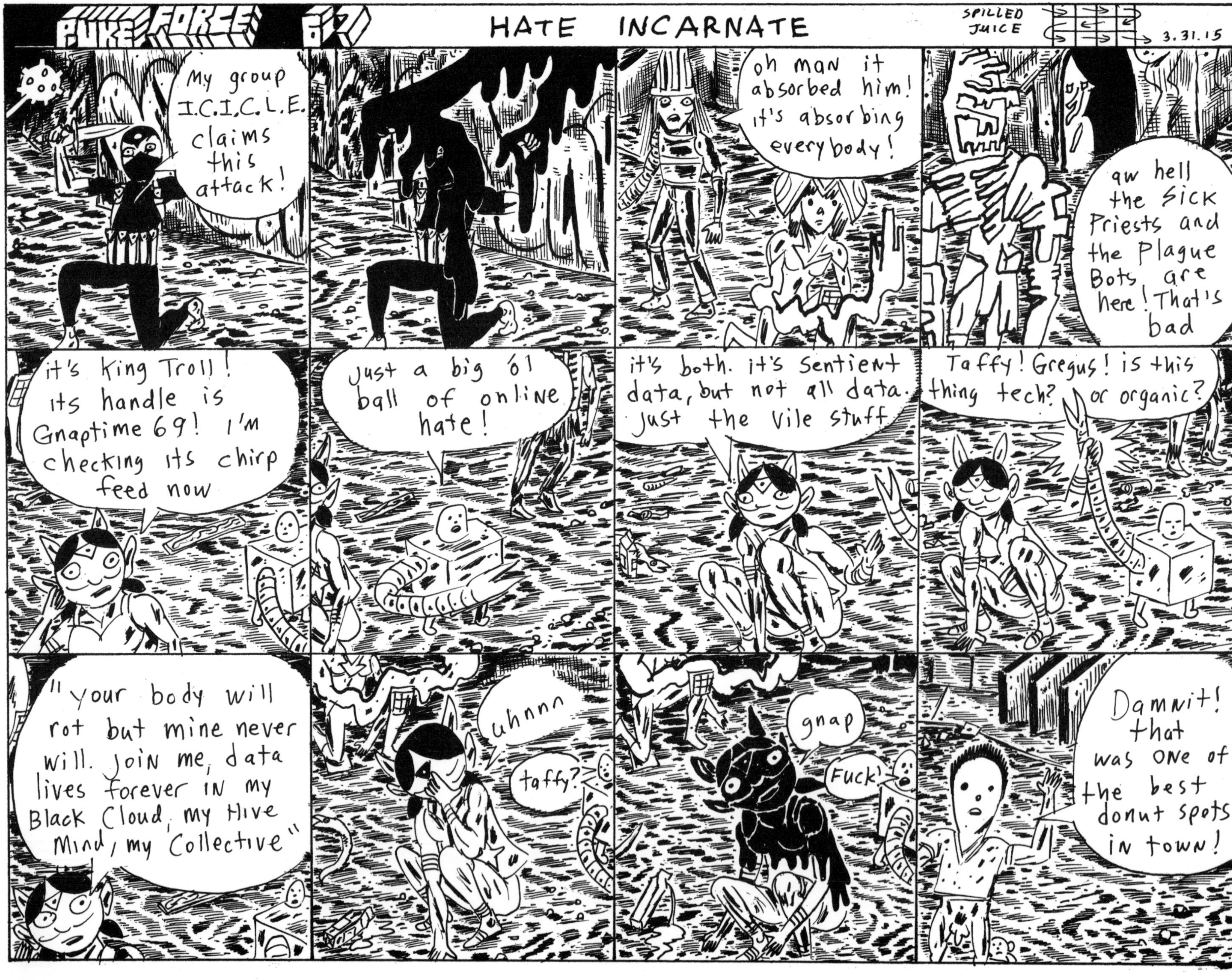

HATE INCARNATE
SPILLED JUICE
3.31.15
My group I.C.I.C.L.E. claims this attack!
oh man it absorbed him! it's absorbing everybody!
aw hell the Sick Priests and the Plague Bots are here! That's bad
it's King Troll! its handle is Gnaptime 69! I'm checking its chirp feed now
just a big 'ol ball of online hate!
it's both. it's sentient data, but not all data. just the vile stuff
Taffy! Gregus! is this thing tech? or organic?
"your body will rot but mine never will. join me, data lives forever in my Black Cloud, my Hive Mind, my Collective"
uhnnn
taffy?
gnap
Fuck!
Damnit! that was one of the best donut spots in town!

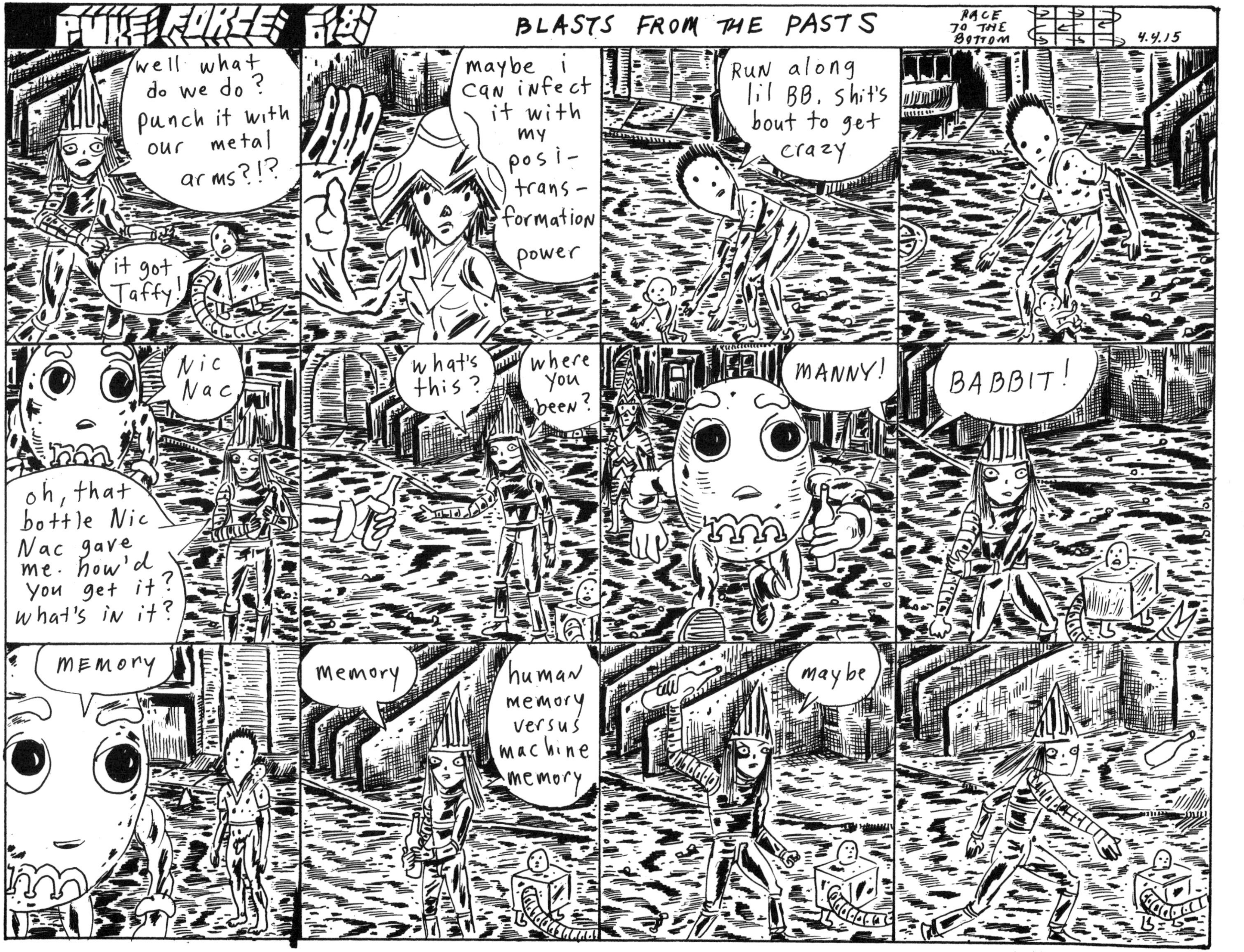
PUKE FORCE
BLASTS FROM THE PASTS
RACE TO THE BOTTOM
4.4.15
well what do we do? punch it with our metal arms?!?
it got Taffy!
maybe i can infect it with my posi-trans-formation power
RUN along lil BB. shit's bout to get crazy
BABBIT!
MANNY!
what's this?
where you been?
Nic Nac
oh, that bottle Nic Nac gave me. how'd you get it? what's in it?
MEMORY
memory
human memory versus machine memory
maybe

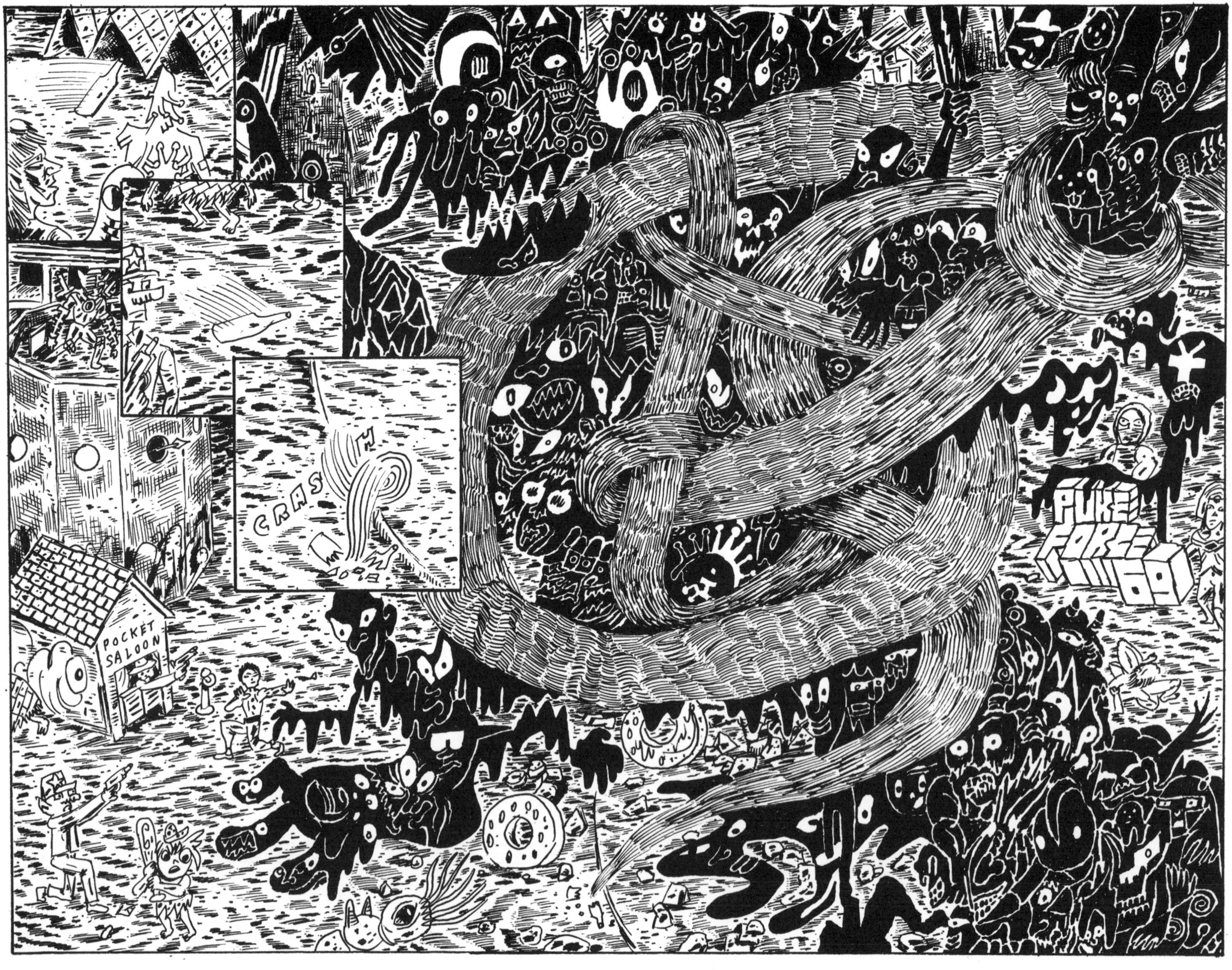
CRAS
POCKET SALOON
PUKE FORCE

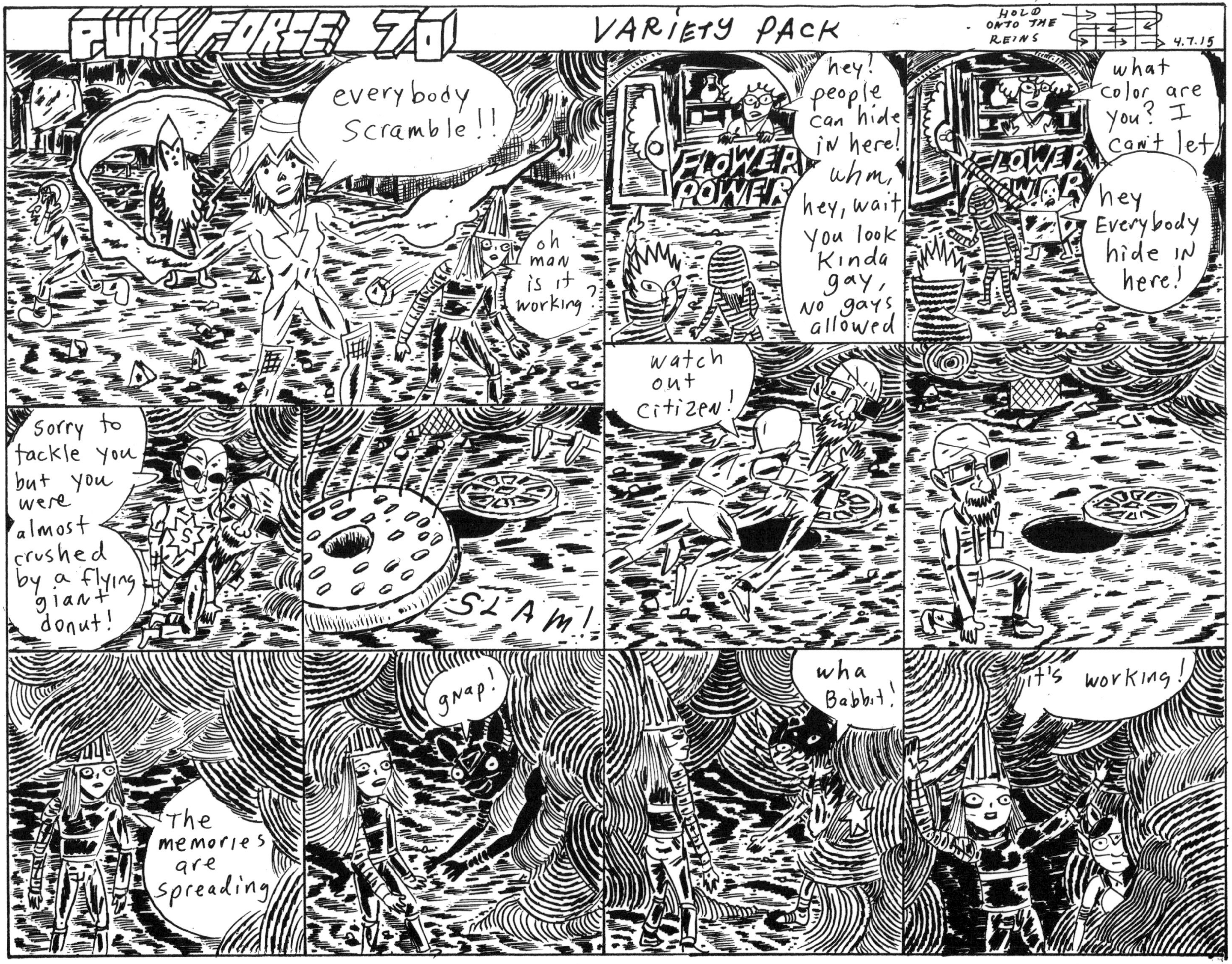
PUKE FORCE 70
VARIETY PACK
HOLD ONTO THE REINS
4.7.15
everybody Scramble!!
oh man is it working?
hey! people can hide in here!
FLOWER POWER
uhm, hey, wait, you look kinda gay, no gays allowed
what color are you? I can't tel
hey Everybody hide in here!
watch out citizen!
Sorry to tackle you but you were almost crushed by a flying giant donut!
SLAM!
The memories are spreading
gnap!
wha Babbit!
it's working!

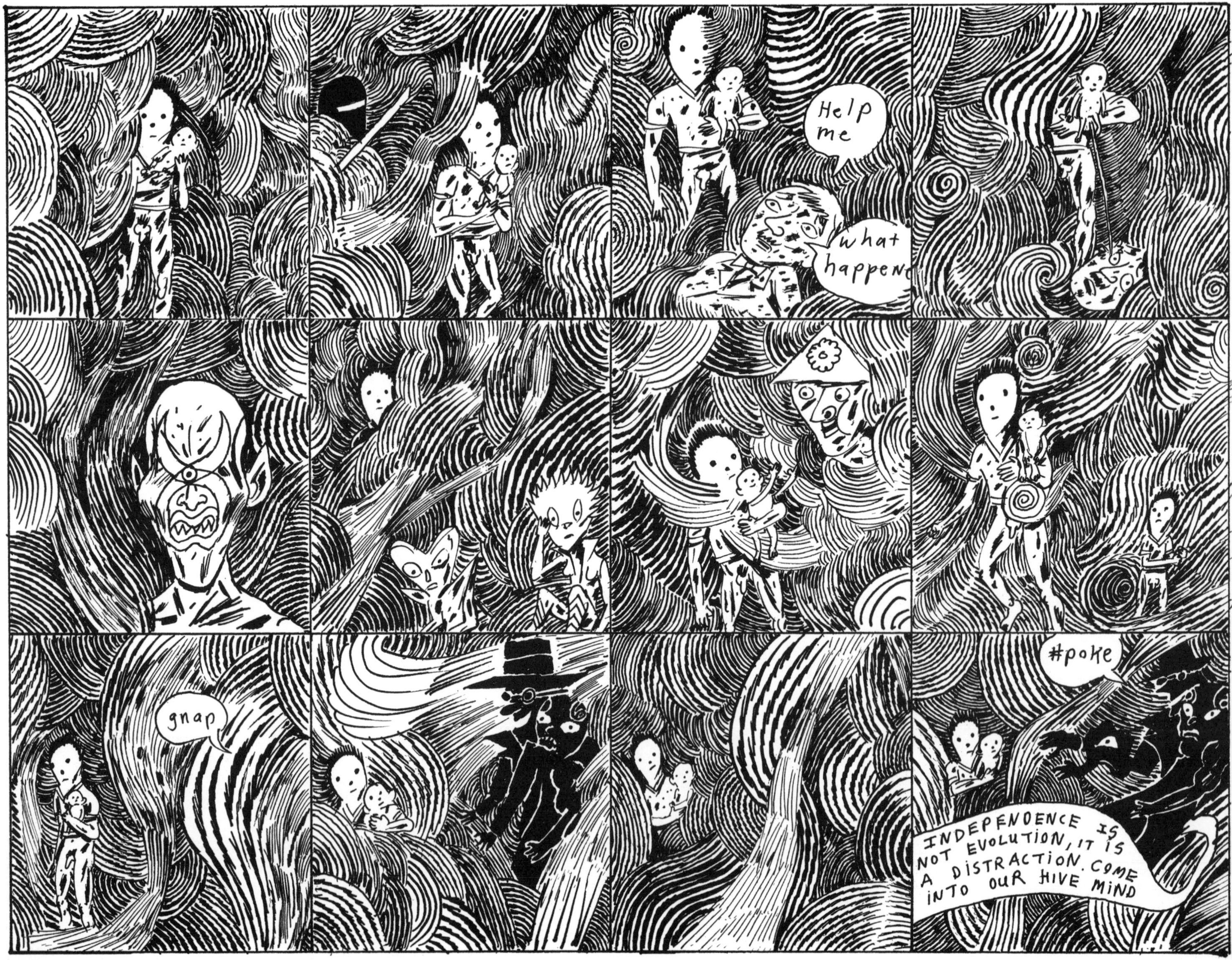

Help me
what happen
gnap
#poke
INDEPENDENCE IS NOT EVOLUTION, IT IS A DISTRACTION. COME INTO OUR HIVE MIND

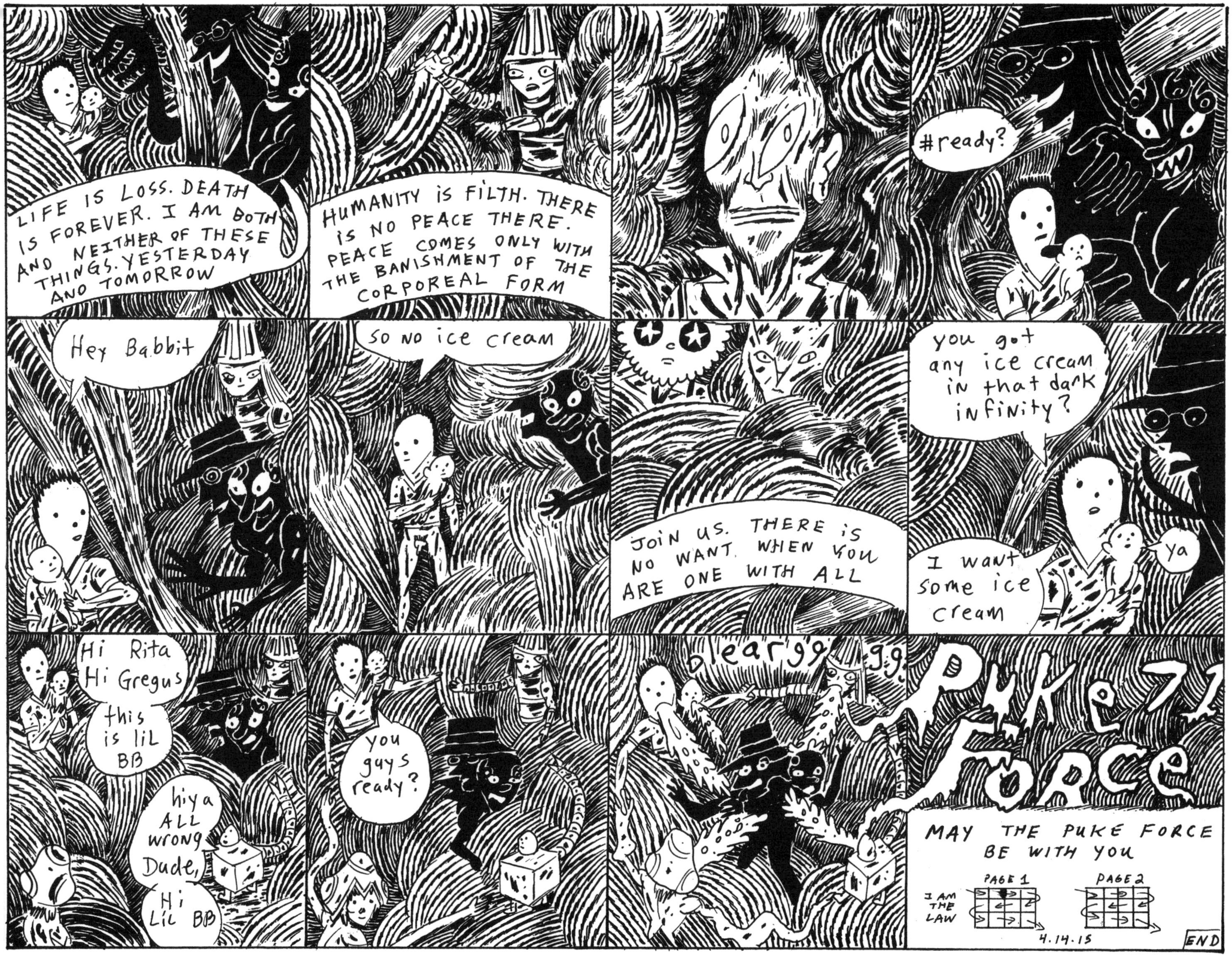
LIFE IS LOSS. DEATH IS FOREVER. I AM BOTH AND NEITHER OF THESE THINGS. YESTERDAY AND TOMORROW
HUMANITY IS FILTH. THERE IS NO PEACE THERE. PEACE COMES ONLY WITH THE BANISHMENT OF THE CORPOREAL FORM
#ready?
Hey Babbit
so no ice cream
JOIN US. THERE IS NO WANT WHEN YOU ARE ONE WITH ALL
you got any ice cream in that dark infinity?
I want some ice cream
ya
Hi Rita
Hi Gregus
this is lil BB
hiya ALL WRONG Dude,
Hi Lil BB
you guys ready?
blearggg ggg
Puke Force 71
MAY THE PUKE FORCE BE WITH YOU
I AM THE LAW
PAGE 1
PAGE 2
4.14.15
END

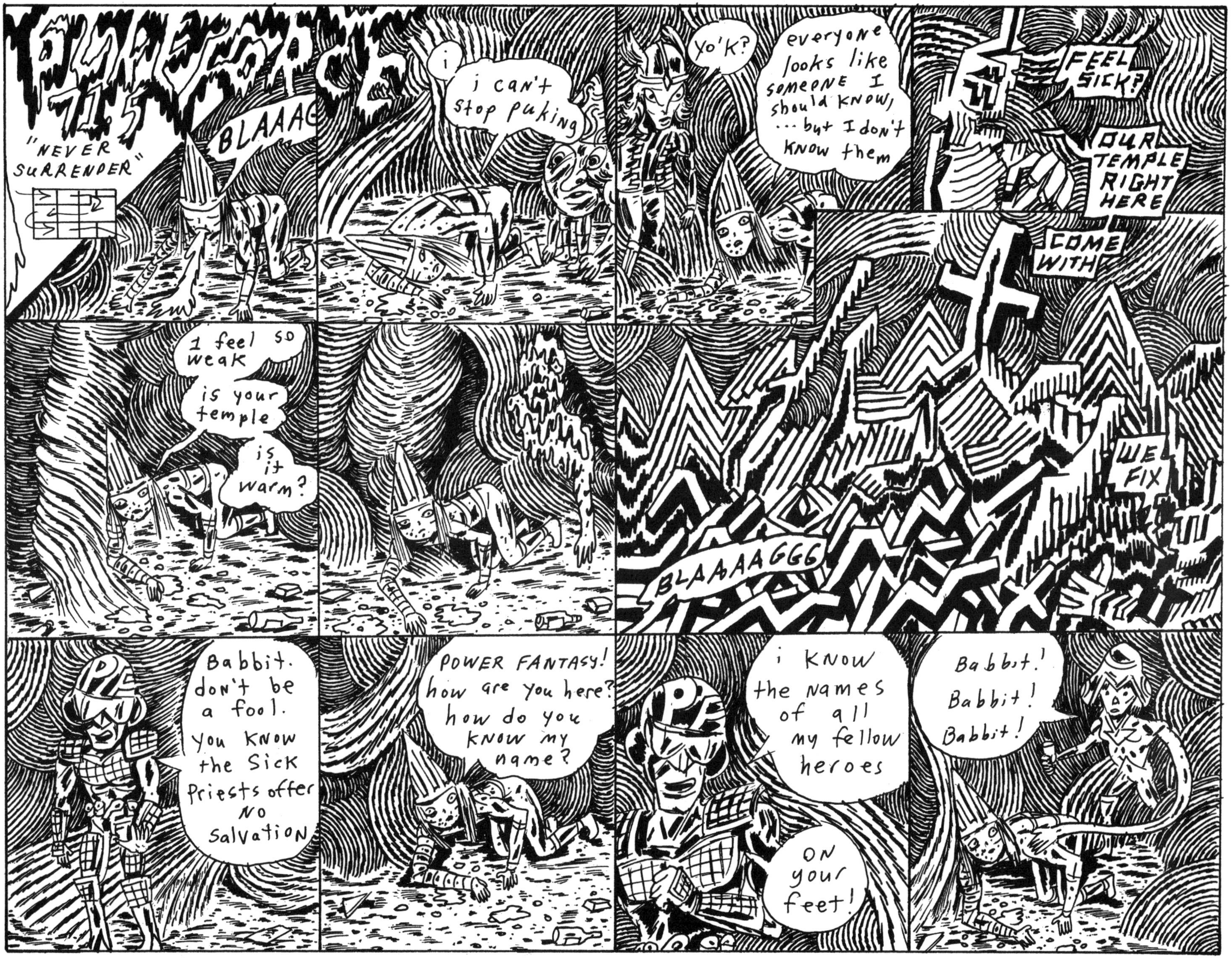
115
"NEVER SURRENDER"
BLAAAG
i
i can't stop puking
Yo'K?
everyone looks like someone I should know, ...but I don't know them
FEEL SICK?
OUR TEMPLE RIGHT HERE
COME WITH
1 feel so weak
is your temple
is it warm?
WE FIX
BLAAAAGGG
Babbit. don't be a fool. You know the Sick Priests offer NO salvation
POWER FANTASY! how are you here? how do you know my name?
i know the names of all my fellow heroes
ON your feet!
Babbit! Babbit! Babbit!

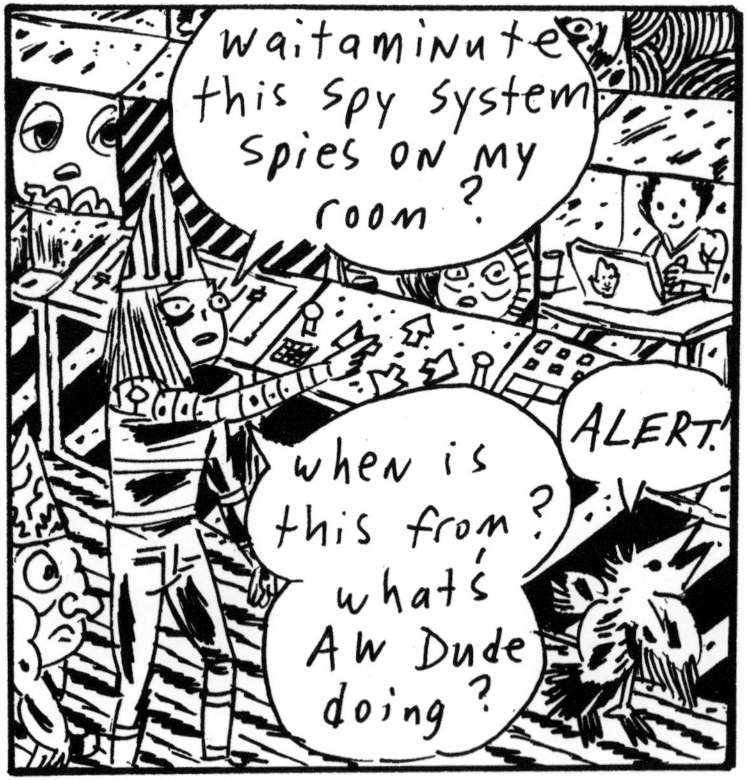
waitaminute this spy system spies on my room?
when is this from? what's Aw Dude doing?
ALERT!

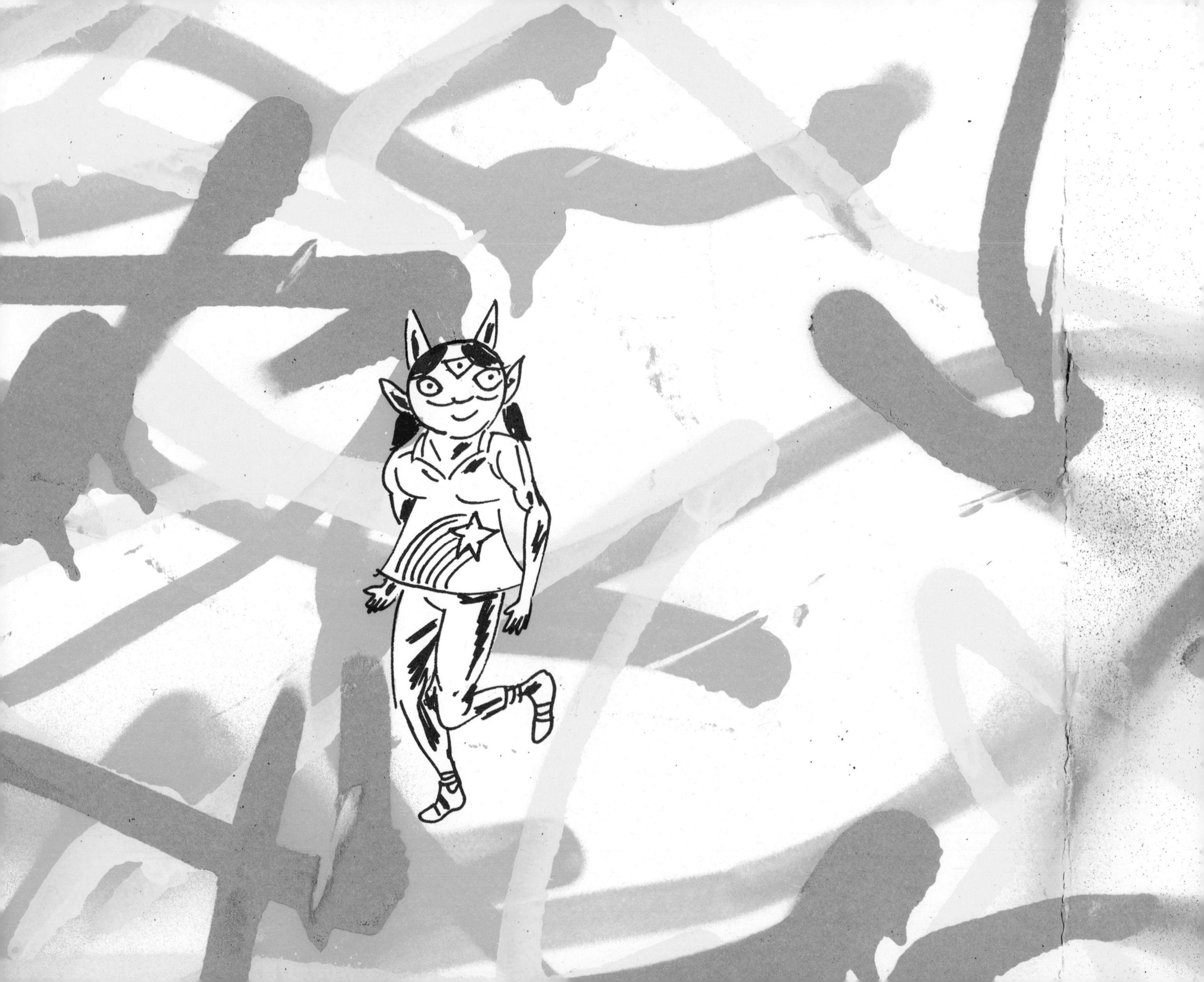